speaking yo...

Confident
German

Berlitz Publishing

New York   London   Singapore

Contacting the Editors
Every effort has been made to provide accurate information in this publication, but changes are inevitable. The publisher cannot be responsible for any resulting loss, inconvenience or injury. We would appreciate it if readers would call our attention to any errors or outdated information, please contact us at:
comments@berlitzpublishing.com

First printing: 2014

Berlitz Trademark Reg. U.S. Patent Office and other countries. Marca Registrada.
Used under license from Berlitz Investment Corporation

Senior Commissioning Editor: Kate Drynan
Design: Beverley Speight
Picture research: Beverley Speight
German Editor: Vincent Docherty
Cover photos: © APA Publications (UK) Ltd. & istockphotos
Interior photos: © All APA Publications (UK) Ltd. except istockphotos on p13,19,30,43,59,69,83,93,163,178,210,223,239.

Distribution

Worldwide
APA Publications GmbH & Co. Verlag KG
(Singapore branch)
7030 Ang Mo Kio Ave 5
08-65 Northstar @ AMK, Singapore 569880
Email: apasin@singnet.com.sg

UK and Ireland
Dorling Kindersley Ltd
(a Penguin Company)
80 Strand, London, WC2R ORL, UK
Email: sales@uk.dk.com

US
Ingram Publisher Services
One Ingram Blvd,
PO Box 3006
La Vergne, TN 37086-1986
Email: ips@ingramcontent.com

Australia
Woodslane
10 Apollo St
Warriewood, NSW 2102
Email: info@woodslane.com.au

Contents

Introduction

This course is designed for advanced beginner learners or for those who have already had some introduction to German. It is divided into sections so that you can easily build up your language skills at your own pace. By the end of the course, you should have a good understanding of the language. You will be able to speak, write and understand basic German and you will have the grammar and vocabulary foundations to help you to progress with ease.

How to Use this Book

Listen to the dialogue at the beginning of each lesson. You can follow along with the book which contains the dialogue in German and the English translation.

You can then move on to the grammar section. Here you will learn how to build sentences and what each component means and how to use it.

Next you will find the vocabulary section. When studying the vocabulary, it is useful to write the words down - this will help you to memorize them faster. Another tip is to try to create sentences that contain the word. This way you will remember the word, what it means, and how to use it. For more on the vocabulary section, see the Online Content section below.

Finally, you will come across the exercises. These are important to complete in order to progress as they allow you the opportunity to put into practice what you have learnt. Do not go on to the next section until you have successfully completed each one. You can refer back to the dialogue and the vocabulary sections to help you. You will be able to check your answers against the Answer Key at the end of the book on page 244.

Online Content

You will notice that each of the vocabulary sections has an audio symbol. You can download the audio version online from our website at **www.berlitzpublishing.com**. Each word is read once in English, and then in German. This will help you to memorize words and to build your vocabulary more quickly. It will also help you to work on your pronunciation.

The dialogues from the audio CD are also available for download in MP3 version, direct to your device at **www.berlitzpublishing.com**.

Pronunciation

This section is designed to make you familiar with the sounds of German using our simplified phonetic transcription. You'll find the pronunciation of the German letters and sounds explained in this section, together with their "imitated" equivalents. This system is used in the beginning of this course from Lesson 1 through to Lesson 4; simply read the pronunciation as if it were English, noting any special rules below.

1. Spelling

Use of capital letters

In German the following words are written with a capital letter:

— the first word in a sentence

Ich komme aus Japan.	I come from Japan.

— all nouns

Tee, Computer, Foto...	tea, computer, photo...

— nominalized verbs

das Lesen, das Schwimmen...	reading, swimming...

— nominalized adjectives

etwas Gutes,	something good,
das Schönste...	the most beautiful thing...

— pronouns (polite forms)

Sie, Ihnen, Ihr:

Wie heißen Sie?	What's your name?
Wie geht es Ihnen?	How are you?
Ist das Ihr Gepäck?	Is this your luggage?

Use of lower case letters

The following words are written with a lower case letter:

– verbs

heißen, trinken, kommen... to be called, to drink, to come...

– adjectives

groß, klein... large, small...

– pronouns

ich, du, er... mein, dein... I, you, he... my, your...

– conjunctions

und, oder, aber... and, or, but...

– adverbs

da, dort, bald... there, there, soon...

– prepositions

an, auf, unter, in... on, on, under, in...

ß and ss

ß is found

– after long vowels:

Straße, Spaß, grüßen... street, fun, greet...

ss is found

– after short vowels:

Kuss, muss, dass... kiss, must, that...

2. Pronunciation

Long vowels

- a doubled vowel is long:

  Tee, Zoo...   tea, zoo...

- a vowel followed by an **h** is long:

  Jahr, fahren, ihr...   year, to drive, her...

- a vowel is long when it is followed by a consonant and then by a vowel:

  fragen, hören, Rose...   ask, hear, rose...

- when an **e** follows an **i**, the **i** is long:

  Sie, wie, viel...   you, how, much...

Short vowels

- a vowel at the end of a word is short:

  Taxi, Katze, lese...   taxi, cat, read ...

- a vowel is usually short when two or more consonants follow:

  Ostern, morgens, Herbst...   Easter, in the morning, autumn...

Consonants

Specific characteristics

-ch:

After **i** and **e**, after **l**, **r**, **n** and with the ending **-ig**, **ch** is formed at the front of the mouth:

ich, sprechen...   I, to speak...

After **a**, **o** and **u**, **ch** is formed at the back of the mouth:

machen, noch, Buch, auch...   make, still, book, also...

st and sp

St- or **-sp-** at the beginning of a word or syllable is pronounced **sch**:

stehen, Gespräch...   to stand, conversation

Plurals

To indicate the plural of a noun, the following conventions are used:

– singular and plural are identical

Example:

Zimmer, das, – room   ***Zimmer*** rooms

– + letter add that letter to the end of the word

Example:

Rose, die, –n rose   ***Rosen*** roses

–¨ replace the **a, o,** or **u** closest to the end of the word with that letter's umlaut (**ä, ö, ü**)

Example:

Bruder, der, –¨ brother   ***Brüder*** brothers

Exception: an **au** construction becomes **äu**

Example:

Maus, die, –¨e mouse   ***Mäuse*** mice

–¨ + letter(s) replace the final **a, o,** or **u** with its umlaut, and add the letter(s) to the end of the word

Example:

Wort, das, –¨er word   ***Wörter*** words

1. Guten Tag!

Welcome to Germany. Be prepared to immerse yourself in the German language, starting with an overview of the basics. Listen to the audio, become accustomed to the rhythm of the language and just start speaking – don't forget to download the audio vocabulary online too.

GUTEN TAG! HELLO!

Herr Schmidt	**Guten Tag, Paul!**
	Hello, Paul.
Paul	**Guten Tag, Herr Schmidt! Wie geht es Ihnen?**
	Hello, Mr. Schmidt. How are you?
Herr Schmidt	**Danke, mir geht es gut. Und wie geht es Ihnen, Paul?**
	Thanks, I'm fine. And how are you, Paul?
Paul	**Sehr gut, danke.**
	Very well, thank you.
Herr Schmidt	**Eine Frage, Paul!**
	Can I ask you something, Paul?
Paul	**Ja?**
	Yes?
Herr Schmidt	**Was ist das? Ist das ein Kugelschreiber?**
	What's that? Is it a pen?
Paul	**Ja. Das ist ein Kugelschreiber.**
	Yes. It's a pen.
Herr Schmidt	**Und das? Ist dies ein Kugelschreiber oder ein Bleistift?**
	And this? Is this a pen or a pencil?

Paul	**Das ist ein Bleistift!**
	It's a pencil.
Herr Schmidt	**Ach so! Aber ist das auch ein Bleistift?**
	I see! But is that a pencil, too?
Paul	**Nein. Das ist kein Bleistift!**
	No. That's not a pencil!
Herr Schmidt	**Und was ist das?**
	What is it?
Paul	**Das ist ein Laserpointer!**
	It's a laser pointer!
Herr Schmidt	**Verstehe. Danke, Paul! Auf Wiedersehen!**
	Oh, I see. Thanks, Paul. Goodbye!
Paul	**Auf Wiedersehen, Herr Schmidt!**
	Bis demnächst!
	Goodbye, Mr. Schmidt. See you soon!

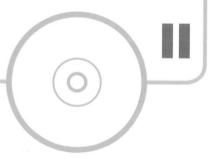

Grammatik/Grammar

1. FRAGEN UND ANTWORTEN

Was ist das?
What's that?

Das ist ein Kugelschreiber.
It's a pen.

Was ist das?

Das ist ein Buch.
It's a book.

Was ist das?

Das ist ein Schreibtisch.
It's a desk.

2. JA ODER NEIN?

Ist das ein Schreibtisch?
Is that a desk?

Ja.
Yes, it is.

Ja, das ist ein Schreibtisch.
Yes, it's a desk.

Ist das ein Kugelschreiber?
Is that a pen?

Ja, das ist ein Kugelschreiber.
Yes, it's a pen.

Ist das ein Kugelschreiber?
Is that a pen?

Nein.
No, it's not.

Nein, das ist kein Kugelschreiber.
No, it's not a pen.

3. DER, DIE ODER DAS?

There are three genders in German – *masculine, feminine* and *neuter* – and three words for **the** – **der**, **die**, and **das**. Nouns are used with **der** when they are *masculine*; they take **die** when they are *feminine*, and **das** when they are *neuter*.

Because the grammatical gender of a noun cannot always be worked out logically, it is best to learn the gender of the word *(masculine, feminine or neuter)* at the same time as you learn the word itself (not just **Buch** but **das Buch** *(neuter)*, not just **Schreibtisch**, but **der Schreibtisch** *(masculine)*, etc.).

All German nouns (**Buch**, **Schreibtisch**, etc.) begin with a capital letter.

Here are some words that take **die** *(feminine)*:

die Schachtel **die Frage** **die Antwort**
the box the question the answer

Ist das eine Schachtel?
Is this a box?

Nein, das ist keine Schachtel.
No, it's not a box.

Ist das ein Bleistift oder ein Kugelschreiber?
Is that a pencil *or* a pen?

Das, meaning **it** as in **was ist das?**, is used where something has not been introduced before. (**Es** also meaning **it** can be used where you have already talked about the object.)

Was ist das?
What's that?

Das ist ein Kugelschreiber.
It's a pen.

Wer ist das?
Who's that?

Das ist Herr Schmidt!
That's Mr. Schmidt.

4. EIN ODER EINE? / THE INDEFINITE ARTICLE

The indefinite article **a** or **an** is translated into German by:

ein when the noun is masculine or neuter; eine when the noun is feminine.

The negative forms **not a** and **not an** are expressed by one word in German: kein for masculine or neuter nouns, and keine for feminine nouns.

Both the indefinite (**a**) and definite (**the**) articles in German decline. This means that they change their endings depending on how the noun is used in the sentence. We will examine these changes, and the plural **the** (die), in later lessons.

Wortschatz/Vocabulary

der Wortschatz: *the vocabulary*
die Grammatik: *the grammar*
guten Tag: *hello*
guten Morgen: *hello/good morning*
guten Abend: *hello/good evening*
grüß Gott: *hello (in Southern Germany, Austria and Switzerland)*
auf Wiedersehen: *goodbye, bye*
bis demnächst: *see you soon*
der Herr: *the man, the gentleman*
Frau Schmidt: *Ms. Schmidt or Mrs. Schmidt*
Fräulein Schmidt *meaning Miss Schmidt is now obsolete in German. In cases where first names are not used, stick with* **Frau** *plus the woman's family name.*
die Frau: *the woman*

klein (or kleiner, kleine, kleines): *small/little*
groß (or großer, große, großes): *big/large*
das Gespräch: *the conversation*
ein Gespräch: *a conversation*
die Frage: *the question*
eine Frage: *a question*
die Antwort: *the answer*
eine Antwort: *an answer*
ja: *yes*
nein: *no*
danke: *thank you, thanks*
dies: *this*
das: *that, it*
wie geht's?: *how are things?*
gut: *good/well*

ach so: *I see*

verstehe: *I get it*

schlecht: *bad/badly*

sehr: *very*

sehr gut: *very well/very good*

sehr schlecht: *very bad/very badly*

wie geht es Ihnen?: *how are you?*

wie: *how*

Sie: *you (polite form)*

Ihnen: *you, to you*

der Schreibtisch: *the desk*

ein Schreibtisch: *a desk*

der Kugelschreiber: *the pen*

ein Kugelschreiber: *a pen*

das Buch: *the book*

ein Buch: *a book*

der Bleistift: *the pencil*

ein Bleistift: *a pencil*

der Laserpointer: *the laser pointer*

ein Laserpointer: *a laser pointer*

die Schachtel: *the box*

eine Schachtel: *a box*

der Stuhl: *the chair*

ein Stuhl: *a chair*

andere: *other (plural)*

das Wort: *the word*

ein Wort: *a word*

eine Lektion: *a lesson*

der Lehrer: *the teacher*

und: *and*

was?: *what?*

wer?: *who?*

oder: *or*

auch: *also*

bald: *soon*

demnächst: *soon, in the near future*

bis: *until*

die Übung: *exercise*

aus: *out of, from*

Übungen/Exercises

Exercise A

DER, DIE oder DAS?

1. .... der .... Stuhl   6. .... Bleistift

2. .... Frage   7. .... Buch

3. .... Schreibtisch   8. .... Herr

4. .... Gespräch   9. .... Antwort

5. .... Schachtel   10. .... Kugelschreiber

Exercise B

DAS IST oder DAS IST NICHT?

1. Ja, ... das ist .... Paul!

2. Nein, ... Ulrike!

3. Ja, ... Herr Schmidt!

4. Ja, ... der Lehrer!

5. Nein, ... Frau Schmidt!

Exercise C

WAS IST DAS?

1. A pen: .... ein Kugelschreiber ....

2. A box: ....

3. A gentleman: ....

4. A book: ....

5. An answer ....

2. Introductions

In this lesson you will continue with basic introductions. You will learn the essential verbs you need to form a solid foundation for speaking German and you will increase your knowledge and understanding of German grammar and vocabulary.

   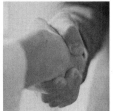

DARF ICH VORSTELLEN ... MAY I INTRODUCE ...

Herr Schmidt	**Guten Tag! Ich bin Thomas Schmidt. Und wer sind Sie?** Hello! I'm Thomas Schmidt. And who are you?
Frau Constanze	**Ich bin Ulrike Constanze. Ich bin Deutsche. Und Sie?** I'm Ulrike Constanze. I'm German. What about you?
Herr Schmidt	**Ich bin kein Deutscher. Ich bin kein Schweizer und auch kein Holländer!** I'm not a German. I'm not Swiss, nor am I a Dutchman.
Frau Constanze	**Was sind Sie denn?** What nationality are you then?
Herr Schmidt	**Ich bin Österreicher. Aber ich wohne in Berlin. Wo kommen Sie her?** I'm from Austria. But I live in Berlin. Where do you come from?
Frau Constanze	**Ich bin aus Hamburg. Jetzt arbeite ich hier in Berlin, in einer Bank. Es ist eine sehr große Bank. Wo arbeiten Sie?** I'm from Hamburg. I'm working here in Berlin at the moment, in a bank. It's a very large bank. Where do you work?
Herr Schmidt	**Ich arbeite in einer Schule. Ich bin Lehrer.** I work in a school. I'm a teacher.

Frau Constanze	Und wer ist dieser junge Mann?
	And who is this young man?
Herr Schmidt	Er heißt Paul. Er ist Engländer und lernt Deutsch. Paul! Paul, bitte kommen Sie her!
	His name is Paul. He's English and he's learning German. Paul! Paul, come over here, please.
Paul	Guten Tag, Herr Schmidt! Guten Tag!
	Hello, Mr. Schmidt! Hello.
Herr Schmidt	Frau Constanze, darf ich Ihnen Paul vorstellen? Paul, darf ich Ihnen Frau Constanze vorstellen?
	Ms. Constanze, I want you to meet Paul. Paul, I want you to meet Ms. Constanze.
Paul	Freut mich sehr!
	Pleased to meet you.
Frau Constanze	Freut mich sehr!
	Pleased to meet you.

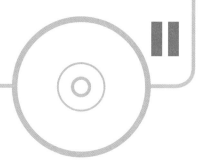

Grammatik/Grammar

1. ICH BIN/ICH BIN NICHT

When describing your profession, you do not use the indefinite article in German. So in the audio dialogue, Herr Schmidt says: **Ich bin Lehrer** and not **Ich bin ein Lehrer**.

Ich bin Thomas Schmidt.
I'm Thomas Schmidt.

Ich bin Ulrike Constanze.
I'm Ulrike Constanze.

The negative is formed in general by putting nicht after the verb of the sentence (as above). However, as stated in the last chapter, not a and not an are expressed by **kein** or **keine**, as in:
das ist ein Kugelschreiber – das ist kein Bleistift (it's a pen – it's not a pencil).

Ich bin nicht Paul.
I'm not Paul.

Ich bin nicht Frau Schmidt
I am not Mrs. Schmidt.

2. SIE SIND/SIE SIND NICHT

Sind Sie Thomas Schmidt?
Are you Thomas Schmidt?

Sind Sie Ulrike Constanze?
Are you Ulrike Constanze?

Questions based on the above examples are formed by inverting the personal subject pronoun (Sie = the polite form of **you** – written with a capital S) and the verb (sind). **Sind Sie?**

Sie sind Deutscher.   Sind Sie Deutscher?
You're German.   Are you German?

Another way to form the interrogative is by putting oder (**or**) after a statement. Some Germans use nicht wahr? – often shortened to just nicht? – after a statement. In Southern Germany the most common addition is gell? In all such cases the speaker generally assumes the answer to be positive.

Sie sind Amerikaner.   Sie sind Amerikaner, nicht?/Sie sind Amerikaner, oder?
You're an American.   You're (an) American, aren't you?

Other examples:

Sie sind Thomas Schmidt, nicht wahr?
You're Thomas Schmidt, aren't you?

Sie sind Paul, oder?
You're Paul, aren't you?

3. NATIONALITIES

Sie sind Kanadier, oder?
You're Canadian, aren't you?

Aha! Sie sind kein Kanadier.
Oh! You're not Canadian.

Sind Sie Amerikaner?
Are you American?

Nein? Also was sind Sie denn?
No? So what nationality are you then?

Ich bin Italiener.
I'm Italian.

In all the examples given so far, the nationality referred to has been **masculine**. The **feminine** form is generally the masculine word plus **-in** at the end. The definite article is **die**.

e.g.

der Amerikaner (masculine) the American (male)	**die Amerikanerin** (feminine) the American (female)
der Kanadier (masculine) the Canadian (male)	**die Kanadierin** (feminine) the Canadian (female)
Ich bin Spanier. I'm a Spaniard/I'm Spanish.	**Ich bin Spanierin.** I am a Spaniard/I'm Spanish.
Ich bin Engländer. I'm an Englishman/I'm English.	**Ich bin Engländerin.** I'm an English woman/ I'm English.
Ich bin Japaner. I'm Japanese.	**Ich bin Japanerin.** I'm Japanese.
Ich bin Deutscher. I'm German.	**Ich bin Deutsche.** I'm German.

The **female** form in the last example is an exception, as **Deutscher**/**Deutsche** derives from the adjective **deutsch** (see below).

The feminine forms of nouns describing people's professions are created in the same way. For example:

der Lehrer the teacher (male)	**die Lehrerin** the teacher (female)
der Arbeiter the worker (male)	**die Arbeiterin** the worker (female)

4. ER IST/ER IST NICHT/ER IST KEIN

er ist	**er ist nicht**	**er ist kein**
he is	he's not	he's not a/an

Herr Schmidt ist Österreicher.
Mr. Schmidt is Austrian.

Er ist Österreicher.
He's Austrian.

Er ist kein Japaner.
He's not Japanese.

Er ist kein Russe.
He's not Russian.

Er ist nicht Paul.
He's not Paul.

5. SIE IST/SIE IST NICHT/SIE IST KEINE

sie ist	sie ist nicht	sie ist keine
she is	she's not	she's not a/an

Ist Frau Constanze Russin?
Is Ms. Constanze Russian?

Nein, Sie ist keine Russin.
No, she's not Russian.

Frau Constanze ist Deutsche, oder?
Ms. Constanze is German, isn't she?

Sie ist nicht Frau Schmidt.
She's not Mrs. Schmidt.

Welche Staatsangehörigkeit hat sie?
What nationality is she?

Sie ist Deutsche.
She's German.

6. LANGUAGES

In many of the above examples, nouns have been used to describe nationality. The nouns that refer to languages in German are usually identical to the adjective used for things from that country. As these are nouns, they are always written with a capital letter.

Sie spricht Deutsch.
She speaks German.

Sprechen Sie Russisch?
Do you speak Russian?

Ich lerne Italienisch.
I'm learning Italian.

7. AGREEMENT OF ADJECTIVES

Adjectives in German have to **agree** with the noun that they refer to. This means that, when the adjective appears before the noun, it is modified in certain defined ways: it is *declined*. So, when the noun is the subject of the sentence, any accompanying adjective must reflect this. Adjectives in German are written in the lower case.

der amerikanische Junge   the American boy

When the noun is *masculine*, -**e** is added after the definite article (**the**) and -**er** is added to the adjective after the indefinite article (**a/an**) in the nominative case singular. This is the case used for the subject of a sentence.

ein amerikanisch**er** Junge   an American boy

definite article	indefinite article
der klein**e** Herr the small/short gentleman	ein klein**er** Herr a small/short gentleman
der groß**e** Junge the big boy	ein groß**er** Junge a big boy
der rund**e** Tisch the round table	ein rund**er** Tisch a round table

When the noun is *feminine*, -**e** is added on to the adjective after both the definite and the indefinite article in the nominative case singular:

definite article	indefinite article
die klug**e** Frau the intelligent woman	eine klug**e** Frau an intelligent woman
die kurz**e** Frage the quick question	eine kurz**e** Frage a quick question
die deutsch**e** Stadt the German town	eine deutsch**e** Stadt a German town

When the noun is *neuter*, -**e** is added on to the adjective after the definite article, and -**es** is added on after the indefinite article in the nominative case singular:

definite article	indefinite article
das interessant**e** Gespräch the interesting conversation	ein interessant**es** Gespräch an interesting conversation
das groß**e** Land the big country	ein groß**es** Land a big country
das klein**e** Kind the small child	ein klein**es** Kind a small child

8. VERBEN/VERBS

sein to be

ich bin	ich bin nicht	bin ich?
du bist	du bist nicht	bist du?
er/sie/es ist	er/sie/es ist nicht	ist er/sie/es?
wir sind	sie ist nicht	ist sie?
irh seid	seid ihr nicht	ihr seid?
Sie sind	Sie sind nicht	sind Sie?

Paul ist nicht groß.
Paul is not tall.

Ist er klug?
Is he intelligent?

kommen to come

ich komme	ich komme nicht	komme ich?
er kommt	er kommt nicht	kommt er?
sie kommt	sie kommt nicht	kommt sie?
es kommt	es kommt nicht	kommt es?
Sie kommen	Sie kommen nicht	kommen Sie?

Kommen Sie aus Berlin?
Do you come from Berlin?

Ulrike Constanze kommt aus Hamburg.
Ulrike Constanze comes from Hamburg.

From is usually **von** in German, but to say someone comes from a town, city or country, use **aus**.

arbeiten to work

ich arbeite	ich arbeite nicht	arbeite ich?
er arbeitet	er arbeitet nicht	arbeitet er?
sie arbeitet	sie arbeitet nicht	arbeitet sie?
es arbeitet	es arbeitet nicht	arbeitet es?
Sie arbeiten	Sie arbeiten nicht	arbeiten Sie?

Thomas arbeitet nicht in der Bank.
Thomas doesn't work in the bank.

Wo arbeitet er?
Where does he work?

lernen to learn

ich lerne	ich lerne nicht	lerne ich?
er lernt	er lernt nicht	lernt er?
sie lernt	sie lernt nicht	lernt sie?
es lernt	es lernt nicht	lernt es?
Sie lernen	Sie lernen nicht	lernen Sie?

Lernen Sie Italienisch oder Spanisch?
Are you learning Italian or Spanish?

Paul lernt Deutsch.
Paul is learning German.

sprechen to speak

ich spreche	ich spreche nicht	spreche ich?
er spricht	er spricht nicht	spricht er?
sie spricht	sie spricht nicht	spricht sie?
es spricht	es spricht nicht	spricht es?
Sie sprechen	Sie sprechen nicht	sprechen Sie?

Ich spreche Deutsch.
I speak German.

Sprechen Sie Russisch?
Do you speak Russian?

Wortschatz/Vocabulary

die Vorstellung: *the introduction*
die Vorstellungen: *the introductions*
wie: *how*
wo kommen Sie her?:
where do you come from?
auch: *also, too*
gut: *good*
die Staatsangehörigkeit: *the nationality*
der Amerikaner/die Amerikanerin:
the American man/the American woman
der Deutsche/die Deutsche: *the German man/the German woman*
der Franzose/die Französin: *the Frenchman/the French woman*
der Engländer/die Engländerin: *the Englishman/the English woman*
der Holländer/die Holländerin: *the Dutchman/the Dutch woman*
der Italiener/die Italienerin: *the Italian man/the Italian woman*
der Japaner/die Japanerin: *the Japanese man/the Japanese woman*
der Kanadier/die Kanadierin: *the Canadian man/the Canadian woman*
der Österreicher/die Österreicherin: *the Austrian man/the Austrian woman*
der Russe/die Russin: *the Russian man/the Russian woman*
der Schweizer/die Schweizerin: *the Swiss man/the Swiss woman*
der Spanier/die Spanierin: *the Spanish man/the Spanish woman*
deutsch: *German (adjective)*
Deutsch: *German (language)*
amerikanisch: *American (adjective)*

russisch: *Russian (adjective)*
Russisch: *Russian (language)*
japanisch: *Japanese (adjective)*
Japanisch: *Japanese (language)*
spanisch: *Spanish (adjective)*
Spanisch: *Spanish (language)*
österreichisch: *Austrian (adjective)*
er/sie/es hat: *he/she/it has*
der junge Mann: *the young man*
jung: *young*
die Schule: *the school*
in die Schule: *to school*
das Kind: *the child*
die Bank: *the bank*
wohnen: *to live (in a place)*
groß: *large, big*
klein: *small, little*
kurz: *short, brief, quick*
rund: *round*
das Beispiel: *the example*
Wien: *Vienna*
vorstellen: *to introduce*
darf ich Ihnen X vorstellen: *may I introduce X to you/I want you to meet X*
freut mich sehr: *pleased to meet you*
bitte: *please*
bitte kommen Sie her: *could you come over here, please?*
was heißt x auf Deutsch?: *what is x in German?*
er heißt Paul: *his name is Paul*
die Sprache: *the language*
nicht?: *is that not so?/isn't it?*
der Lehrer/die Lehrerin: *the teacher*
der Arbeiter/die Arbeiterin: *the worker*

der Tisch: *the table*	**lesen:** *to read*
klug: *intelligent*	**der Mann:** *the man*
die Stadt: *the town*	**also:** *so, therefore*
das Gespräch: *the conversation*	**denn:** *then; for (conjunction)*
das Land: *the country*	**hier:** *here*
das Auto: *the car*	**da:** *there*
sein: *to be*	**hier ist:** *here is*
kommen: *to come*	**hin:** *a word indicating a direction or movement*
arbeiten: *to work*	*away from the speaker*
noch yet: *still*	**her:** *a word indicating a direction or movement*
lernen: *to learn*	*towards the speaker*
(also means to study at school)	**woher:** *where from?*
die Übung: *the exercise*	**dieser/diese/dieses:** *this*
das Buch: *the book*	**jener/jene/jenes:** *that*
sprechen: *to speak*	

Übungen/Exercises

Exercise A

ANSWER THE FOLLOWING QUESTIONS

Sind Sie Lehrer?

Nein, ich bin kein Lehrer

1. **Kommen Sie aus Berlin?**

   ....

2. **Kommen Sie aus Wien?**

   ....

3. **Sind Sie Deutscher/Deutsche?**

   ....

4. Arbeiten Sie in Hamburg?

....

5. Lernen Sie Deutsch?

....

6. Sprechen Sie Spanisch?

....

Exercise B

INSERT THE CORRECT OPTION

Hier ist eine <u>kleine</u> Übung. (kleiner/kleine/kleines)

1. Carmen ist .... (Spanier/Spanierin)

2. Herr Giuseppe Rossini ist kein .... (Engländer/Engländerin)

3. Ist Frau Schmidt .... ? (Deutscher/Deutsche)

4. Sie lesen ein .... Buch. (deutscher/deutsche/deutsches)

5. Ist sie eine .... Frau? (kluger/kluge/kluges)

6. Berlin ist eine sehr .... Stadt. (großer/große/großes)

3. Getting Around

Lesson 3 introduces more verbs to aid your conversation skills. The dialogue focuses on travel and the vocabulary you need to talk about it. You will learn how to say things in the negative and you will get used to asking questions.

ULRIKE MACHT EINE REISE ULRIKE GOES ON A TRIP

Paul	**Ulrike, haben Sie Ihr Ticket?**
	Ulrike, do you have your plane ticket?
Ulrike	**Ja, Paul. Ich habe das Ticket in der Tasche.**
	Yes, Paul. I've got the ticket in my bag.
Paul	**Sie haben auch einen Koffer, oder?**
	You've got a a suitcase, too, haven't you?
Ulrike	**Ja, selbstverständlich! Ich reise immer mit einem großen Koffer.**
	Yes of course! I always travel with a big suitcase.
Paul	**Haben Sie einen Reisepass?**
	Do you have a passport?
Ulrike	**Nein, ich habe keinen Reisepass, nur einen Personalausweis.**
	No, I don't have a passport, only an identity card.
Paul	**Ach so! Und wohin fliegen Sie? Nach Frankfurt?**
	Ah, I see. And where are you flying to? To Frankfurt?
Ulrike	**Nein, ich fliege nicht nach Frankfurt. Ich fliege nach München.**
	No, I'm not flying to Frankfurt. I'm flying to Munich.
Paul	**Wollen Sie mit der U-Bahn zum Flughafen fahren?**
	Are you going to use the underground to get to the airport?

Ulrike	Nein, ich fahre mit dem Taxi.
	No, I'm going by cab.
Paul	Und wann reisen Sie? Heute?
	And when are you travelling? Today?
Ulrike	Nein, ich reise morgen Nachmittag.
	No, I'm travelling tomorrow afternoon.
Paul	Um wie viel Uhr?
	At what time?
Ulrike	Um zehn Uhr. Aber Sie wollen wirklich alles wissen, Paul!
	At ten a.m. You really do want to know everything, Paul, don't you!
Paul	Warum nicht? Sie kommen bald zurück, oder?
	Why not? You're coming back soon, aren't you?
Ulrike	Ja, ich bin in einer Woche zurück. Ich habe hier viel zu tun. Noch etwas?
	Yes. I'll be back in a week. I have a lot to do here. Anything else?
Paul	Ja. Gute Reise, Ulrike. Auf Wiedersehen!
	Yes. Have a good trip, Ulrike. Goodbye!
Ulrike	Auf Wiedersehen, Paul!
	Goodbye, Paul.

Grammatik/Grammar

1. THE ACCUSATIVE CASE

In the previous lesson, the nominative case was shown. Below are examples of the accusative case, which is used for the direct object in a sentence. These examples show the effect of the accusative case on **ein** and **eine**, **kein** and **keine**. It can be summarized as follows:

	masculine		feminine		neuter	
Nominative	ein	kein	eine	keine	ein	kein
Accusative	einen	keinen	eine	keine	ein	kein

Only the masculine accusative form is different from the nominative form.

2. ICH HABE/ICH HABE KEINEN, KEINE, KEIN

Ich <u>habe einen</u> Koffer.
I have a suitcase.

Ich <u>habe keinen</u> Koffer.
I don't have a suitcase.

Ich <u>habe keine</u> Tasche.
I don't have a bag.

Ich <u>habe kein</u> Smartphone.
I don't have a smartphone.

3. SIE HABEN / SIE HABEN KEINEN, KEINE, KEIN

<u>Haben</u> Sie <u>einen</u> Reisepass?
Do you have a passport?

<u>Haben</u> Sie <u>eine</u> Tasche?
Do you have a bag?

Sie <u>haben kein</u> Buch.
You don't have a book.

Notice that German speakers often use the definite (**der, die, das**) and indefinite articles (**ein, eine, ein**) to mean **my, etc.**

Was <u>haben</u> Sie <u>in der</u> Tasche?
What do you have in your bag?

Ich <u>habe ein</u> Ticket.
I have a plane ticket.

4. ER HAT / ER HAT KEINEN, KEINE, KEIN

Herr Schmidt <u>hat einen</u> Schlüssel.
Mr. Schmidt has a key.

Er <u>hat keine</u> Tasche.
He doesn't have a bag.

Er <u>hat kein</u> Buch.
He doesn't have a book.

5. SIE HAT / SIE HAT KEINEN, KEINE, KEIN

Hat Ulrike einen Reisepass?
Does Ulrike have a passport?

Hat sie eine Tasche?
Does she have a bag?

Ja, sie hat eine Tasche.
Yes, she has a bag.

Sie hat kein Buch.
She doesn't have a book.

6. ES HAT / ES HAT KEINEN, KEINE, KEIN

Das Kind hat keinen Koffer.
The child doesn't have a suitcase.

Es hat keinen Koffer.
He/She does not have a suitcase.

Note that Kind is neuter in German, regardless of whther the child is male or female.

Es hat eine Tasche.
He/She has a bag.

Es hat kein Smartphone.
He/She doesn't have a smartphone.

7. DER, DIE AND DAS IN THE ACCUSATIVE

	masculine	feminine	neuter
Nominative	der	die	das
Accusative	den	die	das

Like ein, eine, kein and keine, der, die and das are used in the accusative. The table above shows that the only change is in masculine nouns.

8. WELCHER, DIESER, JENER/**WHICH, THIS, THAT**

As we have seen, **der** (**the**) indicates a masculine noun. **Welcher** (**which**), **dieser** (**this**) and **jener** (**that**) are also used for masculine words.

der Mantel	welcher Mantel?	dieser Mantel
at	which coat?	this coat
der Schlüssel	welcher Schlüssel?	jener Schlüssel
the key	which key?	that key

Other examples of the masculine:

Dies ist ein Koffer. Er ist ein großer Koffer.
This is a suitcase. It's a big suitcase.

Hier ist der Schreibtisch. Er ist ein sehr großer Schreibtisch.
Here is the desk. It's a very big desk.

die indicates a feminine noun, as do **welche**, **diese** and **jene**:

die Tasche	welche Tasche?	jene Tasche
the bag	which bag?	that bag
eine Frage	welche Frage?	diese Frage
a question	which question?	this question

Other examples of the feminine:

Die junge Frau heißt Ulrike. Sie heißt Ulrike.
The young lady is called Ulrike. She's called Ulrike./Her name is Ulrike.

Wo ist die kleine Schachtel? Die kleine Schachtel ist hier.
Where's the little box? The little box is here.

das, **welches**, **dieses** and **jenes** indicate a neuter noun:

das Buch	welches Buch? dieses Buch
the book	which book? this book
das Land	welches Land? jenes Land
the country	which country? that country

Other examples of the neuter:

Das Kind ist sehr klug. Es ist ein kluges Kind.
The child is very intelligent. He's/She's a very intelligent child.

Das Haus ist neu. Es ist ein neues Haus.
The house is new. It is a new house.

Dies und jenes for **this** and **that**, approximate the English meanings, though **dies** sometimes refers to something further away and would be **that** in English. The Germans also say **dies und das** for **this and that**.

9. VERBEN/ VERBS

---

haben to have

ich habe	ich habe nicht	habe ich …?
er hat	er hat nicht	hat er …?
sie hat	sie hat nicht	hat sie …?
es hat	es hat nicht	hat es …?
Sie haben	Sie haben nicht	haben Sie …?

Ich habe kein Buch.
I don't have a book/I have no book.

Hat sie eine Tasche?
Does she have a bag?

Ich habe es nicht.
I don't have it.

Sie hat keine Tasche.
She doesn't have a bag.

---

reisen to travel (go on a journey)

ich reise	ich reise nicht	reise ich …?
er reist	er reist nicht	reist er …?
sie reist	sie reist nicht	reist sie …?
es reist	es reist nicht	reist es …?
Sie reisen	Sie reisen nicht	reisen Sie …?

Just like **arbeiten** and **lernen** in the previous lesson, **reisen** is a **regular weak verb** (a verb whose stem – the part without the -en – remains unchanged whatever verb endings are added).

Ulrike reist immer mit einem großen Koffer.
Ulrike always travels with a big suitcase.

Notice the preposition **mit**, meaning **with**, changes the ending of the article (not **ein** or **einen**, but **einem**). We will explain this later.

---

fahren to go, to drive, to travel (in a vehicle)

ich fahre	ich fahre nicht	fahre ich …?
er fährt	er fährt nicht	fährt er …?
sie fährt	sie fährt nicht	fährt sie …?
es fährt	es fährt nicht	fährt es …?
Sie fahren	Sie fahren nicht	fahren Sie …?

Fahren is an **irregular strong verb** (a verb whose stem vowel sometimes changes).

Ich fahre mit dem Bus.
I'm going by bus.

Ulrike fährt Paul nach Hause.
Ulrike drives Paul home.

---

gehen to go

ich gehe	ich gehe nicht	gehe ich …?
er geht	er geht nicht	geht er …?
sie geht	sie geht nicht	geht sie …?
es geht	es geht nicht	geht es …?
Sie gehen	Sie gehen nicht	gehen Sie …?

The verb **gehen** is used to mean **to go** (as the opposite of **to come**):

Sie gehen in die Stadt.
They're going into town.

Ich gehe in die Arbeit.
I'm going to work.

Note that Germans often use other verbs to mean **go** which also express the means used **to go**, e.g. to go by plane = to fly = **fliegen**.
to go by car = to drive = **fahren**.

Wie geht es Ihnen? (How are you? – see **Lesson 1**) is an idiomatic expression that uses the verb **gehen** in a figurative way. Here are some more examples of the figurative use of gehen:

Das Geschäft geht gut.
The business is going well.

Mir geht es gut.
I'm fine.

gehen is an important verb in German and we will be introducing other examples of its use in later lessons.

10. THE DATIVE CASE

zu	von	mit	in	an
to	from	with	in	at

Ulrike fährt mit dem Taxi.
Ulrike is going by cab.

Sie arbeitet in einer Bank.
She works in a bank.

Herr Schmidt arbeitet am Schreibtisch.
Mr. Schmidt is working at his desk.

Paul geht zur Schule.
Paul goes to school.

Ulrike reist mit einem großen Koffer.
Ulrike travels with a big suitcase.

Herr Schmidt kommt vom Flughafen.
Mr. Schmidt is coming from the airport.

Ulrike fährt zum Flughafen.
Ulrike drives to the airport.

You will notice in the above examples as well as the dialogue, that the prepositions **zu** (**to**), **von** (**from**), **an** (**at** or **on**), **mit** (**with**), **in** (**in**) used here make both the definite and indefinite articles change from the nominative and accusative forms you saw earlier, to another form, which is known as the *dative* case. There is no English equivalent of this case.

With masculine nouns, the definite article **der** becomes **dem**:

der Mantel	mit dem Mantel	(with the coat)
der Lehrer	von dem Lehrer	(from the teacher)
	or: vom Lehrer	(where von and dem become vom)
der Flughafen	zu dem Flughafen	(to the airport)
	or: zum Flughafen	(where zu and dem become zum)
der Schreibtisch	an dem Schreibtisch	(at the desk)
	or: am Schreibtisch	(where an and dem become am)
der Koffer	in dem Koffer	(in the suitcase)
	or: im Koffer	(where in and dem become im)

The masculine indefinite article **ein** becomes **einem**:

ein Mantel	mit einem Mantel	(with a coat)
ein Lehrer	von einem Lehrer	(from a teacher)
ein Flughafen	zu einem Flughafen	(to an airport)
ein Schreibtisch	an einem Schreibtisch	(at a desk)
ein Koffer	in einem Koffer	(in a suitcase)

With feminine nouns, the definite article **die** becomes **der**:

die Frau	mit der Frau	(with the woman)
die Stadt	von der Stadt	(from the town)
die Schule	zur Schule	(to the school)
		(**zu** and **der** become **zur**)
die Wand	an der Wand	(on the wall)
die Tasche	in der Tasche	(in the bag)

The feminine indefinite article **eine** becomes **einer**:

eine Frau	mit einer Frau	(with a woman)
eine Stadt	von einer Stadt	(from a town)
eine Schule	zu einer Schule	(to a school)
eine Wand	an einer Wand	(on a wall)
eine Tasche	in einer Tasche	(in a bag)
die Tasche	in der Tasche	(in the bag)

With neuter nouns, the definite article **das** becomes **dem**:

das Taxi	mit dem Taxi	(by taxi)
das Büro	von dem Büro	(from the office)
	or: vom Büro	(**von** and **dem** become **vom**)
das Haus	zu dem Haus	(to the house)
	or: zum Haus	(**zu** and **dem** become **zum**)
das Ende	an dem Ende	(at the end)
	or: am Ende	(**an** and **dem** become **am**)
das Buch	in dem Buch	(in the book)
	or: im Buch	(**in** and **dem** become **im**)
die Tasche	in der Tasche	(in the bag)

Note: **zum Beispiel** = for example

The neuter indefinite article **ein** becomes **einem**:

ein Taxi	mit einem Taxi	(by taxi)
ein Büro	von einem Büro	(from an office)
ein Haus	zu einem Haus	(to a house)
ein Ende	an einem Ende	(at an end)
ein Buch	in einem Buch	(in a book)

Note: **zu Hause** = at home

1. Adjectives used in the dative case generally take an **-en** at the end.
   e.g. **in dem neuen Koffer:** in the new suitcase
   von der großen Stadt: from the big town
   in einer kleinen neuen Schachtel: in a small new box

2. The prepositions **mit, von** and **zu** are **always** used with the dative. **An** and **in** are sometimes used with the dative to denote a state or fixed location, and with the accusative where a movement is implied.
   e.g. in die Küche: into the kitchen
   an die Wand: onto the wall

   See Lesson 4 for more examples.

3. **Dieser, diese, dieses** (**this**) become **diesem, dieser** and **diesem** in the dative and the same endings are used for **jener** and **welcher**.

Wortschatz/Vocabulary

die Reise: *the trip*
machen: *to make, to do*
eine Reise machen: *to go on a trip*
das Ticket: *the plane ticket*
das Flugzeug: *the plane*
die Tasche: *the bag; the pocket*
der Koffer: *the suitcase*
der Mantel: *the coat*
der Rock: *the skirt*
selbstverständlich: *of course, naturally*
der Reisepass: *the passport*
der Personalausweis: *the identity card*
ach so!: *Ah, O.K.! Oh, I see!*
fliegen: *to fly, to go by plane*
wollen: *to want (to)*
wollen Sie …?: *do you want to/do you intend to …?*
sie will: *she wants to*
die U-Bahn: *the underground, the subway*
das Taxi: *the taxi, the cab*
der Flughafen: *the airport*
heute: *today*
fahren: *to drive, to go (in a vehicle)*
wann: *when*
morgen: *tomorrow*
der Morgen: *the morning*
am Morgen: *in the morning*
der Nachmittag: *the afternoon*
am Nachmittag: *in the afternoon*
morgen Nachmittag: *tomorrow afternoon*
die Uhr: *the time; the clock*
um wie viel Uhr?: *at what time?*
wie viel Uhr ist es?: *what time is it?*
um zehn Uhr: *at ten o'clock*
München: *Munich*

wirklich: *really*
die Woche: *the week*
in einer Woche: *in a week*
zurück: *back*
ich habe viel zu tun: *I have a lot (of work) to do*
gute Reise!: *have a good trip!*
das Haus: *the house*
zu Hause: *at home*
haben: *to have*
dies: *this*
jenes: *that*
das Geschäft: *the business*
die Präposition: *the preposition*
zu: *to (with dative)*
mit: *with (with dative)*
in: *in (with dative); into (with accusative); to (with accusative)*
von: *from (with dative)*
an: *on, at (with dative); onto (with accusative)*
die Stadt: *the town*
die Arbeit: *the work*
die Wand: *the wall*
das Büro: *the office*
das Ende: *the end*
die Küche: *the kitchen*
das Buch: *the book*
das Smartphone: *the smartphone*
der Schlüssel: *the key*
sagen: *to say*
viel: *a lot, much*
viel Arbeit: *a lot of work*
viele Bücher: *a lot of books*
wie: *how*
noch: *still etwas: something*

noch etwas?: *anything else?*
warum?: *why?*
warum nicht?: *why not?*
wohin?: *where to?*

Übungen/Exercises

Exercise A

BITTE ANTWORTEN SIE!

Listen to the dialogue at the beginning of Lesson 3 and answer these questions.

Macht Ulrike eine Reise?

Ja, sie macht eine Reise.

1. **Wohin fliegt sie?**

   ....

2. **Will sie in einer Woche reisen?**

   ....

3. **Wann reist sie?**

   ....

4. **Um wie viel Uhr fliegt sie?**

   ....

5. **Hat sie einen Reisepass oder einen Personalausweis?**

   ....

6. **Hat sie einen Koffer?**

   ....

7. Hat sie einen kleinen Koffer?

....

8. Will Paul mit Ulrike fliegen?

....

9. Hat Ulrike ein Ticket?

....

10. Ist das Ticket im Koffer oder in der Tasche?

....

11. Will Ulrike mit der U-Bahn zum Flughafen fahren?

....

12. Wie fährt sie?

....

13. Wann kommt sie aus München zurück?

....

14. Was sagt Paul?

....

4. Conversations

This lesson focuses on conversation skills and phone calls in particular. It's often harder to converse by phone than to speak to someone face-to-face as you cannot use gestures to help yourself be understood. Take the time to listen to the audio and practice repeating it out loud.

AM TELEFON ON THE TELEPHONE

Clara Schmidt sitzt zu Hause und telefoniert mit einer Bekannten, Heidi Oster.
Clara Schmidt is sitting at home and talking on the phone to Heidi Oster, a lady she knows.

Frau Schmidt	**Frau Oster? Guten Abend! Wie geht es Ihnen? ... Danke, mir geht es gut. Ich bin zu Hause ... Ja, morgen gehen wir ins Theater ... Ja, morgen, am Freitag.**
	Mrs. Oster? Good evening! How are you? .... I'm fine, thanks. I'm at home. Yes, we're going to the theater tomorrow ... Yes, tomorrow, on Friday.
Frau Oster	**Freitag? Aber heute ist nicht Donnerstag. Heute ist schon Freitag!**
	Friday? But today isn't Thursday. Today's Friday already.
Frau Schmidt	**Wie, bitte? Heute ist schon Freitag? Ist das möglich? Ja, Sie haben recht.**
	Pardon? Today's Friday already? Is that possible? Yes, you're right.
Frau Oster	**Gehen Sie alleine ins Theater?**
	Are you going to the theater on your own?
Frau Schmidt	**Nein, mein Mann und ich sind mit einigen Bekannten**

	verabredet. Es sind einige Kollegen aus dem Büro. Das sind sehr nette Leute.
	No, my husband and I have arranged to meet some acquaintances. Some colleagues from the office. They're very nice people.
Frau Oster	Wie schön! Und wohin gehen Sie?
	How nice! And where are you going to?
Frau Schmidt	Wir gehen ins Schiller – Theater. Anschließend essen wir in einem Restaurant am Ku'damm. Aber sagen Sie mal – wie viel Uhr ist es jetzt?
	We're going to the Schiller-Theater. After that we are having a meal in a restaurant on the Ku'damm (a famous street in Berlin). But, tell me, what time is it now?
Frau Oster	Es ist achtzehn Uhr. Sie müssen aber bald los.
	It's six o'clock. You'll have to be going soon.
Frau Schmidt	Was! Schon achtzehn Uhr? Um halb sieben kommen sie ja! Also, auf Wiederhören, Frau Oster!
	What! Six o'clock already? They're coming at half past six. So, goodbye, Mrs. Oster!
Frau Oster	Auf Wiederhören, Frau Schmidt! Viel Vergnügen!
	Goodbye, Mrs. Schmidt! Enjoy yourselves!

Grammatik/Grammar

1. TIPPS/TIPS

The word **friend** can be translated as **der Freund** if the friend is male, **die Freundin** if the friend is female.

However, where the person is more of an acquaintance, the word **der Bekannte** or **die Bekannte** is used. **Bekannte** is treated as an adjective for the purposes of grammar.

Auf Wiederhören (literally, "until we hear one another again") is used to say goodbye only on the phone.

2. DIE MEHRZAHL/THE PLURAL

There are a number of ways of forming the plural of German nouns. Only feminine nouns are fairly predictable, so try to learn the plural of each new word together with its gender and singular form.

In the dative case the plural always ends in an -n, so if the plural ending does not finish in -n, one is added.

The plural ending of each noun will appear after the noun in the vocabulary at the end of this book.

There are several possibilities to express indefinite amounts in the plural. The main ones are:

einige	mehrere	viele
some, a few	several	many, a lot of, lots of
alle	manche	sämtliche
all	some	all (of the)

einige Bücher
some books

mehrere Blumen
several flowers.

manche Männer
some men

If there is an adjective between alle, sämtliche, manche, and the noun, an -en is added on. However, where the plural of the noun is used without any article, the adjective is treated as though it were a definite article. We will study this in more detail later.

ein nettes Geschenk	alle netten Geschenke	nette Geschenke
a nice present	all the nice presents	nice presents
eine gute Idee	sämtliche guten Ideen	gute Ideen
a good idea	all of the good ideas	good ideas

However, adjectives coming after einige, mehrere and viele behave as though these words were not there.

ein neuer Mantel	mehrere neue Mäntel	neue Mäntel
a new coat	several new coats	new coats
eine große Stadt	einige große Städte	große Städte
a big town	some big towns	big towns

Just like in English, nouns can stand on their own in the plural:

Haben Sie Kinder?	Do you have (any) children?
Wie sind Freunde.	We're friends

3. VERBEN/ VERBS

haben to have

ich habe	ich habe nicht	habe ich … ?
er/sie/es hat	er/sie/es hat nicht	hat er/sie/es … ?
Sie haben (you, singular)	Sie haben nicht	haben Sie …?
wir haben	wir haben nicht	haben wir … ?
Sie haben (you, plural)	Sie haben nicht	haben Sie … ?
sie haben	sie haben nicht	haben sie … ?

Ich means **I** and **wir** is the German for **we**.

Notice that the polite form **Sie** (**you**) with a capital **S** can be used for addressing more than one person. The context will tell you whether **Sie** is meant in the singular or the plural.

However, **sie**, with a small "**s**" means **she** in the singular and **they** in the plural.

Haben Sie Tische
Do you have any tables?

Wir haben mehrere gute Freunde.
We have several good friends.

Note:	**Sie haben recht.**	**Sie hat recht.**
	You're right.	She's right.

geben to give

ich gebe	ich gebe nicht	gebe ich …?
er/sie/es gibt	er/sie/es gibt nicht	gibt er/sie/es …?
Sie geben (you, singular)	Sie geben nicht	geben Sie …?
wir geben	wir geben nicht	geben wir …?
Sie geben (you, plural)	Sie geben nicht	geben Sie …?
sie geben	sie geben nicht	geben sie … ?

Examples:

Sie gibt dem Freund einen Kugelschreiber.
She gives her friend a pen.

Note: in German, the phrase with the dative (**dem Freund**) usually comes before the phrase with the accusative (**einen Kugelschreiber**).

Geben Sie heute eine Party?
Are you giving a party today?

4. THERE IS/THERE ARE

es gibt
there is/there are

This is a very common use of the verb **geben**, and differs from the English usage in that it can mean both **there is** and **there are**.

Note: the article of the noun following **es gibt** must be in the accusative.

There are other ways of saying **there is** and **there are**. These will be covered later in the book.

Examples:

Es gibt viel zu tun.
There's a lot to do.

Es gibt noch Kaffee.
There's still some coffee left.

Gibt es hier ein Telefon?
Is there a phone here?

And the idiomatic:

Das gibt es nicht!
I don't believe it!

5. DIE MEHRZAHL/THE PLURAL (CONTINUED)

The definite article in the nominative case plural is always **die**:

Here are some examples:

der Kugelschreiber	**die Kugelschreiber** (the pens)
die Tasche	**die Taschen** (the bags)
das Land	**die Länder** (the countries)

Im Koffer ist ein Mantel.	**Im Koffer sind zwei Mäntel.**
There's a coat in the suitcase.	There are two coats in the suitcase.

6. MORE PREPOSITIONS – THROUGH, AROUND, WITHOUT, INTO, FOR

The examples in the previous lesson showed prepositions which take the dative case, as well as some which sometimes take the dative when describing a state, but take the accusative when describing motion.

Now we will look at some more prepositions which take the accusative, as well as those two from the last lesson.

Der Lehrer kommt ins Zimmer.
The teacher comes into the room.

Ulrike reist ohne Reisepass.
Ulrike travels without her passport.

Paul geht durch das Tor.
Paul goes through the gate.

Herr Schmidt arbeitet rund um die Uhr.
Mr Schmidt works around the clock.

Ich habe einen Brief für den Lehrer.
I have a letter for the teacher.

Sie geht ans Fenster.
She goes to the window.

Note that **in**, **an** and **durch** followed by **das** can be shortened to **ins**, **ans**, **durchs**.

Durch, **ohne** and **um** always take the accusative; **in** and **an** also take the dative when no motion is implied.

7. THE GENITIVE

The genitive is used in German to express the meaning **of** or **belonging to**.

When the genitive is used with proper names only, an **-s** is added.

Examples:

Ulrikes Tasche
Ulrike's bag

Pauls Buch
Paul's book

The masculine and neuter definite article in the genitive changes to **des**.

An **-s** or **-es** is added to most nouns.

The feminine definite article in the genitive changes to **der**, as does the plural and nothing is added to the noun. The indefinite articles follow the same pattern.

Examples:

masculine

die Preis des Mantels
the price of the overcoat

die Preis eines Mantels
the price of an overcoat

feminine

der Preis der Tasche
the price of the bag

der Preis einer Tasche
the price of a bag

neuter

der Preis des Buchs
the price of the books

der Preis der Bücher
the price of the books

plural

der Preis der Koffer
the price of the cases

The ending of adjectives with a definite or indefinite article in the genitive is always -**en**.

For example:

masculine

des großen Schreibtisches
of the big desk

feminine

der teuren Tasche
of the expensive bag

neuter

des interessanten Buches
of the interesting book

plural

der kleinen Städte
of the small towns

The meaning **of** can also be expressed with the preposition **von** and the dative.

Von also means **from**.

der Hund von meinem Freund   my friend's dog

Study the system of genders and case endings carefully. They are essential for you to be able to make sense of a German sentence or phrase.

8. NUMBERS

1	2	3	4	5
eins	zwei	drei	vier	fünf
one	two	three	four	five

6	7	8	9	10
sechs	sieben	acht	neun	zehn
six	seven	eight	nine	ten

In dieser Schachtel sind sieben Kugelschreiber.
There are seven pens in this box.

Sind wir jetzt auf Seite vier? Nein.
Are we now on page four? No.

20	25
zwanzig	fünfundzwanzig
twenty	twenty five

Note that for numbers from **21** to **99**, follow the system used for 25 above, i.e. five and twenty.

Ulrike hat einundzwanzig Euro in der Tasche.
Ulrike has twenty one euros in her bag.

9. WIE VIEL UHR IST ES? / WHAT TIME IS IT?

Es ist zwei Uhr.
It's two o'clock/it's two.

Es ist fünf Minuten nach zwei.
It's five minutes past two/five past two.

Es ist zehn Minuten nach zwei.
It's ten minutes past two/ten past two.

Es ist Viertel nach zwei.
It's quarter past two.

Es ist zwanzig Minuten nach zwei.
It's twenty past two.

Es ist fünfundzwanzig Minuten nach zwei/Es ist fünf vor halb drei.
It's twenty five past two.

Es ist halb drei.
It's half past two.

Es ist fünf Minuten vor drei.
It's five minutes to three.

Es ist zehn Minuten vor drei.
It's ten minutes to three.

Es ist Viertel vor drei.
It's quarter to three.

Es ist zwanzig Minuten vor drei.
It's twenty minutes to three.

Es ist fünfundzwanzig Minuten vor drei./Es ist fünf nach halb drei.
It's twenty-five to three.

Es ist drei Uhr.
It's three o'clock.

There are several ways of expressing what time of day it is in German:

morgens is used for **in the morning** (before work starts, e.g. before 9.00 a.m.).

vormittags is used for the period before lunch (usually before 1.00 p.m.).

mittags is used for the period between 1.00 p.m. and 3.00 p.m.

nachmittags means **in the afternoon** or **p.m.** as in English.

abends means **in the evening** or **p.m.** as in English.

nachts means **at night**.

So

sieben Uhr morgens = 7:00 a.m.
elf Uhr vormittags = 11:00 a.m.

halb vier Uhr nachmittags = 3:30 p.m.
Viertel vor acht abends = 7:45 p.m.

To say **at one o'clock** etc. place **um** before the time:

Um fünf nach halb zehn (vormittags).
At twenty-five to ten in the morning.

Nachmittags um zwanzig vor vier.
At twenty minutes to four in the afternoon.

Note:

Das ist eine Uhr.
That's a clock.

Es ist ein Uhr.
It's one o'clock

10. VERBEN/VERBS

---

sein to be

ich bin	ich bin nicht	bin ich … ?
er/sie/es ist	er/sie/es ist nicht	ist er/sie/es … ?
Sie sind (you polite singular)	Sie sind nicht	sind Sie … ?
wir sind	wir sind nicht	sind wir… ?
Sie sind (you polite plural)	Sie sind nicht	sind Sie … ?
sie sind	sie sind nicht	sind sie … ?

Wir sind nicht müde.
We aren't tired.

Sind wir schon in Frankfurt?
Are we in Frankfurt already?

11. DIES IST/DIES SIND/DAS IST/DAS SIND/THIS IS/ THESE ARE/ THAT IS/ THOSE ARE

---

dies ist	dies sind
this is	these are
das ist	das sind
that is	those are

Das ist ein hübsches Haus.
That's a pretty house.

Das sind hübsche Häuser.
Those are pretty houses.

Dies ist Pauls Koffer.
This is Paul's suitcase.

Das sind Pauls Koffer.
Those are Paul's suitcases.

12. DIES IST NICHT/THIS IS NOT

dies ist nicht	dies sind nicht
this is not	these are not
das ist nicht	das sind nicht
that is not	those are not

Das ist nicht Ulrikes Rock.
That is not Ulrike's skirt.

Das sind nicht Ulrikes Röcke.
Those are not Ulrike's skirts.

Dies ist keine neue Tasche.
This isn't a new bag.

Dies sind keine neuen Taschen.
These are not new bags.

Sind dies die Büroschlüssel?
Are these the office keys?

Nein, das sind nicht die Büroschlüssel.
No, those are not the office keys.

13. ADJECTIVES WITH NOUNS – A SUMMARY

If the adjective appears in another part of the sentence from the noun (e.g. after the verb), then it does not change.

If one or more adjectives are placed immediately between a noun and its **indefinite** article, then -er is added on in the masculine nominative; -e is added in the feminine nominative and accusative; -es is added in the neuter nominative and accusative.

Otherwise an -en is added in both singular and plural.

If one or more adjectives are placed before a noun **without either a definite or an indefinite article**, are declined as if there were an indefinite article before them. The same applies to adjectives after einige, mehrere and viele.

If one or more adjectives are placed between a noun and its **definite** article, then -e is added in the masculine, feminine and neuter nominative, and the feminine and neuter accusative. Otherwise, -en is added in both the singular and the plural.

Dieser/diese/dieses, jener/jene/jenes and welcher/welche/welches, as well as alle, manche, and sämtliche are treated as if they were definite articles.

Examples:

Der Koffer ist groß.
The suitcase is big.

Das ist ein großer Koffer.
That's a big suitcase.

Er hat einen großen Koffer.
He has a big suitcase.

Die Stadt ist klein.
The town is small.

Die Bücher sind alt.
The books are old.

Es sind alte Bücher.
They are old books.

Sie hat viele alte Bücher.
She has lots of old books.

14. VERBEN/VERBS

gehen to go

ich gehe	ich gehe nicht	gehe ich …?
Sie gehen (you, singular)	Sie gehen nicht	gehen Sie …?
er/sie/es geht	er/sie/es geht nicht	geht er/sie/es …?
wir gehen	wir gehen nicht	gehen wir …?
Sie gehen (you, plural)	Sie gehen nicht	gehen Sie …?
sie gehen	sie gehen nicht	gehen sie …?

Wohin gehen Sie?
Where are you going?

Wir gehen nach Hause.
We're going home.

Note:

Die Uhr geht nicht.
The clock is not working.

kommen to come

ich komme	ich komme nicht	komme ich …?
Sie kommen (you, singular)	Sie kommen nicht	kommen Sie …?
er/sie/es kommt	er/sie/es kommt nicht	kommt er/sie/es …?
wir kommen	wir kommen nicht	kommen wir …?
Sie kommen (you, plural)	Sie kommen nicht	kommen Sie …?
sie kommen	sie kommen nicht	kommen sie …?

Kommen Sie mit?
Are you coming with me/us?

Claras Bekannte kommen um halb sieben.
Clara's friends are coming at half past six.

Wortschatz/Vocabulary

das Telefon: *the telephone*

am Telefon: *on the phone*

ans Telefon gehen: *to go and answer the phone*

telefonieren: *to telephone, to be on the phone with*

das Haus: *the house*

zu Hause: *at home*

nach Hause gehen: *to go home*

das Theater: *the theater*

ins Theater gehen: *to go to the theater*

der Bekannte: *the (male) acquaintance, someone you know*

die Bekannte: *the (female) acquaintance, someone you know*

heute: *today*

gestern: *yesterday*

morgen: *tomorrow*

der Abend: *the evening*

heute Abend: *this evening*

einige: *some*

der Tag: *the day*

(der) Donnerstag: *Thursday*

(der) Freitag: *Friday*

das kann nicht sein!: *it can't be!*

möglich: *possible*

schon: *already*

Sie haben recht: *you're right*

der Freund: *the friend (male); the boyfriend*

die Freundin: *the friend (female); the girlfriend*

das heißt: *that is to say/that means*

mit (+ *dative*) **x verabredet sein:** *to have arranged to meet x*

der Kollege: *the colleague, coworker (male)*

die Kollegin: *the colleague, coworker (female)*

nett: *nice*

die Leute (*plural*)**:** *people*

schön: *beautiful, nice*

wo gehen sie hin?: *where are they going to?*

wie: *how*

zuerst: *first of all*

anschließend: *after that*

das Restaurant: *the restaurant*

auf Wiederhören!: *goodbye (used on the phone)*

das Vergnügen: *pleasure, enjoyment*

viel Vergnügen!: *enjoy yourself/yourselves*

die Aussprache: *the pronunciation*

Sie müssen aber bald los!: *you'll have to be going soon*

es gibt: *there is/there are* (+ *accusative*)

die Mehrzahl: *the plural*

die Zahl: *the number*

einige: *some, several, a few*

manche: *some, many a*

viele: *many*

sämtliche: *all of (the)*

alle: *all (the)*
mehrere: *several*
weitere: *further, additional, more*
die Präposition: *the preposition*
der Genitiv: *the genitive*
die Fortsetzung: *the continuation*
durch *(+ accusative)*: *through*
um *(+ accusative)*: *around*
ohne *(+ accusative)*: *without*
rund: *round*
rund um *(+ accusative)*: *all around*
der Brief: *the letter*
das Fenster: *the window*
der Mann: *the man*
kommen: *to come*
das Zimmer: *the room*
das Tor: *the gate*
hübsch: *pretty*
brav: *well-behaved*
wichtig: *important, weighty*
der Preis: *the price*
der Koffer: *the case, the suitcase*
das Gewicht: *the weight*
die Größe: *the size*

teuer: *expensive*
interessant: *interesting*
zählen: *to count*
achtzehn: *eighteen*
zwanzig: *twenty*
fünfundzwanzig: *twenty-five*
zahlen: *to pay*
die Seite: *the side; the page*
wie viel Uhr ist es?: *what time is it?*
die Uhr: *the clock, the watch*
halb: *half*
morgens: *in the morning (e.g. before 9.00 a.m.)*
vormittags: *in the morning, a.m., before lunch (e.g. before 1.00 p.m.)*
mittags: *at midday (between 12.00 a.m. and 1.30 p.m.)*
nachmittags: *in the afternoon, p.m.*
abends: *in the evening*
nachts: *by night*
wann?: *when?*
richtig: *right, correct*
natürlich: *naturally, of course*

Übungen/Exercises

Exercise A

ZÄHLEN SIE VON EINS BIS ZEHN (NATÜRLICH AUF DEUTSCH)

Count from 1 to 10 (in German, of course!).

....

....

....

Exercise B

WIE VIEL UHR IST ES?

1. **(A) quarter to ten.**

   ....

2. **Half past seven.**

   ....

3. **Five to one.**

   ....

4. **Twenty past five/Five twenty.**

   ....

5. **Twenty-five to nine.**

   ....

Exercise C

BITTE ANTWORTEN SIE!

Go through the dialogue at the beginning of the lesson and answer these questions:

1. **Ist Frau Schmidt zu Hause oder in der U-Bahn?**

   ....

2. **Telefoniert sie mit Herrn Schmidt oder mit einer Bekannten?**

   ....

3. **Ist Frau Schmidt mit einigen Bekannten verabredet?**

   ....

4. **Wann ist sie verabredet? Abends oder vormittags?**

   ....

5. **Sind die Kollegen nette Leute?**

   ....

6. **Wo gehen sie hin?**

   ....

7. **Wo ist das Restaurant?**

   ....

8. **Wann kommen die Kollegen aus dem Büro?**

   ....

5. Communications

Lesson 5 focuses on written and spoken communications and you will learn more complex sentence structures. Listen to the vocabulary audio as you go through the list and repeat it – this will help you to memorize the words and to perfect your pronunciation.

IM BÜRO AT THE OFFICE

der Chef	**Guten Morgen, Herr Heinze! Sie sind sehr pünktlich heute.**
	Good morning, Mr. Heinze! You're very punctual today.
der Büroangestellte	**Guten Morgen, Herr Busch! Ja, ich fange immer sehr früh an.**
	Good morning, Mr. Busch! Yes, I always start very early.
der Chef	**Sie haben heute eine ganze Menge Arbeit.**
	You have a whole lot of work today.
der Büroangestellte	**Ja, ich weiß. Wir müssen diese Briefe absenden.**
	Yes, I know. We have to send these letters off.
der Chef	**Wie viele Briefe müssen Sie verschicken?**
	How many letters do you have to send off?
der Büroangestellte	**Es sind hundertfünfundzwanzig Briefe, Herr Busch.**
	There are a hundred and twenty-five letters, Mr. Busch.
der Chef	**Hundertfünfundzwanzig! Da haben Sie aber viel Arbeit!**
	A hundred and twenty-five! You have a lot of work there!
der Büroangestellte	**Stimmt, Herr Busch! Ich habe eine lange Kundenliste.**
	That's right, Mr. Busch. I have a long customer list.
der Chef	**Dann fangen Sie sofort an. Melden Sie sich, wenn Sie fertig sind.**
	Then get started right away. Let me know when you're finished.
der Büroangestellte	**Natürlich!**
	Of course!

Grammatik/Grammar

1. VERBEN/VERBS

wissen to know (something)

ich weiß	ich weiß nicht	weiß ich …?
er/sie/es weiß	er/sie/es weiß nicht	weiß er/sie/es …?
Sie wissen	Sie wissen nicht	wissen Sie …?
wir wissen	wir wissen nicht	wissen wir …?
Sie wissen	Sie wissen nicht	wissen Sie …?
sie wissen	sie wissen nicht	wissen sie …?

Er weiß Bescheid.
He knows all about it.

Wir wissen nichts damit anzufangen.
We don't know what to make of it.

Wissen Sie, wo meine Sekretärin ist?
Do you know where my secretary is?

Ja, ich weiß.
Yes, I know.

Ich weiß nicht recht.
I'm not sure.

Was weiß ich?
How should I know?

When the verb **to know** refers to people (i.e. to know a person), we use another verb: KENNEN. We will come back to this in lesson 9 on page 98.

können can/to be able to

ich kann	ich kann nicht	kann ich …?
er/sie/es kann	er /sie/es kann nicht	kann er/sie/es …?
Sie können	Sie können nicht	können Sie …?
wir können	wir können nicht	können wir …?
Sie können	Sie können nicht	können Sie …?
sie können	sie können nicht	können sie …?

The verb **können** is usually used with the infinitive of another verb. It is one of a number of so-called **auxiliary verbs**. However, it can be used on its own in idiomatic expressions (see first example).

Note that when **können** is used in conjunction with the infinitive of another verb, it sends that verb to the **end** of the sentence or clause. See the third and fourth examples.

Paul kann Deutsch.
Paul can speak German.

Können Sie kommen?
Can you come?

Wir können mit der U-Bahn fahren.
We can go by underground/subway.

Das Kind kann schon gut sprechen.
The child can speak well already.

---

müssen must/to have to

ich muss	ich muss nicht	muss ich …?
er/sie/es muss	er /sie/es muss nicht	muss er/sie/es …?
Sie müssen	Sie müssen nicht	müssen Sie …?
wir müssen	wir müssen nicht	müssen wir …?
Sie müssen	Sie müssen nicht	müssen Sie …?
sie müssen	sie müssen nicht	müssen sie …?

The verb **müssen** is used with the infinitive of another verb, but can also be used by itself in idiomatic expressions, like **können**. It also sends the other verb to the **end** of the sentence or clause. See the, third and fourth examples.

Ich muss nach Berlin.
I have to go to Berlin.

Sie muss nach Hause.
She has to go home.

Ich muss diese Briefe absenden.
I have to send these letters off.

Wir müssen pünktlich sein.
We must be punctual.

2. NUMBERS (CONTINUED)

11	12	13	14	15
elf	**zwölf**	**dreizehn**	**vierzehn**	**fünfzehn**
eleven	twelve	thirteen	fourteen	fifteen

16	17	18	19	
sechzehn	**siebzehn**	**achtzehn**	**neunzehn**	
sixteen	seventeen	eighteen	nineteen	

20	30	40	50	60
zwanzig	dreißig	vierzig	fünfzig	sechzig
twenty	thirty	forty	fifty	sixty

70	80	90	95	
siebzig	achtzig	neunzig	fünfundneunzig	
seventy	eighty	ninety	ninety-five	

100	125	150
hundert	hundertfünfundzwanzig	hundertfünfzig
a/one hundred	a hundred and twenty-five	a hundred and fifty

3. WIE VIEL/WIE VIELE ...?/HOW MUCH?/HOW MANY?

Wie viele/Wie viel?
How many?/How much?

Wie viele Briefe sind auf dem Schreibtisch?
How many letters are on the desk?

Wie viele Einwohner hat die Stadt?
How many inhabitants does the town have?

Wie viel bin ich Ihnen schuldig?
How much do I owe you?

Wie viel Geld haben Sie?
How much money do you have?

Wie viele is used when the noun is countable (e.g. **Briefe**).

Wie viel is used when the noun is not countable (e.g. **Geld**).

In the same way, the word **viele** is used when the noun is countable, **viel** is used when the noun is not countable.

Examples:

viel Arbeit
a lot of work

viele Bücher
lots of books

nicht viel Zeit
not much time

4. VERBEN/VERBS

heißen to be called, to name

ich heiße	ich heiße nicht	heiße ich …?
Sie heißen	Sie heißen nicht	heißen Sie …?
er/sie/es heißt	er/sie/es heißt nicht	heißt er/sie/es …?
wir heißen	wir heißen nicht	heißen wir …?
Sie heißen	Sie heißen nicht	heißen Sie …?
sie heißen	sie heißen nicht	heißen sie …?

Der junge Mann heißt Paul. **Er heißt Paul.**
The young man's name is Paul. He's called Paul.

Heißen Sie Thomas Schmidt?
Is your name Thomas Schmidt?

Wie heißen Sie? **Ich heiße Ulrike.**
What's your name? My name is Ulrike.

Note: **das heißt** is the equivalent of **i.e.** in English. It is often abbreviated to **d.h.**

senden to send

ich sende	ich sende nicht	sende ich …?
Sie senden	Sie senden nicht	senden Sie …?
er/sie/es sendet	er/sie/es sendet nicht	sendet er/sie/es …?
wir senden	wir senden nicht	senden wir …?
Sie senden	Sie senden nicht	senden Sie …?
sie senden	sie senden nicht	senden sie …?

Senden Sie diesen Brief per Einschreiben?
Are you sending this letter by registered mail?

absenden means **to send off** and behaves like **anfangen** below.

Anfangen is one of a large number of verbs in German which are formed from a **base verb** (in this case **fangen** – to catch) plus a preposition (an). The verb splits into its two parts in sentences with **normal word order***, and the preposition usually goes to the end of the sentence.

*Other grammatical rules can change normal word order. These will be explained later in the book.

anfangen to begin/to start

ich fange an	ich fange nicht an	fange ich …an?
er/sie/es fängt an	er/sie/es fängt nicht an	fängt er/sie/es …an?
Sie fangen an	Sie fangen nicht an	fangen Sie …an?
wir fangen an	wir fangen nicht an	fangen wir …an?
Sie fangen an	Sie fangen nicht an	fangen Sie …an?
sie fangen an	sie fangen nicht an	fangen sie …an?

Sie fängt an zu sprechen.
She is beginning to speak.

Wir müssen pünktlich anfangen.
We have to start punctually.

Wann fängt die Schule an?
When does school begin?

schließen to close/to shut/to end

ich schließe	ich schließe nicht	schließe ich …?
er/sie/es schließt	er/sie/es schließt nicht	schließt er/sie/es .?
Sie schließen	Sie schließen nicht	schließen Sie …?
wir schließen	wir schließen nicht	schließen wir …?
Sie schließen	Sie schließen nicht	schließen Sie …?
sie schließen	sie schließen nicht	schließen sie …?

Wann schließt das Büro?
When does the office close?

Wir schließen um sechs Uhr abends.
We close at six o'clock in the evening.

5. DIESER/DIESE/DIESES/DIESE/THIS

Nominative	Accusative	Genitive	Dative
dieser	diesen	dieses	diesem when the following noun is **masculine**
diese	diese	dieser	dieser when the following noun is **feminine**
dieses	dieses	dieses	diesem when the following noun is **neuter**
diese	diese	dieser	diese when the following noun is **plural**

Wer ist dieser Herr?
Who is this gentleman?

Am Ende dieses Jahres.
At the end of this year.

Muss ich diese Arbeit machen?
Do I have to do this job?

Wie viel wiegen diese Briefe?
How much do these letters weigh?

6. DER IMPERATIV/ THE IMPERATIVE

Bitte, fangen Sie an!
Please begin.

Kommen Sie hierher!
Come here.

Lernen Sie diese Wörter!
Learn these words.

Fahren Sie mit dem Taxi!
Go by taxi.

Bitte beantworten Sie diese Frage!
Please answer this question.

Schließen Sie das Fenster!
Close the window.

Wiederholen Sie die Lektion!
Repeat the lesson.

What do all these have in common? They are all commands. They are the command (or imperative) form of the verbs. The imperative is identical with the **Sie** form of the verb.

Suggestions can be made with the **wir** form.

Gehen wir!	**Fahren wir hin!**	**Fangen wir an!**
Let's go.	Let's drive there.	Let's begin.

Wortschatz/Vocabulary

der Chef: *the boss*
der Büroangestellte: *the office worker, the employee*
der Angestellte: *the salaried employee, the white collar worker*
pünktlich: *punctual, on time*
die Menge: *the quantity*

eine ganze Menge: *a whole lot*

absenden: *to send off*
verschicken: *to send (off)*
senden: *to send*
wissen: *to know*
wie viel?: *how much?*
wie viele?: *how many?*
Hundert: *a hundred*
da haben Sie viel Arbeit: *you have a lot of work there*
da: *there*
hier und da: *here and there*
die Kundenliste: *the customer list*
der Kunde: *the customer (male)*
die Kundin: *the customer (female)*
die Liste: *the list*

stimmt!: *that's right*
sofort: *immediately*
Bescheid wissen über (+ *accusative*)**:** *to know all about*
schon: *already*
kennen: *to know (a person, a place)*
können: *can, to be able*
müssen: *must, to have to*
mitkommen: *to come along*
nach Hause gehen: *to go home*
wie viel bin ich Ihnen schuldig?: *how much do I owe you?*
der Einwohner: *the inhabitant*
heißen: *to be called*
das heißt: *i.e., that is*
die Frage beantworten: *to answer the question*
beantworten: *to answer*
anfangen: *to begin*
schließen: *to close, shut, end*
hierher: *here (towards the speaker)*
dorthin: *there (away from the speaker)*
das Wort: *the word*
wiegen: *to weigh*
die Zeit: *the time*

Übungen/Exercises

Exercise A

Write out hte numbers from 1 to 20 in German

....

....

....

Exercise B

Write the following numbers:

23: .... dreiundzwanzig ....

25: ....

30: ....

35: ....

40: ....

57: ....

60: ....

64: ....

70: ....

80: ....

90: ....

99: ....

100: ....

122: ....

Exercise C

Refer to the dialogue at the beginning of the lesson and answer these questions.

1. **Ist der Büroangestellte pünktlich?**

   ....

2. **Hat er heute viel Arbeit?**

   ....

3. **Muss der Büroangestellte Briefe oder E-Mails verschicken?**

   ....

4. **Wie viele Briefe sind es?**

   ....

5. **Hat der Büroangestellte eine Kundenliste?**

   ....

6. Review of Lessons 1 to 5

This review section is a revision of what you have learnt so far. Listen to the audio dialogues again and see how much you can understand without turning back to the English versions in the previous chapters! Don't forget to do the short exercise section too!

1. Wortschatz/Vocabulary

die Wiederholung: *the repetition, the recapitulation*
die Seite: *the page; the side*
das Gespräch: *the conversation, the dialogue*
die Übung: *the exercise*
der Satz: *the sentence*
ergänzen: *to complete, to fill in*
ergänzen Sie diese Sätze: *complete these sentences*
wählen: *to choose*
wählen Sie!: *choose*
das Adjektiv: *the adjective*
die Eigenschaft: *the quality, the feature, the characteristic*

das Eigenschaftswort: *the adjective*
antworten: *to answer*
männlich: *masculine*
weiblich: *feminine*
sächlich: *neuter*
die Sache: *the thing*
der Artikel: *the article*
die Präposition: *the preposition*
das Verhältniswort: *the preposition*
das Verhältnis: *the proportion, the relationship*
passend: *appropriate, suitable*
das Beispiel: *the example*

Übungen/Exercises

Exercise A

BITTE WÄHLEN SIE DEN PASSENDEN ARTIKEL: DER, DIE, DAS ODER DIE (PLURAL)

Beispiel: die Frage   das Gespräch   der Flughafen   die Seiten

1. .... Haus	13. .... Buch	25. .... Schreibtisch
2. .... Schachtel	14. .... Abend	26. .... Städte
3. .... Schule	15. .... Restaurants	27. .... Freund
4. .... Lehrerin	16. .... Reisepass	28. .... Freundin
5. .... Kundenliste	17. .... Leute	29. .... Wortschatz
6. .... Mantel	18. .... Frauen	30. .... Wort
7. ....Telefon	19. .... Häuser	31. .... Geschäft
8. .... U-Bahn	20. .... Stuhl	32. .... Antwort
9. .... Taxi	21. .... Theater	33. .... Sätze
10. .... Uhr	22. .... Arbeit	34. .... Smartphone
11. .... Tage	23. .... Chef	
12. .... Woche	24. .... Briefe	

Exercise B

BITTE ERGÄNZEN SIE DIESE SÄTZE

Complete these sentences.

(wissen) Ich weiß es nicht.   (lernen) Wir lernen Deutsch.

1. (machen) Ulrike .... eine Reise.

2. (sein) Wie viel Uhr .... es?

3. (fahren) Wir .... mit dem Taxi.

4. (gehen) Ulrike .... nach Hause.

5. (haben) Ich .... viel zu tun.

6. (arbeiten) Wo .... Sie?

7. (fliegen) Wohin .... er?

8. (sein) Ich .... heute Abend mit einigen Freunden verabredet.

9. (arbeiten) Thomas Schmidt .... rund um die Uhr.

10. (müssen) .... ich Deutsch lernen?

11. (müssen) Ja, Sie .... Deutsch lernen.

12. (fahren) Wann .... Ulrike zum Flughafen?

13. (geben) .... er heute eine Party?

14. (können) .... Sie diese Fragen beantworten?

Exercise C

BITTE WÄHLEN SIE DAS PASSENDE WORT

Ulrike arbeitet in <u>einer</u> Bank. (eine, einer, einen)

1. Welche .... haben Sie?   (Schreibtisch/Staatsangehörigkeit/Mantel)

2. Ich bin keine Spanierin und .... keine Italienerin. (nicht/auch/von)

3. Ulrike fliegt .... München. (nach/zu/an)

4. Dieser Herr hat .... Personalausweis. (zwei/keinen/nicht)

5. Wer ist .... junge Mann? (diese/dieser/dieses)

6. Ich reise immer .... einem großen Koffer. (mit/in/ohne)

7. Mein .... ist in der Tasche. (Freund/Reisepass/Schachtel)

8. Heute ist .... Freitag. (auch/nicht/um)

9. Die Kollegen sind sehr .... Leute. (großen/viel/nette)

10. Es ist fünf .... halb zehn. (vor/mit/zu)

7. Dining In & Out

Lesson 7 is all about food! Learn how to order food and drinks out and about and the vocabulary you need to talk about it at home. You will also learn to use the verbs mögen and wollen (to like/want), as well as personal pronouns, helping you to further develop your language skills.

DAS FRÜHSTÜCK BREAKFAST

Es ist halb zehn an einem Sonntagvormittag. Ulrike und ein Freund, Wolfgang, sitzen zusammen in einem Café. Sie frühstücken.
It's half past nine on a Sunday morning. Ulrike and a friend, Wolfgang, are sitting together in a café. They are having breakfast.

Der Kellner	**Guten Morgen! Was darf's denn sein?**
	Good morning! What would you like to have?
Ulrike	**Guten Morgen! Ich nehme einen Tee mit Zitrone, zwei Brötchen und Aprikosenmarmelade.**
	Good morning. I'll have a tea with lemon, two bread rolls and some apricot jam.
Der Kellner	**Und für den Herrn?**
	And for the gentleman?
Wolfgang	**Für mich einen Kaffee, Käse und Brot, bitte.**
	For me, a coffee, cheese and bread, please.
Der Kellner	**Sofort.**
	I'll be right back.
Wolfgang	**Ulrike, was machst du heute Nachmittag?**

	Ulrike, what are you doing this afternoon?
Ulrike	**Nichts Besonderes. Und du?**
	Nothing in particular. What about you?
Wolfgang	**Ich habe auch nichts Besonderes vor. Aber "Die Lupe" ist gleich um die Ecke. Wollen wir hingehen? Sie zeigen den neuen Bond-Film.**
	I haven't anything planned special either. But "Die Lupe" (a cinema in Berlin) is just round the corner. Shall we go there? They're showing the new James Bond film.
Ulrike	**Ja, einverstanden! Weißt du, wann der Film beginnt?**
	Yes, sure! Do you know when the film begins?
Wolfgang	**Ja. Um halb drei. Bis dann können wir vielleicht den Trödelmarkt besuchen. Es gibt da immer etwas Interessantes zu sehen.**
	Yes. At two-thirty. Until then, we can perhaps go to the flea market. There's always something interesting to see there.
Ulrike	**Eine gute Idee! Wollen wir gleich nach dem Frühstück hingehen?**
	Good idea! Shall we go straight after breakfast?
Wolfgang	**Ja, warum nicht? Ah, der Kellner kommt schon ... Vielen Dank. Können wir gleich zahlen, bitte?**
	Yes, why not? Ah, here comes the waiter. Thank you very much. Can we pay now, please?
der Kellner	**Ja, selbstverständlich. Zusammen oder getrennt?**
	Yes, of course. Are you paying together or separately?
Wolfgang	**Zusammen.**
	Together.
der Kellner	**Also, zusammen macht das neunzehn Euro fünfzig.**
	So. Together that comes to nineteen euros fifty.

Grammatik/Grammar

1. VERBEN/VERBS

machen to do/make

ich mache	ich mache nicht	mache ich ...?
Sie machen	Sie machen nicht	machen Sie ...?
(2nd person singular, polite form)		
du machst	du machst nicht	machst du ...?
(2nd person singular, familiar form, see below)		
er/sie/es macht	er /sie/es macht nicht	macht er/sie/es ...?
wir machen	wir machen nicht	machen wir ...?
Sie machen	Sie machen nicht	machen Sie ...?
(2nd person plural)		
sie machen	sie machen nicht	machen sie ...?

Sie macht das Essen.
She's preparing the meal.

Wie viel macht das?
How much does it come to?

Was macht das?
How much does it come to?

Das macht nichts! (often shortened to **macht nichts**)
Never mind!/Don't worry about it!

Was macht das Studium?
How are you getting along with your studies?

2. DU/THE FAMILIAR "YOU"

Sie is used to mean **you**, when addressing one person or a group of people. As students of German, you are well advised to stick to this form until you are sure that you can use the familiar **du** without causing offence. Germans, especially of the older generation, are very particular about this. The **Sie** form is also used in the business world as the normal form to address someone. Always wait until someone addresses you in the familiar **du** form before you use it yourself.

However, **du** is the form generally used for **you** when talking to friends and partners and close relatives, as well as children under 16. It's also usual for university students to address one another as **du**. Children will, however, address an older person as **Sie**, except for members of the same family.

The verb form following **du** is generally **-st** (sometimes **-est**) plus the stem of the verb.

Examples

du machst	you do, make
du fängst an	you begin
du hast	you have
du gehst	you go

Where there is a stem change in irregular verbs, the **du** form also reflects this change:

geben	(to give)
du gibst	you give

Note also:

du bist	you are
du kannst	you can

You saw the familiar **you** being used between close friends in the dialogue.

In the plural, the familiar **you** is **ihr**. This form is in general based on the stem of the verb (the part without **-en**), to which **-t** is added.

Examples

machen	du machst (singular)	ihr macht (plural)
gehen	du gehst (singular)	ihr geht (plural)
können	du kannst (singular)	ihr könnt (plural)
haben	du hast (singular)	ihr habt (plural)
sein	du bist (singular)	ihr seid (plural)

Be aware of its existence, but there is no need for you to learn it now!

3. VERBEN

nehmen to take

ich nehme	ich nehme nicht	nehme ich …?
Sie nehmen	Sie nehmen nicht	nehmen Sie …?
du nimmst	du nimmst nicht	nimmst du …?
er/sie/es nimmt	er /sie/es nimmt nicht	nimmt er/sie/es …?
wir nehmen	wir nehmen nicht	nehmen wir …?
Sie nehmen	Sie nehmen nicht	nehmen Sie …?
sie nehmen	sie nehmen nicht	nehmen sie …?

Ich nehme einen Tee mit Zitrone.
I'll have a tea with lemon.

Sie nimmt den Kugelschreiber vom Tisch.
She takes the pen from the table.

Sie können den Bus/das Taxi zum Flughafen nehmen.
You can take the bus/the taxi to the airport.

Etwas unter die Lupe nehmen.
To examine something closely.

---

wollen to want (to)/to wish

ich will	ich will nicht	will ich ...?
Sie wollen	Sie wollen nicht	wollen Sie ...?
du willst	du willst nicht	willst du ...?
er/sie/es will	er /sie/es will nicht	will er/sie/es ...?
wir wollen	wir wollen nicht	wollen wir ...?
Sie wollen	Sie wollen nicht	wollen Sie ...?
sie wollen	sie wollen nicht	wollen sie ...?

Wollen Sie Wurst?
Would you like (some) sausage?

Ich will nicht ins Kino gehen.
I don't want to go to the cinema.

Er weiß, was er will.
He knows what he wants.

Wollen wir hier frühstücken?
Shall we have breakfast here?

Note: In the second and fourth examples, **wollen** is used, like **können** and **müssen**, as an auxiliary verb (with other verbs).

---

mögen to want (to), like to

ich möchte	ich möchte nicht	möchte ich ...?
Sie möchten	Sie möchten nicht	möchten Sie ...?
du möchtest	du möchtest nicht	möchtest du ...?
er/sie/es möchte	er /sie/es möchte nicht	möchte er/sie/es ...?
wir möchten	wir möchten nicht	möchten wir ...?
Sie möchten	Sie möchten nicht	möchten Sie ...?
sie möchten	sie möchten nicht	möchten sie ...?

Mögen is used as a softer and more polite version of **wollen** in many cases.

It can also be used as an auxiliary verb.

Examples

Was möchten Sie?
What would you like?

Compare: Was wollen Sie?
What do you want?

Ich möchte jetzt nach Hause gehen.
I'd like to go home now.

Wir möchten zwei Kaffee, bitte.
We would like two coffees, please.

4. PERSONAL PRONOUNS

These are the accusative form of the respective personal pronouns where:

> **ich** becomes **mich**   **er** becomes **ihn**
> **du** becomes **dich**   **sie** (she), **Sie** (you), **sie** (they) stay as they are
> **wir** becomes **uns**   **es** stays as **es**

Einen Kaffee mit Milch für mich, bitte.
A coffee with milk for me, please.

Ist der Tee für mich?
Is the tea for me?

Nein, er ist für ihn. (er refers to **der Tee)**
No, it is for him.

5. ETWAS/SOMETHING/ANYTHING

This is a word that can be used in a variety of situations:

> **Gibt es etwas für mich?**
> Is there anything for me?

Ich will Ihnen etwas sagen.
I want to tell you something.

Ich möchte noch etwas trinken.
I would like to have another drink.

Es gibt immer etwas Interessantes zu sehen.
There's always something interesting to see.

Jetzt zu etwas anderem. (dative!)
Now to something else.

Das Buch ist etwas teuer.
The book is rather expensive.

Bitte sprechen Sie etwas langsamer!
Please speak a little more slowly.

In spoken German **etwas** is sometimes shortened to **was**:

So was gibt's nicht!/So etwas gibt es nicht!
I don't believe it!

6. OPPOSITES

ja	nein
der Vormittag	der Nachmittag/der Abend
der Tag	die Nacht
groß	klein
teuer	billig
beginnen	aufhören
öffnen	schließen
gehen	kommen
geben	nehmen
viel	wenig little
etwas	nichts nothing
wahr/richtig	falsch wrong
gut	schlecht bad

You will have encountered most of them by now, in the dialogues.

Here are two more prepositions

auf   on

unter   under

Examples of their uses:

Das Buch liegt auf dem Tisch (dative gives the position).
The book is on the table.

Die Schachtel steht unter dem Tisch (dative).
The box stands is under the table.

Stellen Sie das Buch auf den Tisch! (accusative gives the direction)
Put the book on the table

Stellen Sie die Schachtel unter den Tisch! (accusative)
Put the box under the table.

Note: we saw with the verb **to go** that German is often more specific about the means of **going**. When it comes to things **being** somewhere, the verb used in German usually indicates more precisely what is meant (liegen = **to lie**, stehen = **to stand**).

7. DIE WOCHENTAGE / THE DAYS OF THE WEEK

der Sonntag	Sunday
der Montag	Monday
der Dienstag	Tuesday
der Mittwoch	Wednesday
der Donnerstag	Thursday
der Freitag	Friday
der Sonnabend	Saturday (in Northern Germany)
der Samstag	Saturday (in the rest of Germany, Austria and Switzerland)

Wortschatz/Vocabulary

das Frühstück: *the breakfast*

der Vormittag: *the morning*

der Nachmittag: *the afternoon*

das Café: *the cafe*

frühstücken: *to have breakfast*

der Kellner: *the waiter*

den Herrn (accusative)**:** *the gentleman (note that -n is added in accusative)*

sitzen: *to sit*

zusammen: *together*

was darf's denn sein? *what would you like to have?*

mich: *me*

dich: *you (familiar form)*

ihn: *him*

uns: *us*

nehmen: *to take*

der Tee: *the tea*

die Zitrone: *the lemon*

das Essen: *the meal; the food*

das Brot: *(the) bread*

das Brötchen: *the bread roll*

die Aprikose: *the apricot*

die Marmelade: *(the) jam*

der Kaffee: *the coffee*

der Käse: *(the) cheese*

bitte: *please*

nichts: *nothing*

besonders: *especially*

nichts Besonderes: *nothing special*

nach *(+ dative)*: *after*

vorhaben: *to have planned*

die Lupe: *the magnifying glass*

gleich: *immediately, at once*

die Ecke: *the corner*

um die Ecke: *around the corner*

wollen: *to want (to)*

hingehen: *to go (to somewhere away from the speaker)*

herkommen: *to come (towards the speaker)*

zeigen: *to show*

der Film: *the film, the movie*

einverstanden!: *agreed! all right!*

einverstanden sein: *to agree to*

beginnen, anfangen: *to begin*

vielleicht: *perhaps, maybe*

der Trödelmarkt: *the flea market*

besuchen: *to visit, to go to*

da: *there*

interessant: *interesting*

sehen: *to see*

die Idee: *the idea*

warum: *why*

warum nicht?: *why not?*

zurück: *back*

vielen Dank: *many thanks/thank you very much*

selbstverständlich: *of course*

die Rechnung: *the bill, the check*

das Studium: *the studies (plural)*

anders: *different*

etwas anderes: *something else*

billig: *cheap, inexpensive*

aufhören: *to cease, come to an end*

wenig: *a little*

falsch: *wrong, false*

schlecht: *bad*

unter: *under*

auf: *on*

immer: *always*

wann? *when?*

zahlen: *to pay*

dorthin: *there (away from the speaker)*

nett: *nice*

getrennt: *separate, separately*

bestellen: *to order*

die Scheibe: *the slice*

Übungen/Exercises

Exercise A

BITTE BEANTWORTEN SIE DIESE FRAGEN!

Answer these questions by looking at the dialogue.

1. **Wo sitzen Ulrike und Wolfgang zusammen?**

   ....

2. **Was nimmt Ulrike?**

   ....

3. **Was bestellt Wolfgang?**

   ....

4. **Hat Wolfgang etwas Besonderes vor?**

   ....

5. **Um wie viel Uhr fängt der Film an?**

   ....

6. **Wann gehen Wolfgang und Ulrike zum Trödelmarkt?**

   ....

Exercise B

Name the days of the week.

Sie heißen...

1. ....Montag...

2. ....

3. ....

4. ....

5. ....

6. .... oder ....

7. ....

Exercise C

Complete the following sentences.

1. Ich möchte .... Scheibe Brot.

2. Ich nehme .... Tee mit Zitrone.

3. Wissen Sie, ... der Film anfängt?

4. Ich .... nichts Besonderes vor.

Exercise D

Complete these sentences with the opposite of the underlined words.

Ich gehe heute Abend nicht ins Büro. Ich gehe morgen Vormittag dorthin.

1. Herr Schmidt reist wenig, aber er arbeitet ....

2. Das ist nicht richtig! Das ist ....

3. Die Stadt ist nicht groß. Sie ist ....

4. Das Buch liegt nicht unter dem Schreibtisch. Es liegt .... dem Schreibtisch.

5. Ist etwas in der Schachtel? Nein, es ist .... in der Schachtel.

8. Reservations

Lesson 8 covers making hotel reservations. Again, listen to the audio to immerse yourself in the language so that you become accustomed to making sentences – this will also help you to absorb the grammar easily. Finally, you will learn some new verbs and vocabulary.

IM HOTEL IN THE HOTEL

Herr Schmidt ist heute in Hannover. Er hat ein Zimmer in einem Hotel der mittleren Preisklasse reserviert. Er spricht gerade mit der Empfangsdame.
Mr. Schmidt is in Hanover today. He has reserved a room in a medium-priced hotel. He's talking to the receptionist right now.

Herr Schmidt	Guten Tag. Ich habe ein Zimmer reserviert.
	Good afternoon. I've booked a room.
Die Empfangsdame	Guten Tag. Wie ist Ihr Name?
	Good afternoon. Can I ask you for your name, please?
Herr Schmidt	Mein Name ist Thomas Schmidt.
	My name is Thomas Schmidt.
Die Empfangsdame	Schauen wir mal ... Eine Reservierung für eine Nacht?
	Let's have a look. A reservation for one night?
Herr Schmidt	Genau, für eine Nacht. Ich reise morgen Vormittag ab.
	Exactly, for one night. I'm leaving tomorrow morning.
Die Empfangsdame	Wunderbar. Wollen Sie sich bitte eintragen? Haben Sie Gepäck?
	Sie können Ihre Koffer dem jungen Mann geben.

	Wonderful. Would you sign in, please? Do you have any luggage? You can give your cases to the young man.
Herr Schmidt	**Danke. Ich habe nur diesen kleinen Koffer. In welchem Stock ist das Zimmer, bitte?**
	Thank you. I have only this small suitcase. Which floor is the room on, please?
Die Empfangsdame	**Im dritten Stock. Der Aufzug ist direkt hinter Ihnen.**
	On the third floor. The elevator's right behind you.
Herr Schmidt	**Danke schön. Wie kann ich von meinem Zimmer nach draußen telefonieren?**
	Thank you. How can I get an outside line from my room?
Die Empfangsdame	**Wählen Sie einfach eine "9" vor. Ihr Schlüssel, bitte sehr. Sie haben Zimmer 372.**
	Just dial "9" beforehand. Here's your key. You're in room 372.
Herr Schmidt	**Danke. Bis wie viel Uhr servieren Sie morgens das Frühstück?**
	Thank you. Until what time in the morning do you serve breakfast?
Die Empfangsdame	**Bis zehn Uhr. Das Frühstückszimmer ist dort drüben.**
	Until ten o'clock. The breakfast room is over there.
Herr Schmidt	**Schönen Dank.**
	Thank you very much.
Die Empfangsdame	**Bitte schön. Guten Aufenthalt!**
	You're welcome. Enjoy your stay!

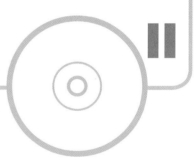

Grammatik/Grammar

1. POSSESSIVE ADJECTIVES (MY, YOUR, HIS, HER, OUR, THEIR)

mein	my
Ihr	your (singular or plural – polite form)
dein	your (singular – familiar form)
sein	his or its
ihr	her
unser	our
euer	your (plural– familiar form)
ihr	their

Possessive adjectives, like other adjectives, agree in gender and number with the noun they modify. They take the same endings as the indefinite article.

nominative

mein Chef	(**Chef** being **masculine**) my boss
meine Kollegin	(**Kollegin** being **feminine**) my colleague
mein Kind	(**Kind** being **neuter**) my child
meine Freunde	(**Freunde** being **plural**) my friends

accusative

seinen Chef	his boss
seine Kollegin	his colleague
sein Kind	his child
seine Freunde	his friends

genitive

ihres Chefs	of her boss
ihrer Kollegin	of her colleague
ihres Kindes	of her child
ihrer Freunde	of her friends

dative

unserem Chef	to our boss
unserer Kollegin	to our colleague
unserem Kind	to our child
unseren Freunden	to our friends

So possessive adjectives in German indicate, as do the articles, the gender and grammatical situation of whatever is being referred to.

Examples:

Ihr Gepäck ist noch in Ihrem Zimmer.
Your luggage is still in your room.

Er gibt dem jungen Mann seinen Koffer.
He gives his case to the young man.

Unser Chef sitzt in seinem Büro.
Our boss is in his office.

Sie trinkt mit ihrem Mann Tee.
She is having tea with her husband.

2. EIGEN/OWN

A useful word to go with these possessive adjectives is **eigen-**, meaning **own**. The endings are the same as those that follow **kein(e)**:

Mein eigenes Haus.
My own house.

Seine eigenen Bücher.
His own books.

Ihre eigene Idee.
Her own idea.

3. VERBEN/VERBS

sitzen to sit

ich sitze	ich sitze nicht	sitze ich …?
Sie sitzen	Sie sitzen nicht	sitzen Sie …?
du sitzt	du sitzt nicht	sitzt du …?
er/sie/es sitzt	er/sie/es sitzt nicht	sitzt er/sie/es …?
wir sitzen	wir sitzen nicht	sitzen wir …?
Sie sitzen	Sie sitzen nicht	sitzen Sie …?
sie sitzen	sie sitzen nicht	sitzen sie …?

Wo wollen Sie sitzen?
Where do you want to sit?

Er sitzt im falschen Zug.
He's sitting in the wrong train.

Sie sitzt vor dem Fernseher.
She's sitting in front of the television.

Sie sitzen beim Kaffee.
They're having coffee.

Der Mantel sitzt gut.
The coat fits well.

Bitte setzen Sie sich!
Please sit down!

servieren to serve

ich serviere	ich serviere nicht	serviere ich …?
Sie servieren	Sie servieren nicht	servieren Sie …?
du servierst	du servierst nicht	servierst du …?
er/sie/es serviert	er/sie/es serviert nicht	serviert er/sie/es …?
wir servieren	wir servieren nicht	servieren wir …?
Sie servieren	Sie servieren nicht	servieren Sie …?
sie servieren	sie servieren nicht	servieren sie …?

Der Kellner serviert das Frühstück.
The waiter serves breakfast.

Es ist serviert!
Dinner is served!

Reservieren (to reserve, book) follows the same pattern:

Ich möchte ein Zimmer reservieren.
I would like to reserve a room.

Diese Plätze sind für uns reserviert.
These seats are reserved for us.

Serviert in the 2nd example is a past participle – more on this in Lesson 11 on page 127.

Verbs with **-ieren** on the end are mostly of non-German origin (deriving from English and French).

Some examples are:

addieren	to add
reservieren	to reserve
studieren	to study (at university)
telefonieren	to telephone

dürfen to be allowed to/to be permitted to

ich darf	ich darf nicht	darf ich …?
Sie dürfen	Sie dürfen nicht	dürfen Sie …?
du darfst	du darfst nicht	darfst du …?
er/sie/es darf	er /sie/es darf nicht	darf er/sie/es …?
wir dürfen	wir dürfen nicht	dürfen wir …?
Sie dürfen	Sie dürfen nicht	dürfen Sie …?
sie dürfen	sie dürfen nicht	dürfen sie …?

This is an important verb, and is used in German both by itself and as an auxiliary verb in conjunction with other verbs.

Das dürfen Sie nicht!
You're not allowed to do that!

Darf ich Ihnen noch etwas Kaffee anbieten?
Can I offer you some more coffee?

Sie darf keine Schokolade essen.
She's not allowed to eat chocolate.

4. BITTE, DANKE, VERZEIHUNG/PLEASE, THANK YOU, SORRY

Bitte, meaning **please**, comes from the verb **bitten**, and means literally **I request**.

The verb **bitten** (**to request something**) itself is used with the preposition **um** (+ the accusative):

Darf ich Sie um Ihren Namen bitten?
Can I ask you for your name please?

bitte or **bitte sehr** can mean **here you are**.

Example:

Bitte sehr, Ihr Kaffee.
Here's your coffee.

Note:

Ich bitte um Verzeihung.	is usually shortened to	**Verzeihung!**
Please forgive me.		I'm sorry!
Ich bitte um Entschuldigung.	is usually shortened to	**Entschuldigung!**
Please excuse me.		Sorry!

Danke, meaning **thank you**, comes from the verb **danken**, and means literally **I thank**.
When you say **danke** (**thanks**) or **danke schön** (**thank you**) or **vielen Dank** (**many thanks**),
the German speaker will often say **bitte** or **bitte schön** in reply. This means something like **don't
mention it**, or **you're welcome**.

danke can also mean **No, thank you,** often accompanied by a declining gesture.

Noch Kaffee? Danke! (Nein, danke.)
Some more coffee? No, thanks.

5. NUMBERS

Cardinal Number	Ordinal Number	
1 (eins)	der/die/das erste	the first
2 (zwei)	der/die/das zweite	the second
3 (drei)	der/die/das dritte	the third
4 (vier)	der/die/das vierte	the fourth
5 (fünf)	der/die/das fünfte	the fifth
6 (sechs)	der/die/das sechste	the sixth
7 (sieben)	der/die/das siebte	the seventh
8 (acht)	der/die/das achte	the eighth
9 (neun)	der/die/das neunte	the ninth
10 (zehn)	der/die/das zehnte	the tenth

Ordinal numbers behave in general as if they were adjectives.

Examples:

Sind wir bei Lektion Nummer drei? Ist dies die dritte Lektion?
Are we doing lesson number three? Is this the third lesson?

Nein, wir sind bei der achten Lektion!
No, we're doing the eighth lesson! das zweite Zimmer
the second room

sein erster Computer
his first computer

unser drittes Kind
our third child

But

im dritten Stock
on the third floor

6. VERBEN/VERBS

verstehen to understand

ich verstehe	ich verstehe nicht	verstehe ich. ...?
Sie verstehen	Sie verstehen nicht	verstehen Sie ...?
du verstehst	du verstehst nicht	verstehst du ...?
er/sie/es versteht	er/sie/es versteht nicht	versteht er/sie/es ...?
wir verstehen	wir verstehen nicht	verstehen wir ...?
Sie verstehen	Sie verstehen nicht	verstehen Sie ...?
sie verstehen	sie verstehen nicht	verstehen sie ...?

Verstehen Sie Deutsch?
Do you understand German?

Ich verstehe kein Wort.
I don't understand a word.

Jetzt verstehe ich!
Now I understand!

Note that the verb **stehen** **to stand** is declined in exactly the same way.

Wortschatz/Vocabulary

der mittleren Preisklasse: *in the medium price range*
mittel: *moderate, medium (usually used in the form **mittler-**)*
der Preis: *the price*
die Preisklasse: *the price bracket*
das Zimmer: *the room*
die Empfangsdame: *the receptionist*
der Name: *the name*
wie?: *how?*
wie ist Ihr Name?: *what's your name?*
die Reservierung: *the reservation*
reservieren: *to reserve*
schauen wir mal: *let's have a look*

die Nacht: *the night*
genau: *exact (adjective), **exactly** (adverb)*
wollen Sie sich bitte eintragen?: *would you please sign the register?*
sich eintragen: *to enter one's name*
das Gepäck: *the luggage*
nur: *only, just*
der Stock: *the stor(e)y, the floor*
in welchem Stock?: *on which floor?*
der Aufzug: *the elevator, the lift*
danke: *thanks*
danke schön: *thank you*
bitte schön: *don't mention it, you're welcome*

Verzeihung!: *I'm sorry, excuse me*
Entschuldigung!: *sorry!, I beg your pardon*
selbstverständlich: *of course, naturally*
vorwählen: *to dial beforehand*
wählen: *to choose, to dial (a telephone number)*
die Nummer: *the number*
servieren: *to serve*
morgens: *in the morning*
das Frühstückszimmer: *the breakfast room*
dort drüben: *over there*
wunderbar: *wonderful*
schönen Dank: *thank you very much*
der Aufenthalt: *stay*
guten Aufenthalt!: *enjoy your stay*
mein: *my*
dein: *your (familiar form)*
sein: *his*
ihr: *her, theirs*
Ihr: *your (polite form)*

die Tasse: *the cup*
der Mann: *the man; the husband*
die Frau: *the woman; the wife*
der Computer: *the computer*
anbieten: *to offer*
die Schokolade: *the chocolate*
eigener, eigene, eigenes: *own (adjective)*
zusammen: *together*
der Fernseher: *the television*
bei *(+ dative)***:** *near, by, at*
der Zug: *the train*
der Platz: *the place, space, seat*
studieren: *to study (at university)*
addieren: *to add*
telefonieren: *to telephone*
dürfen: *to be allowed to*
darf ich ...?: *may I ...?*
bitte sehr!: *here you are*
richtig: *correct*

Übungen/Exercises

Exercise A

BITTE BEANTWORTEN SIE DIESE FRAGEN!

Answer these questions relating to the dialogue on page 83.

1. **In welcher Stadt ist Herr Schmidt?**

   ....

2. **Hat er eine Reservierung für eine Nacht oder für zwei Nächte?**

   ....

3. **Mit wem** *(with whom)* **spricht er?**

   ....

4. Wann *(when)* reist er ab?

....

5. Muss Thomas Schmidt seinen Namen eintragen?

....

6. Hat er viel Gepäck?

....

7. Gibt es einen Aufzug im Hotel?

....

8. Bis wie viel Uhr servieren sie das Frühstück?

....

Exercise B

ERGÄNZEN SIE DIESE SÄTZE MIT DEM RICHTIGEN POSSESSIVADJEKTIV!

Complete these sentences with the correct possessive adjective.

Beispiel: Ich habe <u>mein</u> Ticket und <u>meinen</u> Personalausweis.

1. Der Chef sitzt in .... Büro an .... Schreibtisch.

2. Wir haben .... Koffer *(singular)* .... und Taschen.

3. Sie ist erst 18, aber sie hat .... eigene Wohnung und .... eigenes Auto.

Exercise C

ERGÄNZEN SIE DIESE SÄTZE:

Die Seite Nummer 6 ist <u>die sechste Seite</u>.

1. Die Lektion Nummer 1 ist ....

2. Die Frage Nummer 9 ist ....

3. Die Antwort Nummer 3 ist ....

9. The Post Office

Lesson 9 introduces some general daily activities such as running errands. Here, we use the example of the post office but remember that much of the vocabulary is transferrable and can apply to many other situations too. You will also learn the future tense.

PAUL AUF DER POST PAUL AT THE POST OFFICE

Paul	**Guten Tag. Ich brauche eine Briefmarke für eine Postkarte, bitte.**
	Hello. I need a stamp to send a postcard, please.
Die Beamtin	**Inland oder Ausland?**
	Domestic or overseas?
Paul	**Inland. Ich habe auch zwei Briefe. Dieser geht nach England, der andere in die USA. Bitte sehr.**
	Domestic. I also have two letters. This one is going to England, the other to the U.S.A. Here you are.

Die Beamtin nimmt die Briefe und wiegt sie auf der Waage. Anschließend gibt sie Paul die entsprechenden Briefmarken.
The clerk takes the letters and weighs them on the scales. After that, she gives Paul the appropriate stamps.

Die Beamtin	**Bitte sehr. Diese Marke ist für Ihren Brief nach England, die andere für Ihren Brief in die USA.**
	Here you are. This stamp is for your letter to England. The other is for your letter to the U.S.A.

Paul	**Danke. Ich möchte dieses Paket nach Kanada verschicken. Wie lange wird es dauern?**
	Thank you. I'd like to send this parcel to Canada. How long will it take?
Die Beamtin	**Normalerweise ungefähr eine Woche.**
	As a rule, about a week.
Paul	**In Ordnung. Bitte.**
	Fine. Here it is.
Die Beamtin	**Bevor Sie das Paket absenden können, müssen Sie dieses Formular ausfüllen. Bitte.**
	Before you can send the parcel, you have to fill out this form. Here you are.
Paul	**Danke.**
Die Beamtin	**Schreiben Sie hier den Namen und die Adresse des Absenders sowie Name und Adresse des Empfängers.**
	Write here the name and the address of the sender as well as the name and the address of the addressee.
Paul	**Mache ich! ... Hoffentlich können Sie meine Handschrift lesen!**
	I'll do it! ... I hope you can read my writing!
Die Beamtin	**Lassen Sie mal sehen! Ja, das geht.**
	Let me see. Yes, that's fine.
Paul	**Was soll ich hier schreiben?**
	What should I write here?
Die Beamtin	**Sie müssen den Inhalt sowie dessen ungefähren Wert angeben.**
	You must specify the contents as well as the approximate value.
Paul	**Gut. Bitte sehr. Wie viel macht das alles zusammen?**
	Good. Here you are. How much does that all come to?

Die Beamtin wiegt das Paket und rechnet alles zusammen. Paul klebt die Briefmarken auf seine Briefe.
The official weighs the parcel and totals everything up. Paul sticks the stamps on his letters.

Die Beamtin	**Das macht zusammen zweiundzwanzig Euro neunzig. Haben Sie es passend?**
	That'll be twenty two euros ninety all together. Do you have the right money?
Paul	**Einen Augenblick! Ich sehe nach. Ja, habe ich. Bitte.**
	Just a moment. I'll have a look. Yes, I have. Here you are.
Die Beamtin	**Danke. Stimmt. Schönen Tag noch!**
	Thanks. It's just right. Have a nice day!
Paul	**Ihnen auch.**
	You, too

Grammatik/Grammar

1. VERBEN/VERBS

brauchen to need

ich brauche	ich brauche nicht	brauche ich ... ?
Sie brauchen	Sie brauchen nicht	brauchen Sie ... ?
du brauchst	du brauchst nicht	brauchst du ... ?
er/sie/es braucht	er/sie/es braucht nicht	braucht er/sie/es ...?
wir brauchen	wir brauchen nicht	brauchen wir ... ?
Sie brauchen	Sie brauchen nicht	brauchen Sie ... ?
ihr braucht	ihr braucht nicht	braucht ihr ... ?
sie brauchen	sie brauchen nicht	brauchen sie ... ?

Sie braucht einen neuen Koffer.
She needs a new suitcase.

Sie brauchen nicht zu kommen.
You needn't come/You don't have to come.

Er braucht drei Stunden, um mit dem Auto nach Berlin zu fahren.
It takes him three hours by car to drive to Berlin.

2. PRONOUNS - ZU

zu
to, at, of, on; too; closed

Wie komme ich hier <u>zum</u> Bahnhof?
How do I get **to** the station from here?

Wolfgang fährt <u>zu</u> seinen Eltern.
Wolfgang is going **to see** his parents.

Äpfel <u>zu</u> 3 Euro 20 das Kilo
apples **at** 3 euros 20 a kilo

Wir fahren <u>zu</u> dritt ins Grüne.
The three **of** us are going into the country.

Wir gehen <u>zu</u> Fuß.
We're going **on** foot.

<u>zum</u> ersten Mal

for the first time

Ich habe sie nur <u>zum</u> Teil verstanden.
I only her partly understood.
(**der Teil** the part, the share)

<u>zum</u> Wohl!   **<u>zu</u> Hilfe!**
Good health!   Help!

Die Rechnung ist sofort <u>zu</u> bezahlen.
The bill must be paid immediately.

Herr Schmidt machte eine Reise, ohne viel Gepäck mit<u>zu</u>nehmen.
Mr. Schmidt went on a trip without taking much luggage with him.

Der Mantel ist <u>zu</u> groß. Die Jacke ist <u>zu</u> klein.
The coat is **too** big. The jacket is too small.

Die Tür ist <u>zu</u>.
The door is **closed**.

Wir haben heute <u>zu</u>.
We're closed today.

Zu is also used with verbs – see the next lesson.

3. UM

> um
> around, at, about

Es geht mir nicht <u>ums</u> Geld.
I'm not concerned **about** the money.

Wir müssen <u>um</u> jeden Preis gewinnen.
We must win **at** all costs.

<u>Um</u> Gottes willen!
For goodness' sake!

4. UM ... ZU

> um ... zu
> to, in order to

Ich bin hierher gekommen, <u>um</u> mit dem Chef <u>zu</u> sprechen.
I have come here **in order to** speak to the manager.

Sie ist heute Abend zu müde, <u>um</u> ins Theater mit<u>zu</u>kommen.
She is too tired **to** come with us to the theater this evening.

5. VERBEN/VERBS

angeben to state

ich gebe an	ich gebe nicht an	gebe ich ... an?
Sie geben an	Sie geben nicht an	geben Sie ... an?
du gibst an	du gibst nicht an	gibst du ... an?
er/sie/es gibt an	er /sie/es gibt nicht an	gibt er/sie/es ... an?
wir geben an	wir geben nicht an	geben wir ... an?
Sie geben an	Sie geben nicht an	geben Sie ... an?
ihr gebt an	ihr gebt nicht an	gebt ihr ... an?
sie geben an	sie geben nicht an	geben sie ... an?

This verb contains the verb **geben** – **to give** and is one of a large number of verbs which can be formed from the base verb and a preposition. It behaves just as **anfangen** in Lesson 5.

Others are: **zugeben** to admit, to allow

nachgeben to give way, to give in

zurückgeben to give back, to return (something)

Examples:

Bitte geben sie Ihren Namen und Ihre Adresse an.
Please state your name and address.

angeben also means "**to boast**":

Geben Sie doch nicht so an!
Don't boast so much!

Other examples of verbs formed from a base verb and a preposition in the dialogue are:

ausfüllen   to fill out, fill in

zusammenrechnen   to add up, total up

6. DIRECT OBJECT PRONOUNS

You are familiar with the pronouns **ich**, **Sie**, **du**, **er**, **sie**, **es**, **wir**, **Sie**, **ihr**, **sie**, to mean **I**, **you**, **you** *(familiar)*, **he**, **she**, **it**, **we**, **you** *(plural)*, **you** *(familiar plural)*, **they**.

However, you also need to be able to say me, you, him, her, them, etc. using the pronouns as **direct objects**.

You do this by putting the pronouns into their accusative form.

Examples using kennen (to know):

Ulrike kennt mich.
Ulrike knows me.

Ich kenne Ulrike.
I know Ulrike.

Ich kenne sie.
I know her.

Sie kennen dich.
They know you *(familiar)*.

Wir kennen Herrn Schmidt.
We know Mr. Schmidt.

Wir kennen ihn.
We know him.

Er kennt Ulrike und mich.
He knows Ulrike and me.

Er kennt uns.
He knows us.

Kennen Sie Herrn und Frau Schmidt?
Do you know Mr. and Mrs. Schmidt?

Kennen Sie sie?
Do you know them?

Note also:

Sie kennen sich.
They know each other.

These are all examples of pronouns being used as the **direct object**.

However, when you say **to me**, **to him**, **to us**, you use **indirect object** pronouns which require the dative case.

Examples:

Paul gibt mir den Brief.
Paul gives me the letter/he gives the letter to me.

Die Beamtin gibt Paul die Briefmarken.
The official gives Paul the stamps.

Sie gibt sie ihm.
She gives them to him.

Wolfgang schreibt Ulrike einen Brief.
Wolfgang is writing Ulrike a letter.

Er schreibt ihr einen Brief.
He's writing a letter to her.

Ich schreibe dir bald.
I'll write to you *(familiar)* soon.

Unsere Freunde schreiben uns oft.
Our friends often write to us.

Wir schreiben ihnen ab und zu.
We write to them now and again.

Ich schreibe Ihnen bald.
I'll write to you *(polite form)* soon.

Frau Schmidt schreibt euch einem Brief.
Mrs. Schmidt is writing you *(familiar plural)* a letter.

Note:

Wie geht es <u>Ihnen</u>?	**Wie geht es <u>ihr</u>?**
How are you?	How is she?
Wie geht es <u>dir</u>?	**Wie geht es <u>ihm</u>?**
How are you *(familiar singular)*?	How is he?
Wie geht es <u>euch</u>?	**Wie geht es <u>ihnen</u>?**
How are you *(familiar plural)*?	How are they?

Personal pronouns can also be used with prepositions:

Sie kommt mit <u>mir</u> *(dative)*.	**Da ist ein Brief für <u>dich</u>** *(accusative)*.
She's coming with me.	There's a letter for you.
Er geht mit <u>ihr</u> *(dative)*.	**Sie gehen ohne <u>ihn</u>** *(accusative)*.
He's going with her.	They're going without him.

7. VERBEN/VERBS

---

sagen to say/to tell

ich sage	ich sage nicht	sage ich ... ?
Sie sagen	Sie sagen nicht	sagen Sie ... ?
du sagst	du sagst nicht	sagst du ... ?
er/sie/es sagt	er/sie/es sagt nicht	sagt er/sie/es ... ?
wir sagen	wir sagen nicht	sagen wir ... ?
Sie sagen	Sie sagen nicht	sagen Sie ... ?
ihr sagt	ihr sagt nicht	sagt ihr ... ?
sie sagen	sie sagen nicht	sagen sie ... ?

Ulrike sagt Herrn Schmidt guten Morgen.
Ulrike says good morning to Mr. Schmidt.

Die Beamtin sagt dem jungen Mann den Preis der Briefmarken.
The clerk tells the young man the price of the stamps.

Können Sie mir bitte sagen, wann der nächste Bus kommt?
Can you please tell me when the next bus comes?

Was wollen Sie damit sagen?	(**damit** comes from the preposition
What do you mean by that?	**mit** and means "**with it**")

Ich sage Ihnen Bescheid.
I'll let you know.

Another verb which is irregular:

lesen to read

ich lese	ich lese nicht	lese ich ... ?
Sie lesen	Sie lesen nicht	lesen Sie ... ?
du liest	du liest nicht	liest du ... ?
er/sie/es liest	er/sie/es liest nicht	liest er/sie/es ... ?
wir lesen	wir lesen nicht	lesen wir ... ?
Sie lesen	Sie lesen nicht	lesen Sie ... ?
ihr lest	ihr lest nicht	lest ihr ... ?
sie lesen	sie lesen nicht	lesen sie ... ?

Ulrike liest ihr Buch.
Ulrike is reading her book.

Können Sie nicht lesen?
Can't you read?

Verstehen Sie, was Sie lesen?
Do you understand what you are reading?

8. DESSEN/DEREN/WHOSE/WHICH

masculine	feminine	neuter	plural
dessen	deren	dessen	deren

These are relative pronouns, meaning **whose**, **of whom**, and **of which**.

Ist das der Mann, <u>dessen</u> Auto vor meiner Garage steht?
Is that the man whose car is in front of my garage?

Sie ist die Frau, <u>deren</u> Bücher ich gerne lese.
She's the lady **whose** books I love to read.

Das ist das Kind, <u>dessen</u> Vater so reich ist.
That's the child **whose** father is so rich.

The plural is **deren** for all three genders:

Die Kinder, <u>deren</u> Väter reich sind, fahren nicht mit dem Bus.
The children whose fathers are rich do not travel by bus.

9. VERBEN/VERBS

---

sollen ought to/be supposed to/shall

ich soll	ich soll nicht	soll ich … ?
Sie sollen	Sie sollen nicht	sollen Sie … ?
du sollst	du sollst nicht	sollst du … ?
er/sie/es soll	er/sie/es soll nicht	soll er/sie/es … ?
wir sollen	wir sollen nicht	sollen wir … ?
Sie sollen	Sie sollen nicht	sollen Sie … ?
ihr sollt	ihr sollt nicht	sollt ihr … ?
sie sollen	sie sollen nicht	sollen sie … ?

Was soll ich hier schreiben?
What should I write here?

Sie sollen hier Ihren Namen und Ihre Adresse schreiben.
You're supposed to write your name and your address here.

Du sollst nicht mit diesen Kindern spielen!
You shouldn't play with those children! *(said to a child)*

Dieser Brief soll auf die Post.
This letter is to be taken to the post office.

Was soll ich jetzt tun?
What am I to do now?

Er soll hereinkommen!
Tell him to come in.

Was soll das?
What's the idea?/What's the meaning of this?

Sollen is another auxiliary verb and behaves just like **können**, **müssen**, **dürfen** in earlier lessons.

10. DIE ZUKUNFT / THE FUTURE TENSE

As you have already seen in a number of examples, the present tense is often used in German to express the future. More on this in a later chapter. However, there is also a "proper" future tense, which is formed by the use of the auxiliary verb **werden**. It behaves very much like the other auxiliary verbs you have met so far.

werden to become		
ich werde	ich werde nicht	werde ich ... ?
Sie werden	Sie werden nicht	werden Sie ... ?
du wirst	du wirst nicht	wirst du ... ?
er/sie/es wird	er /sie/es wird nicht	wird er/sie/es ... ?
wir werden	wir werden nicht	werden wir ... ?
Sie werden	Sie werden nicht	werden Sie ... ?
ihr werdet	ihr werdet nicht	werdet ihr ... ?
sie werden	sie werden nicht	werden sie ... ?

Sie wird in einer Stunde hier sein.
She'll be here in an hour.

Wir werden sehen.
We'll see./We shall see.

Ich werde am Sonntag nach München fliegen.
I'm flying to Munich on Sunday.

Es wird nicht schwer sein.
It won't be difficult.

Es muss anders werden. (anders otherwise, differently)
Thing have to change./We cannot go on like this.

Werden can also be used on its own, to mean **to become**, **to get**:

Ich werde müde.
I'm getting tired.

Es wird Herbst.
Autumn is coming.

Wortschatz/Vocabulary

die Post: *the post office*
die Briefmarke: *the postage stamp*
die Postkarte: *the postcard*
das Inland: *the home country, the country in which you are*
das Ausland: *the foreign country, overseas*
brauchen: *to need, to require*
die Post: *the mail, the post*
die USA: *the USA*
die Vereinigten Staaten: *the United States*
wiegen: *to weigh*
die Waage: *the scale*
anschließend: *subsequently, after that*
entsprechend: *corresponding, suitable, appropriate*
das Paket: *the parcel*
verschicken: *to send*
die Ordnung: *the order*
in Ordnung: *okay, fine*
senden: *to send*
dauern: *to continue, to take (time)*
wie lange wird es dauern?: *how long will it take?*
normalerweise: *normally, as a rule*
bevor: *before*
das Formular: *the form*
ausfüllen: *to fill out, to fill in*
Sie müssen dieses Formular ausfüllen: *you have to fill out this form*
die Adresse: *the address*
der Absender: *the sender*
der Empfänger: *the recipient*
sowie: *as well as*
mache ich!: *will do!/O.K.*

hoffentlich: *hopefully/I hope/we hope (so)*
die Handschrift: *the handwriting*
lassen Sie mal sehen: *let me see, let me have a look*
sollen: *shall, ought to, to be supposed to*
angeben: *to state, to specify; to boast*
der Inhalt: *the contents (plural)*
die Marke: *the stamp*
kleben: *to stick*
wie viel macht das alles zusammen?: *how much does it come to all together?*
zusammen: *together*
zusammenrechnen: *to add up*
zufällig: *by chance, as it happens*
passend: *suitable, fitting*
haben Sie es passend?: *do you have the right money?*
der Augenblick: *the moment*
einen Augenblick!: *just a moment*
nachsehen: *to have a look*
ich sehe nach: *I'll have a look*
es stimmt: *it's just right; that's right*
gleich *(adverb)***:** *immediately, at once*
gleich *(adjective)***:** *like, identical, same*
der Apfel: *the apple*
das Kilo: *the kilogram (2.2 lbs)*
der Kilometer: *the kilometer (5/8 of a mile)*
zum Wohl!: *good health!*
die Hilfe: *the help*
zum ersten Mal: *for the first time*
der Teil: *the part*
oft: *often*
ab und zu: *now and again*
zum Teil: *partly*

die Tür: *the door*
die Jacke: *the jacket*
nächst... *(it always has an ending):* **next, nearest**
am nächsten Tag: *the next day*
die Zeitung: *the newspaper*
lesen: *to read*
kennen: *to know (someone)*
dessen: *whose, of whom, of which (masculine and neuter)*
deren: *whose (plural of all genders), whose/ of whom (feminine singular)*
der Vater: *the father*
die Mutter: *the mother*
der Bescheid: *the information*

Bescheid sagen: *to let (someone) know*
anders: *otherwise*
ohne: *without*
müde: *tired*
wozu: *what for?*
kaufen: *to buy*
wohin?: *where to?*
bevor: *before*
sonst noch: *apart from that, as well*
einsetzen: *to insert*
verkaufen: *to sell*
die Telefonnummer: *the telephone number*

Übungen/Exercises

Exercise A

BITTE BEANTWORTEN SIE DIESE FRAGEN ZUM TEXT:

Please answer these questions about the dialogue.

1. Will Paul eine Postkarte kaufen?

....

2. Wie viele Briefe muss er absenden?

....

3. Wohin will er die Briefe senden?

....

4. Was tut die Beamtin mit den Briefen?

....

5. Geht das Paket nach Kanada oder in die Vereinigten Staaten?

....

6. Was muss Paul tun, bevor er das Paket absenden kann?

....

7. Was muss er auf das Formular schreiben?

....

8. Kann die Beamtin seine Handschrift lesen?

....

Exercise B

BITTE SETZEN SIE DIE ENTSPRECHENDEN PRONOMEN EIN!

Please insert the appropriate pronouns.

Beispiel: Frau Schmidt kennt den Chef = Sie kennt ihn.

1. Ulrike fährt ohne Wolfgang in die Stadt.   ....

2. Ulrike und Wolfgang gehen mit Paul ins Kino.   ....

3. Die Empfangsdame hat zwei Pakete für Herrn Schmidt und mich. ....

4. Wolfgang gibt Ulrike seine Telefonnummer.   ....

Exercise C

SETZEN SIE DIE VERBEN IN DIE ZUKUNFT!

Put the verbs into the future tense.

Beispiel: Ich fliege nach München. = Ich werde nach München fliegen.

1. Paul schreibt einige Briefe.

....

2. Wir gehen heute Abend ins Theater.

....

3. Wann fliegen Sie nach München?

....

4. Ich gehe heute nicht in die Stadt.

....

5. Ich habe keine Zeit.

....

10. The Weather

Lesson 10 is all about the weather. You will learn new verbs, as well as the months and seasons. You will also improve and build on your language skills by learning how to use direct object pronouns to make more complicated (and natural) sentences.

DAS WETTER THE WEATHER

Herr Schmidt	Und, Paul, fahren Sie am Wochenende ins Grüne? Ich weiß, dass Sie die frische Luft lieben.
	And, Paul, are you going out into the country at the weekend? I know you love the fresh air.
Paul	Nein. Ich bleibe lieber in Berlin.
	No. I prefer to stay in Berlin.
Herr Schmidt	Wirklich? Warum denn? Zu dieser Jahreszeit ist die Landschaft um Berlin doch so schön.
	Really? Why's that? The countryside around Berlin is so lovely at this time of year.
Paul	Das stimmt! Aber auch in Berlin kann ich spazieren gehen, vor allem bei so schönem Frühlingswetter wie heute. Sehen Sie mal den blauen Himmel an! Die Sonne scheint. Es ist fast keine Wolke am Himmel.
	That's true! But I can go for walks in Berlin as well, especially in such lovely spring weather as today. Just look at the blue sky! The sun is shining. There is hardly a cloud in the sky.
Herr Schmidt	Der Wetterbericht sagt aber Regen fürs Wochenende voraus.

Was wollen Sie bei Regenwetter machen? Warten Sie auf besseres Wetter?

But the weather forecast if for rain at the weekend. What do you intend to do if it rains? Are you going to wait for better weather?

Paul Keineswegs! Ich ziehe meinen Regenmantel an, nehme meinen Regenschirm mit und gehe trotzdem spazieren. Oder ich kann billig mit dem Bus fahren. Ich habe eine Abo-Karte, die für drei Monate gültig ist.

Not at all! I'll put on my raincoat, take my umbrella with me and go for a walk all the same. Or I can travel cheaply on the bus. I have a season ticket which is valid for three months.

Herr Schmidt Aber wenn das Wetter kühl wird, bleiben Sie doch bestimmt zu Hause?

But if the weather turns cool, you'll be staying at home, won't you?

Paul Im Gegenteil! Bei kühlem Wetter ziehe ich warme Kleidung an und gehe trotzdem weg. Ich habe viele Freunde, vor allem meine Kommilitonen. Ich kann sie besuchen. Wir können uns gut unterhalten. Wir reden, wir sehen fern, wir hören Musik oder trinken etwas.

On the contrary! If the weather is cool, I put on warm clothes and still go out. I have lots of friends, especially my fellow students. I can visit them. We can have a good time. We talk, we watch T.V., we listen to music or we have a drink.

Herr Schmidt Und wo verbringen Sie die Ferien?

And where do you spend the vacations?

Paul Ich verbringe die Ferien gewöhnlich in Berlin und Umgebung.

I usually spend the vacations in Berlin and the surrounding area.

Herr Schmidt Was mich angeht, so ziehe ich es vor, die Ferien weit entfernt von Berlin zu verbringen. Im Winter fahre ich manchmal in die Berge, und im Sommer fliege ich nach Österreich, um einen guten Wein zu trinken.

As far as I am concerned, I prefer to spend the vacations a long way from Berlin. In the winter, I sometimes go to the mountains and in summer, I fly to Austria to drink good wine.

Paul Das ist auch keine schlechte Idee!

That's not a bad idea either!

Grammatik/Grammar

1. DIE MONATE/THE MONTHS

Wie viele Monate gibt es im Jahr?
How many months are there in the year?

Es gibt zwölf Monate im Jahr.
There are twelve months in the year.

der Januar	January	der Juli	July
der Februar	February	der August	August
der März	March	der September	September
der April	April	der Oktober	October
der Mai	May	der November	November
der Juni	June	der Dezember	December

im Mai
in May

2. DIE JAHRESZEITEN/THE SEASONS

Wie viele Jahreszeiten gibt es in Deutschland?
How many seasons are there in Germany?

In Deutschland gibt es vier Jahreszeiten.
In Germany there are four seasons.

Die Jahreszeiten sind:

der Winter	winter	der Herbst	autumn/fall
der Frühling	spring	im Winter	in winter
das Frühjahr	spring	im Sommer	in summer
der Sommer	summer		

Ich habe den Winter nicht gern.
I don't like winter.

(etwas gern haben **to like something**)

Ich ziehe den Frühling vor.
I prefer spring.

(vorziehen **to prefer**)

3. WIE IST DAS WETTER?/WHAT'S THE WEATHER LIKE?

Im Winter ist es kalt.
It's cold in winter.

Im Sommer ist es warm.
In summer, it's warm.

Im Herbst ist es kühl.
In fall, it's cool.

Im Frühling ist es angenehm.
In spring, it's pleasant.

Zu dieser Jahreszeit ist Berlin so schön.
Berlin is so nice at this time of year.

4. COMPOUND WORDS

In German you can make one noun out of two or more other nouns by merging them together; sometimes a linking -s-, an -es- or an -n- needs to be added to the first noun. Note that the gender is determined by the last word.

Examples:

das Jahr	+	die Zeit	=	die Jahreszeit
				the season
die Woche	+	das Ende	=	das Wochenende
				the weekend
der Frühling	+	das Wetter	=	das Frühlingswetter
				the spring weather
das Wetter	+	der Bericht	=	der Wetterbericht
				the weather report
der Regen	+	das Wetter	=	das Regenwetter
				the rainy weather
der Regen	+	der Mantel	=	der Regenmantel
				the raincoat
der Regen	+	der Schirm	=	der Regenschirm
				the umbrella
die Sonne	+	der Schirm	=	der Sonnenschirm
				the sunshade
die Post	+	die Karte	=	die Postkarte
				the postcard
der Brief	+	die Tasche	=	die Brieftasche
				the wallet

See what nouns you can recognize in other lessons that are made up of two nouns.

Other examples:

| der Arm | + | das Band | + | die Uhr | = | die Armbanduhr |
| (arm) | | (band, tape) | | | | the wristwatch |

die Kraft	+	das Fahrzeug			=	das Kraftfahrzeug
						the motor vehicle
						(often abbreviated to Kfz e.g. in road signs)

5. VERBEN/VERBS

---

ziehen to pull/to draw/to move

ich ziehe	ich ziehe nicht	ziehe ich . . . ?
Sie ziehen	Sie ziehen nicht	ziehen Sie. . . ?
du ziehst	du ziehst nicht	ziehst du. . . ?
er/sie/es zieht	er/sie/es zieht nicht	zieht er/sie/es. . . ?
wir ziehen	wir ziehen nicht	ziehen wir. . . ?
Sie ziehen	Sie ziehen nicht	ziehen Sie. . . ?
ihr zieht	ihr zieht nicht	zieht ihr. . . ?
sie ziehen	sie ziehen nicht	ziehen sie. . . ?

Pflanzen ziehen ihre Nahrung aus dem Boden.
Plants draw their nourishment from the ground.

Das Pferd zieht den Wagen.
The horse is drawing the cart.

Wolfgang zieht seine Brieftasche aus der Tasche.
Wolfgang takes his wallet out of his pocket.

Bitte die Tür schließen! Es zieht.
Please close the door. There's a draft.

Ziehen!
Pull *(on doors)* as opposed to:
Drücken! *(in Germany)*
Stoßen! *(in Austria and Switzerland)*
Push

Ziehen is also used as a basis for many other verbs. Here are some examples, using prepositions you have already encountered.

abziehen to take off

Können Sie etwas vom Preis abziehen?
Can you take something off the price?

anziehen to put on

Paul zieht seinen Regenmantel an.
Paul puts on his raincoat.

Ich habe nichts anzuziehen.
I have nothing to wear.

ausziehen to take off, remove

Ulrike zieht ihren Pullover aus.
Ulrike takes off her sweater.

einziehen move in(to)

Der neue Mieter zieht ein.
The new tenant is moving in.

zuziehen to close; to consult

Frau Schmidt zieht die Gardinen zu.
Mrs. Schmidt draws the curtains.

Ich werde den Arzt zuziehen (or hinzuziehen).
I will consult the doctor.

vorziehen to prefer

Ich ziehe den Frühling vor.
I prefer spring.

Paul zieht es vor, in Berlin zu bleiben.
Paul prefers to stay in Berlin.

hören to hear/to listen

ich höre	ich höre nicht	höre ich … ?
Sie hören	Sie hören nicht	hören Sie … ?
du hörst	du hörst nicht	hörst du … ?
er/sie/es hört	er /sie/es hört nicht	hört er/sie/es … ?
wir hören	wir hören nicht	hören wir … ?
Sie hören	Sie hören nicht	hören Sie … ?
ihr hört	ihr hört nicht	hört ihr … ?
sie hören	sie hören nicht	hören sie … ?

Paul hört Musik.
Paul is listening to music.

Hören Sie?
Can you hear me?

Sie hören in den nächsten Tagen von mir!
You'll be hearing from me in the next few days!

Wie ich höre, fliegt Ulrike am Freitag nach München.
I hear Ulrike is flying to Munich on Friday.

---

sehen to see/to look

ich sehe	ich sehe nicht	sehe ich … ?
Sie sehen	Sie sehen nicht	sehen Sie … ?
du siehst	du siehst nicht	siehst du … ?
er/sie/es sieht	er/sie/es sieht nicht	sieht er/sie/es … ?
wir sehen	wir sehen nicht	sehen wir … ?
Sie sehen	Sie sehen nicht	sehen Sie … ?
ihr seht	ihr seht nicht	seht ihr … ?
sie sehen	sie sehen nicht	sehen sie … ?

Paul sieht Ulrike.
Paul sees Ulrike.

Frau Schmidt sieht aus dem Fenster.
Mrs. Schmidt is looking out of the window.

Darf ich das bitte sehen?
May I have a look at it please?

Wann sehen wir uns wieder?
When shall we see each other again?

Sehen, with a preposition added on in front, can be used to form other verbs.

Two examples of these from the dialogue are **ansehen** and **fernsehen**.

ansehen to look at, view, consider

Sehen Sie mal den blauen Himmel an!
Just look at the blue sky!

Morgen werden wir uns den Film ansehen.
We're going to see the movie tomorrow.

Ich muss mir das ansehen.
I must have a look at that.

fernsehen to watch TV

Paul und seine Kommilitonen sehen fern.
Paul and his fellow students are watching TV.

warten to wait

ich warte	ich warte nicht	warte ich … ?
Sie warten	Sie warten nicht	warten Sie … ?
du wartest	du wartest nicht	wartest du … ?
er/sie/es wartet	er/sie/es wartet nicht	wartet er/sie/es … ?
wir warten	wir warten nicht	warten wir … ?
Sie warten	Sie warten nicht	warten Sie … ?
ihr wartet	ihr wartet nicht	wartet ihr … ?
sie warten	sie warten nicht	warten sie … ?

Ulrike wartet auf den Bus.
Ulrike is waiting for the bus.

Bitte warten Sie!
Hold on please! *(on the telephone)*.

Wir werden bis vier Uhr auf Sie warten.
We will wait until four o'clock for you.

Ich kann warten.
I can wait.

abwarten to wait for

Werden Sie besseres Wetter abwarten?
Are you going to wait for better weather?

Warten Sie ab, bis Sie an die Reihe kommen!
(**die Reihe** row, series, line)
Wait until it is your turn!

Abwarten und Tee trinken!
Wait and see.

6. WORD ORDER WITH DASS, WENN, OB

Dass, **wenn**, and **ob** are used as conjunctions, meaning **that**, **if/when**, and **whether**.

Sie <u>lieben</u> die frische Luft. Ich weiß, dass Sie die frische Luft <u>lieben</u>.
You love the fresh air.   I know you appreciate the fresh air.

Die Kinder <u>sind</u> gar nicht müde. Es ist klar, dass die Kinder gar nicht müde <u>sind</u>.
The children aren't at all tired.   It's clear that the children aren't at all tired.

You have seen that the verb normally comes as the second element of a German sentence, whichever way around the sentence is. However, if part of a sentence begins with **dass**, **wenn** or **ob**, the verb is sent to the end.

If there is an auxiliary verb in the sentence which has already sent the main verb to the end, then putting in **dass** pushes the auxiliary verb right to the end of the sentence.

Sie <u>kommen</u> morgen.	Ich weiß, dass sie morgen <u>kommen</u>.
They're coming tomorrow.	I know that they're coming tomorrow.
Sie <u>werden</u> morgen kommen.	Ich hoffe, dass sie morgen kommen <u>werden</u>.
They'll be coming tomorrow.	I hope that they'll come tomorrow.

Another conjunction, **wenn** (**if**, **when**, **whenever**), also sends the verb to the end of the sentence, just as **dass** does:

Das Wetter <u>wird</u> kühl.
The weather's getting cool.

Wenn das Wetter kühl <u>wird</u>, bleibt Paul zu Hause.
If the weather gets cool, Paul stays at home.

Let us look at the word order of the last sentence a little more closely:

We have already seen that the verb normally comes as the second element in a German sentence. An "element" can be a verb, a noun, a noun with adjectives or a subordinate clause.

The first half of the sentence (the part which begins with **wenn** and ends with the comma) is a subordinate clause, and in the part of a sentence following a subordinate clause, the normal word order is inverted – **bleibt Paul**, as opposed to the normal **Paul bleibt**.

If the subordinate clause comes second, the normal word order remains:

Paul <u>bleibt</u> zu Hause, wenn das Wetter kühl wird.
Paul stays at home if the weather becomes cool.

Similarly, in the following two sentences:

Wenn Ulrike eine Reise macht, <u>fährt</u> sie mit dem Taxi zum Flughafen.
Whenever Ulrike goes on a trip, she travels to the airport by taxi.

Ulrike <u>fährt</u> mit dem Taxi zum Flughafen, wenn sie eine Reise macht.
Ulrike travels to the airport by taxi, whenever she goes on a trip.

Look at these sentences:

Sie <u>bleibt</u> zu Hause.	<u>Bleibt</u> sie zu Hause?
She's staying at home.	Is she staying at home?

And then, with **dass**:

Sie sagt, dass sie zu Hause <u>bleibt</u>.
She says she's staying at home.

Look at what happens when an auxiliary verb such as **werden** is included in the sentences:

Sie <u>wird</u> zu Hause bleiben.	<u>Wird</u> sie zu Hause bleiben?
She's going to stay at home.	Is she going to stay at home?

Sie sagt, dass sie zu Hause bleiben <u>wird</u>.
She says she'll be staying at home.

After **dass**, the **werden** goes to the end.

The conjunction **ob** (**whether**) also has the same effect as **dass** and **wenn**:

Paul <u>bleibt</u> zu Hause.   <u>Bleibt</u> Paul zu Hause?
Paul is staying at home.   Is Paul staying at home?

Es hängt vom Wetter ab, ob Paul zu Hause <u>bleibt</u>.
It depends on the weather, whether Paul stays at home.

Ob Paul zu Hause <u>bleibt</u>, hängt vom Wetter ab.
Whether Paul stays at home, depends on the weather.

(**abhängen von** to depend on)
(**der Umstand** circumstance)

With **werden**:

Paul <u>wird</u> zu Hause bleiben.   <u>Wird</u> Paul zu Hause bleiben?
Paul will be staying at home.   Will Paul be staying at home?

Es hängt vom Wetter ab, ob Paul zu Hause bleiben <u>wird</u>.
It depends on the weather, whether Paul will stay at home.

Ob Paul zu Hause bleiben <u>wird</u>, hängt vom Wetter ab.
Whether Paul will stay at home, depends on the weather.

Und (**and**) is used merely to join two sentences together. The verbs remain in position in both sentences, which are still considered as separate sentences for the purposes of word order.

Ulrike fährt mit dem Taxi zum Flughafen <u>und</u> fliegt nach München.
Ulrike travels by taxi to the airport and flies to Munich.

You can insert an adverb, e.g. **dann**:

Paul zieht seinen Regenmantel an und geht dann spazieren.
Paul puts on his raincoat and then goes for a walk.

The separable verbs used in the examples:

annehmen	to assume
abhängen	to depend on
mitnehmen	to take *(something)* with *(you)*
mitkommen	to come along, to come too
anziehen	to put on

all behave like **anfangen** and **vorziehen**, which you have already met, in that they consist of a separable part, which splits off from its main part, and is sent to the end when the verb is used in a simple sentence.

An diesem Sonntag <u>kommt</u> Paul <u>mit</u>.
This Sunday, Paul is coming too.

Paul <u>zieht</u> seinen Regenmantel <u>an</u>.
Paul is putting on his raincoat.

However, the separable part of the verb joins up with the main part again when it is sent to the end of the part of the sentence which begins with **wenn**, **ob**, **dass**, and similar conjunctions.

Wenn Paul seinen Regenmantel <u>mitnimmt</u>, regnet es nie.

When Paul takes his raincoat with him, it never rains.

Es hängt vom Wetter ab, ob Paul am Sonntag mitkommt.
It depends on the weather, whether Paul comes along on Sunday.

This can also be expressed the other way round:

Ob Paul am Sonntag mitkommt, hängt vom Wetter ab.
Whether Paul comes along on Sunday depends on the weather.

7. TIME, MANNER, AND PLACE

It is important to note that in German sentences, expressions of **time** normally come before expressions of **manner**, which come before expressions of **place**.

Ulrike wird am Freitag mit der Lufthansa nach München fliegen.
                time   manner   place
Ulrike will be flying to Munich on Friday with Lufthansa.

Paul fährt morgen mit dem Bus nach Dahlem.
            time   manner   place
Paul is going to Dahlem by bus tomorrow.

Herr Schmidt kommt jeden Abend müde nach Hause.
                   time   manner   place
Every evening, Mr. Schmidt comes home tired.

When **dass** is placed in front of the above sentence, the time, manner, place order remains while the verb, in this case **kommt**, is sent to the end.

Seine Frau bemerkt, dass Herr Schmidt jeden Abend müde nach Hause kommt.
His wife notices that Mr. Schmidt comes home tired every evening.

8. VERBS THAT TAKE ZU

When **brauchen** (to need/ have to) is used with another verb, **zu** is placed before the second or dependent verb:

Du brauchst es mir nur zu sagen. (nur only)
You only have to tell me.

Sie brauchen es mir nicht zu sagen.
You **don't have to** tell me.

Morgen brauchen wir nicht zu arbeiten, weil Sonntag ist.
We **don't have to** work tomorrow, because it is Sunday.

The 'zu' is placed between the two parts of a separable verb:

Sie brauchen nichts zuzuzahlen. (zuzahlen to pay extra)
You **need not** pay **anything** extra.

Paul braucht nicht mitzukommen, wenn er nicht will.
Paul **does not need to** come along if he doesn't want to.

Vorziehen (to prefer) also needs a 'zu', which is added in front of the verb in the dependent clause. If the verb is separable, 'zu' is inserted in the middle of the verb:

Ich ziehe es vor, früh ins Bett zu gehen.
I prefer to go to bed early.

Paul zieht es vor, mit seinen Kommilitonen fernzusehen.
Paul prefers to go watch TV with his fellow students.

Note the **es** in the above sentences, which is needed, unlike in English.

9. VERBEN/VERBS

Zu is also required when the verbs **lernen (to learn)** and **lehren (to teach)** are used with a dependent clause:

Wir lehren die Kinder, alte Leute mit Nachsicht zu behandeln.
We're teaching the children to treat old people with consideration.

Er muss noch lernen, pünktlich anzukommen.
He still has to learn to get here on time.

Du musst lernen, vorsichtiger zu zein.
You have to learn to be more careful.
(**vorsichtig cautious, careful**; **vorsichtiger more careful**)

Note the following usage:

Er lehrt die Kinder schwimmen.
He's **teaching** the children to swim.

Sie lernt kochen.
She's **learning to** cook.

Die Kinder lernen schwimmen.
The children **are learning to** swim.

10. COMPARITIVE ADJECTIVES

The comparative of an adjective is usually formed by putting **-er** on the end and the superlative by putting **-st** or **-est** on the end. If the vowel is an **a**, **o** or **u**, it may change to **ä**, **ö**, **ü**, in the comparative and the superlative.

Examples:

schön	**so schön wie**	**schöner als**	**am schönsten**
lovely	as lovely as	more lovely than	the loveliest
klein	**so klein wie**	**kleiner als**	**am kleinsten**
small	as small as	smaller than	(the) smallest
klug	**so klug wie**	**klüger als**	**am klügsten**
intelligent	as intelligent as	more intelligent than	(the) most intelligent

but:

gut	so gut wie	besser als	am besten
good	as good as	better than	(the) best

Paul ist der beste Schüler in seiner Klasse.
Paul is the best student in his class.

Wolfgang ist älter als Paul. (alt old)
Wolfgang is older than Paul.

Monika ist so alt wie Ulrike.
Monika is as old as Ulrike.

Diese Schachtel ist größer als jene.
This box is bigger than that one.

Die andere Schachtel ist am größten.
The other box is the biggest of all.

Mit dem Taxi fahren wir am schnellsten zum Flughafen.
The taxi is the fastest means of getting to the airport.

Wortschatz/Vocabulary

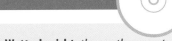

das Wochenende: *the weekend*
am Wochenende: *at/on the weekend*
ins Grüne fahren: *to drive out into the countryside*
die Landschaft: *the countryside*
grün: *green (adjective)*
frisch: *fresh*
die Luft: *the air*
vorziehen: *to prefer*
die Jahreszeit: *the season*
die Zeit: *the time*
spazieren gehen: *to go for a walk*
das Wetter: *the weather*
das Frühlingswetter: *the spring weather*
blau: *blue*
die Sonne: *the sun*
scheinen: *to shine*
die Wolke: *the cloud*

der Wetterbericht: *the weather report*
der Bericht: *the report*
der Regen: *the rain*
voraussagen: *to forecast*
das Regenwetter: *the rainy weather*
besser: *better*
abwarten: *to wait for*
wollen: *to want (to), to intend to, to be going to*
der Regenmantel: *the raincoat*
der Regenschirm: *the umbrella*
mitnehmen: *to take (something) with (you)*
mitkommen: *to come along, to come with (someone)*
die Abo-Karte: *the season ticket*
gültig: *valid*
billig: *cheap*
keineswegs: *by no means, not at all*

doch: *after all, however, still*
der Monat: *the month*
kühl: *cool*
kalt: *cold*
heiß: *hot*
warm: *warm*
bestimmt: *certainly, surely*
bleiben: *to stay, to remain*
im Gegenteil: *on the contrary, quite the reverse*
das Gegenteil: *the opposite*
der Kommilitone: *the fellow student*
weggehen: *to go out*
besuchen: *to visit*
wir unterhalten uns gut: *we have a good time*
sehen: *to see*
fernsehen: *to watch television*
das Fernsehen: *the television*
hören: *to hear; to listen to*
die Musik: *the music*
die Zeitschrift: *the magazine*
die Umgebung: *the surroundings*
angenehm: *pleasant*
die Ferien (plural): *the vacation, the holiday(s)*
angehen: *to concern, to regard*
was mich angeht: *as far as I'm concerned*
weit: *far*
entfernt: *distant*
weit entfernt: *far away*
verbringen: *to spend (time)*
ausgeben: *to spend (money)*
das Jahr: *the year*
der Winter: *the winter*
manchmal: *sometimes*
der Berg: *the mountain*

der Sommer: *the summer*
der Frühling: *the spring*
das Frühjahr: *the spring*
der Herbst: *the fall/the autumn*
gar nicht: *not at all*
zusammengesetzt *(aus + dative)*: *composed of, consisting of*
zusammensetzen: *to put together, to assemble*
das Auge: *the eye*
der Blick: *the glance*
der Augenblick: *the moment*
die Brieftasche: *the wallet, the pocketbook*
die Armbanduhr: *the wristwatch*
das Kraftfahrzeug: *the motor vehicle*
ziehen: *to pull*
die Pflanze: *the plant*
die Nahrung: *the nourishment*
der Boden: *the ground*
das Pferd: *the horse*
der Wagen: *the cart*
stoßen: *to push*
abziehen: *to take off, to withdraw*
anziehen: *to put on; to attract*
ausziehen: *to take off, to remove*
der Pullover: *the pullover*
einziehen: *to enter, to move in(to)*
der Mieter: *the tenant*
zuziehen: *to draw; to consult*
der Arzt: *the doctor*
die Gardine: *the curtain*
das Fenster: *the window*
wie: *as*
ansehen: *to look at, to consider*
das Konzert: *the concert*
der Schüler: *the schoolboy, the student*
die Schülerin: *the schoolgirl, the student*

warten: *to wait*	**behandeln:** *to treat*
abwarten: *to wait for*	**die Nachsicht:** *the consideration*
dass: *that*	**vorsichtig:** *cautious, careful*
wenn: *if, when, whenever*	**schwimmen:** *to swim*
ob: *whether*	**kochen:** *to cook*
dann: *then*	**die Tageskarte:** *the day ticket*
der Mann: *the man; the husband*	**folgend:** *following*
nur: *only*	**abhängen von** *(+ dative):* *to depend on*
alt: *old*	**annehmen:** *to accept*
das Bett: *the bed*	**das Wetter:** *the weather*
zuzahlen: *to pay extra*	
auslachen *(+ accusative):* *to laugh at*	

Übungen/Exercises

Exercise A

BITTE BEANTWORTEN SIE DIE FOLGENDEN FRAGEN ZUM DIALOG:

Answer these questions about the dialogue.

1. **Wird Paul am Wochenende ins Grüne fahren?**

   ....

2. **Zieht Paul es vor, in Berlin zu bleiben?**

   ....

3. **Was macht Paul bei Regenwetter?**

   ....

4. **Wie fährt Paul billiger, mit dem Bus oder mit dem Taxi?**

   ....

5. **Was nimmt Paul mit, wenn er bei Regenwetter spazieren geht?**

   ....

6. Was sagt der Wetterbericht für das Wochenende voraus?

....

7. Zu welcher Jahreszeit ist es am kältesten?

....

8. Was macht Paul, wenn es kühl wird?

....

9. Hat Paul viele Freunde in Berlin?

....

10. Was machen diese jungen Leute, wenn sie zusammen sind?

....

11. Wo verbringt Paul die Ferien?

....

12. Verbringt Herr Schmidt seine Ferien in Berlin?

....

Exercise B

BENUTZEN SIE DASS, WENN, ODER OB IN DEN FOLGENDEN SÄTZEN:

Use **dass**, **wenn**, or **ob** with the following sentences:

Beispiel: Paul geht im Regen spazieren.

    Ich sehe, dass Paul im Regen spazieren geht.

1. **Herr Schmidt wird in die Berge fahren. Ich höre, dass** ....

....

2. **Ulrike zieht ihren Pullover aus. Wolfgang bemerkt, dass** ....

....

3. Kommt Paul mit? – Ich weiß nicht, ob ....

   ....

4. Vielleicht wird es ein Konzert im Park geben. Wir gehen hin, wenn ....

   ....

11. Making Plans

Lesson 11 will further develop your command of natural speech as this chapter revolves around making plans. You will also learn more about the future tense. Don't forget that you can be listening to your vocabulary audio downloads even when you're not using the book.

EIN PICKNICK A PICNIC

Heute wollen Ulrike und Wolfgang ein Picknick machen. Sie wollen mit ihren Freunden ins Grüne fahren.
Today Ulrike and Wolfgang are going to have a picnic. They're going into the country with their friends.

Ulrike	**Wolfgang, hast du mit Monika gesprochen? Kommt sie mit?**
	Wolfgang, did you talk to Monika? Is she coming along?
Wolfgang	**Ja, ich habe gestern Abend mit ihr telefoniert. Sie kommt mit ihrem Freund. Das heißt, wir sind zu viert. Sie wollen den Käse und den Nachtisch mitbringen.**
	Yes, I spoke with her yesterday evening on the phone. She's coming with her boyfriend. That means there are four of us. They're bringing the cheese and the dessert.
Ulrike	**Ich freue mich.**
	That's good.
Wolfgang	**Mm ... Das sieht lecker aus. Was bereitest du für uns zu?**
	Mm ... That looks tasty. What are you making for us?
Ulrike	**Ich bin gerade dabei, einen gemischten Salat zuzubereiten.**
	I'm just preparing a mixed salad.

Wolfgang	Ich verstehe überhaupt nichts vom Kochen. Deshalb habe ich zwei Brathähnchen gekauft. Geht das?
	I don't know anything about cooking, so I've bought two roast chickens. Is that all right?
Ulrike	Großartig! Gib sie her! Ich tue sie in diesen Korb.
	Great! Give them to me! I'll put them in this basket.
Wolfgang	Haben wir alles, was wir brauchen?
	Do we have everything we need?
Ulrike	Noch nicht! Wir haben noch keinen Wein, und außerdem brauchen wir Brot. Beides können wir im Supermarkt kaufen.
	Not yet! We still have no wine, and we also need some bread. We can get both of them in the supermarket.
Wolfgang	Ich gehe schnell mal hin.
	I'll just go down there quickly.
Ulrike	Das ist nett. Zum Supermarkt ist es nicht weit. Du weißt ja Bescheid, nicht?
	That's nice of you. It's not far to the supermarket. You do know where it is, don't you?
Wolfgang	Ja, weiß ich. Bis gleich!
	Yes, I know. See you in a few minutes!
Ulrike	Mach schnell! Sobald Monika und ihr Freund ankommen, müssen wir losfahren.
	Hurry up! As soon as Monika and her friend get here, we have to go.

Grammatik/Grammar

1. DIE ZUKUNFT/ THE FUTURE TENSE (CONTINUED)

You have already seen the use of werden to form the future tense. However, the simplest way to express a future intention in German is by using the present tense. This way is often preferred when it is obvious from the context that the action is in the future:

Examples:

Ich bin gleich da.
I'll be right with you.

Ich komme bald zurück.
I'll be back shortly.

Nächsten Dienstag fahre ich nach Berlin.
I'm going to Berlin next Tuesday.

2. INSEPARABLE PREFIXES

Certain prefixes **never** separate from the verb. There are eight of these prefixes in German.

suchen	to search	+	be-	=	besuchen	to visit
stehen	to stand	+	ent-	=	entstehen	to arise
fehlen	to be missing	+	emp-	=	empfehlen	to recommend
warten	to wait	+	er-	=	erwarten	to expect
fallen	to fall	+	ge-	=	gefallen	to please
achten	to respect	+	miss-	=	missachten	to disregard
geben	to give	+	ver-	=	vergeben	to forgive
brechen	to break	+	zer-	=	zerbrechen	to smash

Examples:

Sie müssen das Ägyptische Museum besuchen.
You must visit the Egyptian Museum.

Ich erwarte Ihren Anruf.
I'll wait for him your call.

Dein neues Kleid gefällt mir.
I like your new dress.

Du musst dir nicht den Kopf darüber zerbrechen.
Don't worry your head about it.

Ich kann Ihnen dieses Buch wärmstens empfehlen.
I can warmly recommend this book to you.

Er hat die Vorfahrt missachtet.
He ignored the right of way.

Hier entsteht eine neue Bibliothek.
A new library is being built here.

Das wird er mir nie vergeben.
He'll never forgive me for that.

Die Stelle ist schon vergeben. (die Stelle post, position)
The position is already filled.

To illustrate how verbs change their meaning when inseparable prefixes are added on, consider the following:

halten	to hold, to keep	denken	to think
behalten	to keep	bedenken	to consider
enthalten	to contain	gedenken	to think of, to remember
verhalten	to keep back	sich verhalten	to behave

3. DIE VERGANGENHEIT/THE PAST TENSE

The past or perfect tense is usually formed with the present tense of **haben**, plus the **past participle** of the verb being placed in the past. Some verbs use **sein** instead of **haben**. The past participle is placed at the **end** of a simple sentence.

The perfect tense is the most commonly used past tense in German, especially in the spoken language.

Ich habe zwei Glas Wein getrunken.
I had two glasses of wine.

Ich habe recht behalten.
I was right after all.

Ulrike hat einen gemischten Salat zubereitet.
Ulrike prepared a mixed salad.

Ich habe nach dem Weg gefragt.
I asked for directions.

Ich habe vergessen anzurufen.
I forgot to call.

Ich bin mit dem Taxi gefahren.
I went by taxi.

Wir sind in Dresden gewesen.
We were in Dresden.

Sometimes, the past participle of the verb is formed from the **stem** of the verb (the part minus the **-en** ending).

There are several types of verb, and they form the past participle in different ways.

Strong verbs where the stem changes:

The stem takes a **ge-** on the front. The past participle ends in **-en**.

The stem itself undergoes certain modifications.

infinitive		past participle	
essen	to eat	gegessen	eaten
sitzen	to sit	gesessen	sat
trinken	to drink	getrunken	drunk
schreiben	to write	geschrieben	written
fliegen	to fly	geflogen	flown
treffen	to meet	getroffen	met
nehmen	to take	genommen	taken
tun	to do	getan	done
werden	to become	geworden	become
finden	to find	gefunden	found
sein	to be	gewesen	been
gehen	to go	gegangen	gone
stehen	to stand	gestanden	stood

Strong verbs where the stem does not change:

The stem takes a **ge-** on the front. The past participle ends in **-en**.

The stem itself remains unchanged.

infinitive		past participle	
lassen	to let, to leave	gelassen	let, left
fahren	to travel, to go	gefahren	travelled, gone
rufen	to call	gerufen	called
kommen	to come	gekommen	come
lesen	to read	gelesen	read
geben	to give	gegeben	given
fangen	to catch	gefangen	caught

Strong verbs with separable prefixes:

The prefix stays on the front of the verb.

A **-ge-** is added between the separable prefix and the root verb. The past participle ends in **-en**.

infinitive		past participle	
mitnehmen	to take along	mitgenommen	taken along
anfangen	to begin	angefangen	begun
mitkommen	to come along	mitgekommen	come along
eintreffen	to arrive, to happen	eingetroffen	arrived, happened
ankommen	to arrive	angekommen	arrived
ausgehen	to go out	ausgegangen	gone out
zurückkommen	to come back	zurückgekommen	come back

Strong verbs with inseparable prefixes:

No ge- is added to the verb. The inseparable prefix stays.

The stem changes or not, the same as the root verb. The past participle ends in -en.

infinitive		past participle	
verstehen	to understand	verstanden	understood
vergeben	to forgive	vergeben	forgiven
empfehlen	to recommend	empfohlen	recommended
zerbrechen	to smash	zerbrochen	smashed
entstehen	to arise	entstanden	arisen
behalten	to keep, to retain	behalten	kept, retained

Strong verbs with inseparable prefix ge-:

The ge- is retained. The stem may change. The past participle ends in -en.

infinitive		past participle	
gestehen	to confess	gestanden	confessed
genießen	to enjoy	genossen	enjoyed
geschehen	to happen	geschehen	happened
gelingen	to succeed	gelungen	succeeded

Regular weak verbs:

The stem remains unchanged. A **ge-** is added on to the front. The past participle ends in **-t**.

infinitive		past participle	
stellen	to put	gestellt	put
machen	to do, to make	gemacht	done, made
setzen	to set, to place	gesetzt	set, placed
hören	to hear	gehört	heard
haben	to have	gehabt	had
brauchen	to need	gebraucht	needed
mischen	to mix	gemischt	mixed
reisen	to travel	gereist	travelled

Regular weak verbs with a stem ending in **-t** or **-d**:

The stem remains unchanged. A **ge-** is added on to the front. The past participle ends in **-et**.

infinitive		past participle	
warten	to wait	gewartet	waited
arbeiten	to work	gearbeitet	worked
senden	to send	gesendet	sent

Irregular weak verbs:

The stem undergoes some modification. A **ge-** is added on to the front. The past participle ends in **-t**.

infinitive		past participle	
müssen	to have to	gemusst	had to
können	to be able to	gekonnt	been able to
denken	to think	gedacht	thought
wissen	to know *(facts)*	gewusst	known
kennen	to know *(people)*	gekannt	known
bringen	to bring	gebracht	brought

Weak verbs with separable prefixes:

The stem is modified or not, depending on whether the root verb is regular or irregular (see above).

A -ge- is added between the separable prefix and the stem. The past participle ends in -t or -et.

Examples (regular):

infinitive		past participle	
abreisen	to depart	abgereist	departed
abwarten	to wait for	abgewartet	waited for
absenden	to send off	abgesendet	sent off

Examples (irregular):

infinitive		past participle	
mitbringen	to bring along	mitgebracht	brought along
umdenken	to rethink	umgedacht	rethought

Weak verbs with inseparable prefixes:

The stem remains unchanged. The inseparable prefix remains on the front. There is no ge- added. The past participle ends in -t or -et.

Examples (regular):

infinitive		past participle	
besuchen	to visit	besucht	visited
verreisen	to travel away	verreist	travelled away
verkaufen	to sell	verkauft	sold
beantworten	to answer	beantwortet	answered
missachten	to disregard	missachtet	disregarded

Examples (irregular):

infinitive		past participle	
verbringen	to spend (time)	verbracht	spent
bedenken	to consider	bedacht	considered

Verbs with inseparable prefixes, to which is added another separable prefix or preposition:

These can be either strong or weak.

The past participle is the same as that of the main verb (whether strong or weak) with the addition of the separable prefix or preposition.

infinitive		past participle	
zubereiten	to prepare	zubereitet	prepared
zurückbekommen	to get back	zurückbekommen	got back

Verbs ending in -ieren:

These are weak verbs and the past participle ends in **-t**. No **ge-** is added at the beginning.

infinitive		past participle	
telefonieren	to phone	telefoniert	phoned
reduzieren	to reduce	reduziert	reduced
studieren	to study	studiert	studied

You must learn the past participle for each irregular verb. Study the categories of verb described above so you are sure of how the past participles are formed in each case.

The past participles of verbs are used in sentences with either **haben** or **sein** to form the past tense.

General guidance for whether **haben** or **sein** is to be used:

Use **haben** with:

1. Verbs which have a direct object or take the accusative case:

Ulrike <u>hat</u> eine Reise gemacht.
Ulrike went on a trip.

Sie <u>hat</u> den Brief gelesen.
She has written the letter.

2. Modal auxiliary verbs (dürfen, können, müssen, mögen, sollen, wollen):

Sie <u>hat</u> die Reise machen können.
She was able to make the journey.

Er <u>hat</u> den Brief schreiben müssen.
He had to write the letter.

Note that in "double infinitive" constructions such as these, neither the main verb nor the auxiliary verb in these sentences is formed as a past participle. This is the case whenever the modal verb is followed by another verb.

Compare these with:

Sie <u>hat</u> es gekonnt.	She was able to do it.
Sie <u>haben</u> es nicht gewollt.	They didn't want to.

where the regular past participle is used.

3. Reflexive verbs (see later in the lesson)

Sie <u>haben</u> sich gesetzt.
They sat down.

Sie <u>hat</u> sich gewaschen.
She got washed.

Use **haben** with most verbs which have no direct object or which take the dative case:

Sie <u>hat</u> ihm geantwortet.
She has given him an answer.

Sie <u>hat</u> gut geschlafen. (schlafen to sleep)
She slept well.

Use **sein** with:

1. most verbs showing a change from one condition or state to another, and verbs describing motion:

Sie <u>ist</u> nach München geflogen.
She flew to Munich.

Sie <u>sind</u> nicht gekommen.
They have not come.

Wir <u>sind</u> spät eingeschlafen. (einschlafen to fall asleep, to get to sleep)
We got to sleep late.

Der Chef <u>ist</u> letztes Jahr gestorben. (sterben to die)
The boss died last year.

Es <u>ist</u> schon spät geworden.
It is already quite late.

2. Past participles of bleiben and sein:

Es <u>ist</u> kalt gewesen.
It was cold.

Er <u>ist</u> zu Hause geblieben.
He stayed at home.

More examples, showing the various types of verb and their usage with **haben** or **sein**:

Ulrike <u>ist</u> in die Stadt <u>gegangen</u>. (strong verb of motion)
Ulrike **went** into town.

Frau Schmidt hat auf ihren Mann gewartet. (weak verb with an indirect object)
Mrs. Schmidt **waited** for her for her husband.

Herr Schmidt hat viel Arbeit nach Hause mitgenommen. (separable strong verb with direct object)
Mr Schmidt **took** a lot of work home with him.

Heidi hat mit Frau Schmidt am Telefon gesprochen. (strong verb with an indirect object)
Heidi **spoke** with Mrs. Schmidt on the phone.

Ich habe alles verstanden. (inseparable strong verb with a direct object)
I **understood** everything.

Ich habe mein Mittagessen genossen. (inseparable strong verb beginning with ge-, with a direct object) (**genießen** to enjoy)
I **enjoyed** my lunch.

Es hat meinen Erwartungen entsprochen. (inseparable strong verb with an indirect object) (**entsprechen** to correspond to, to meet) (**die Erwartung** the expectation)
It **met** my expectations.

Wir sind soeben in Berlin eingetroffen. (separable strong verb of motion, no direct object) (**soeben** just)
We **have** just **arrived** in Berlin.

Ich habe meinen Vater besucht. (inseparable weak verb with direct object)
I **visited** my father.

Ich habe meine Schlüssel zurückbekommen. (inseparable strong verb with added separable prefix with direct object)
I **got** my keys back.

Sentences with inverted word order or questions:

Gestern haben wir viel Deutsch gelernt. (regular weak verb with direct object)
Yesterday, we **learned** a lot of German.

Gestern sind Ulrike und Wolfgang ins Grüne gefahren. (strong verb of motion, no direct object)
Yesterday, Ulrike and Wolfgang **went** into the country.

Sind sie heute zurückgekommen? (separable strong verb of motion, no direct object)
Did they **come** back today?

In the vocabulary at the end of the book, all verbs show (**hat**) if their perfect tense is formed using **haben**, and (**ist**) if they use **sein**. Some verbs can be used with both, and in such cases you will see (**hat/ist**). Usually in such cases **haben** is used if the verb has a **direct object** (**sie hat das Auto gefahren**) and **sein** if it has no direct object (**ich bin nach München gefahren**).

In all the above sentences, the past participle has been placed at the end of the sentence.

However, in sentences containing a dependent clause (one having a conjunction such as **weil** (= **because**), **dass**, **wenn**, **ob**, **wie**) the past participle is placed just before the variant of **haben** or **sein** at the end.

Paul hat gesehen, dass viele Leute ins Kino gegangen sind.

Paul **saw** that many people **went** to the movies.

Wie ich gehört habe, ist Ulrike am Freitag nach München geflogen.
I **heard** is that Ulrike **flew** to Munich on Friday.

Ich weiß nicht, ob Wolfgang die Brathähnchen schon gekauft hat.
I don't know whether Wolfgang **has bought** the roast chickens yet.

Past participles can also be used as adjectives or in other expressions:

ein gebrauchtes Fahrrad (brauchen to need, use)
a used bicycle

eine viel besuchte Stadt.
a much-visited town

ein gut geschriebenes Buch. (schreiben to write)
a well-written book

Some adjectives look like participles and derive from nouns:

Sie ist gut gelaunt. (die Laune the mood)
She is in a good mood.

Note the use of **Rad fahren**, "to cycle":

Ich fahre Rad.   **Ich bin Rad gefahren.**
I am going cycling.   I have been cycling.

4. DER IMPERATIV/THE IMPERATIVE

The imperative of the second person singular (familiar "**you**") is usually formed by leaving the **-en** off the end of the verb.

Mach schnell! (from machen)
Be quick!/Hurry up!

Fahr nicht so schnell! (from fahren)
Don't drive so fast!

Komm her! (from kommen)
Come here.

Sometimes an **-e** is added: if the verb ends in **-eln** or **-ern** or if the stem ends in **-d** or **-t** or in a consonant combined with **-m** or **-n**:

Warte mal! (from warten)
Wait a minute!

Öffne die Tür! (from öffnen)
Open the door.

Some verbs have an irregular imperative:

Sei tapfer! (from sein) (tapfer brave)
Be brave!

Gib's mir! (from **geben**) shortened form for **Gib es mir!**
Give it to me!

Sieh da! (from **sehen**)
Look at that!

Nimm! (from **nehmen**)
Take (it)!

The imperative of verbs with separable prefixes is formed as follows:

Zieh dich an! (**sich anziehen** to get dressed)
Get dressed.

Steh auf! (**aufstehen** to get up)
Get up!

Some advice about when and when not to use the familiar form, whether in the imperative form or otherwise, was given in Lesson 5.

5. VERBEN/VERBS

tun to do

ich tue	ich tue nicht	tue ich ... ?
Sie tun	Sie tun nicht	tun Sie ... ?
du tust	du tust nicht	tust du ...
er/sie/es tut	er /sie/es tut nicht	tut er/sie/es ... ?
wir tun	wir tun nicht	tun wir ... ?
Sie tun	Sie tun nicht	tun Sie ... ?
ihr tut	ihr tut nicht	tut ihr ... ?
sie tun	sie tun nicht	tun sie ... ?

Past participle getan

Was haben Sie heute getan?
What did you do today?

Ich tue sie in diesen Korb.
I'll put them in this basket.

Sie tut ihr Möglichstes. (**möglich** possible)
She's doing everything possible.

Er tut nur so.
He's only pretending.

Es tut nichts zur Sache.
That's of no account.

Er tut seine Pflicht. (die Pflicht duty)
He's doing his duty.

Es tut mir leid.
I'm sorry.

Er/Sie tut mir leid.
I feel sorry for him/her.

Das tut mir gut.
That's doing me good.

Das tut weh.
That hurts.

6. PRONOMEN & REFLEXIVE VERBEN/ PRONOUNS AND REFLEXIVE VERBS

The pronouns you have studied so far:

		accusative		dative	
ich	I	mich	me	mir	to me
Sie	you (singular)	Sie	you	Ihnen	to you
du	you (familiar)	dich	you	dir	to you
er	he	ihn	him	ihm	to him
sie	she	sie	her	ihr	to her
es	it	es	it	ihm	to it
wir	we	uns	us	uns	to us
Sie	you (plural)	Sie	you	Ihnen	to you
ihr	you (familiar plural)	euch	you	euch	to you
sie	they	sie	them	ihnen	to them

These personal pronouns in the accusative and dative cases can also be used with some verbs to translate other shades of meaning relating to the person or persons involved in the action the verb signifies. Verbs used in this way with personal pronouns are called "reflexive" verbs. The English equivalent is "myself", "yourself" etc., though some verbs are reflexive in German but not in English.

There is one important change in the form of the pronouns: Sie, er, sie and es all have the form sich in such cases:

Some verbs can be used both reflexively or not.

Some verbs take the accusative, others take the dative, but note that in many cases, the accusative and dative forms of the personal pronouns are the same.

In the following examples illustrating the difference between a reflexive verb and its irreflexive equivalent, the personal pronoun is in the accusative:

Die Arbeit lohnt sich. (sich lohnen to be worthwhile)
The work is worthwhile.

Die Mühe lohnt sich.
It is worth the trouble/effort.

Ich freue mich.
I'm glad.

Freut mich sehr! (short for **Es freut mich sehr!**)
Pleased to meet you!

Dort teilt sich die Straße.
The street divides there.

Wir müssen uns jetzt trennen.
We must part company now./This is where we say goodbye.

In many cases, the reflexive meaning of a verb is entirely distinct from the meaning of the verb when it is not used reflexively.

Wollen Sie sich bitte eintragen? (reflexive)
Would you sign the register, please?

Das Geschäft trägt wenig ein.
The business brings is not very profitable.

Ich wasche mich jeden Morgen und Abend. (reflexive)
I wash (myself) every morning and evening.

Frau Schmidt wäscht einmal in der Woche.
Mrs. Schmidt does the washing once a week.

Bitte setzen Sie sich! (reflexive)
Please sit down./Please take a seat.

Ich setze viel Wert auf Ordnung.
I place a lot of value on tidiness.

Examples where the personal pronoun is in the dative:

Ich kaufe mir einen neuen Mantel.
I'm buying myself a new coat.

Ich wasche mir schnell die Hände.
I'll wash my hands quickly.

Some reflexive verbs exist only in their reflexive form:

Ulrike begibt sich auf die Reise.
Ulrike is setting out on her journey.

7. PRONOMINAL ADVERBS

To say **with it**, **on it**, etc. in German, you use **da-** placed in front of the relevant preposition.

da- becomes **dar-** before a preposition beginning with a vowel.

mit	with	damit	with it
auf	on	darauf	on it
durch	through	dadurch	through it
neben	near, next to	daneben	near it, next to it
gegen	towards, against	dagegen	towards it, against it
für	for	dafür	for it, in return for it
zu	to, for	dazu	to it, for it
an	at, on	daran	at it, on it
bei	close to, at	dabei	close to it, by it
vor	in front of	davor	in front of it
von	from	davon	from it
in	in	darin	in it

The use of these adverbs cannot always be expressed by these literal translations, so it is best to learn them in various contexts as vocabulary.

Examples:

Ich verstehe nichts vom Kochen. **Ich verstehe nichts <u>davon</u>.**
I know nothing about cooking.   I know nothing about it.

Was ist in der Tasche?   **Mein Reisepass ist <u>darin</u>.**
What's in the bag?   My passport is in it.

Ich warte auf seinen Aruf. **Ich warte <u>darauf</u>, dass er anruft.**
I'm waiting for his call.   I'm waiting for him to call.

Wir sind gegen Ihren Vorschlag. **Wir sind <u>dagegen</u>.** **Die anderen sind <u>dafür</u>.**
We are against your proposal.   We are against it.   The others are in favor of it.

Er hält an seiner Meinung fest. **Er hält <u>daran</u> fest. (festhalten** to stick, to cling to**)**
He's sticking to his opinion.   He's sticking to it.

Er kann nichts <u>dafür</u>.
He can't help it./It isn't his fault.

Ich will <u>damit</u> nichts zu tun haben.
I want to have nothing to do with it.

Mir fehlt das Geld <u>dazu</u>.
I don't have the money for it./I can't afford it.

Ich will nichts <u>davon</u> hören.
I don't want to hear anything about it.

Vor der Garage steht ein Auto.   **<u>Davor</u> steht ein Auto.**
There's a car in front of the garage.   There's a car in front of it.

Lassen wir es <u>dabei</u>!
Let's leave it at that.

These words are also frequently used in other senses and constructions:

dabei ... zu on the point of, about to, in the process of

Ich bin <u>dabei</u>, das Abendessen vorzubereiten.
I'm just preparing dinner.

dabei present, there:

Wer war <u>dabei</u>?
Who was there/present

darauf

Es kommt darauf an.
It depends.

Darauf kommt es an.
That is what matters./That's just the point.

dazu to that end, for that purpose

<u>Dazu</u> sind wir da!
That's what we're here for.

daran to it

Sie sind nahe <u>daran</u>, sich zu trennen.
They are close to separating.

Gehen Sie im Regen spazieren? Ich denke nicht <u>daran</u>. (**denken** to think)
Are you going for a walk in the rain? I wouldn't dream of it.

damit so that

Wir sind gekommen, <u>damit</u> wir helfen können.
We have come so that we can help/to help.

davon on it

Es hängt <u>davon</u> ab, ob es regnet.
It all depends on whether it rains or not.

Note: The words beginning with **da-** as above can only be used with things, not with people.

You say **mit ihm, zu ihr, von ihnen**, etc. when referring to people.

Example:

Wir haben <u>von ihm</u> nichts gehört.
We've heard nothing from him.

Wortschatz/Vocabulary

das Picknick: *the picnic*

gestern: *yesterday*

zu viert: *four of them, four of us*

zu dritt: *three of them, three of us*

der Käse: *the cheese*

der Nachtisch: *the dessert*

ich freue mich: *I'm glad/that's good*

sich freuen: *to be glad, to be pleased*

das sieht lecker aus: *that looks tasty*

aussehen: *to look, to appear*

gemischt: *mixed*

mischen: *to mix*

der Salat: *the salad*

zubereiten: *to prepare*

dabei: *on the point of, in the process of*

gerade: *just, precisely (adverb); straight (adjective)*

nichts: *nothing*

überhaupt nichts: *nothing at all*

das Kochen: *the cooking*

deshalb: *therefore, for that reason*

das Brathähnchen: *the roast chicken*

geht das?: *is that all right?*

großartig!: *great! tremendous!*

der Korb: *the basket*

tun: *to do; to place*

alles: *everything*

noch nicht: *not yet*

der Wein: *the wine*

der Supermarkt: *the supermarket*

außerdem: *as well as that, besides*

das Brot: *the bread*

beides: *both (things)*

beide: *both*

ich gehe schnell mal hin: *I'll just go there*

quickly

nett: *nice*

das ist nett (von dir/von Ihnen): *that's nice of you*

über etwas *(accusative)* **Bescheid wissen:** *to know about something*

du weißt Bescheid?: *do you know about it?*

doch: *yes, I do/we are etc. (in reply to negative questions)*

mach schnell!: *be quick!/hurry up!*

schnell: *fast, quick*

sobald: *as soon as*

eintreffen: *to arrive, to turn up, to appear*

losfahren: *to go off, to leave (in a vehicle)*

gleich: *immediately*

wie: *as*

denken: *to think*

vergessen: *to forget*

rufen: *to call*

anrifen: *to call (on the phone)*

zu spät: *late (in arriving)*

zu früh: *early (in arriving)*

besuchen: *to visit*

fehlen: *to be missing, to be lacking*

empfehlen: *to recommend*

entstehen: *to arise*

die Bibliothek: *the library*

erwarten: *to expect*

der Anruf: *the (phone) call*

achten: *to respect*

missachten: *to disregard*

die Vorfahrt: *the right of way*

brechen: *to break*

zerbrechen: *to smash*

vergeben: *to forgive; to give away*

fehlen: *to be missing*
behalten: *to keep*
gestehen: *to confess*
gelingen *(+ dative)***:** *to succeed*
geschehen: *to happen*
abwarten: *to wait for*
abreisen: *to depart, to leave*
bedenken: *to consider*
verreisen: *to go on a journey*
zurücksenden: *to send back*
zurückbekommen: *to get back*
reduzieren: *to reduce*
schlafen: *to sleep*
einschlafen: *to get to sleep, to fall asleep*
sterben: *to die*
die Erwartung: *the expectation*
entsprechen *(+ dative)***:** *to correspond to, to meet*
essen: *to eat*
trinken: *to drink*
gebraucht: *used*
Rad fahren: *to cycle, to ride a bicycle*
weil: *because*
tapfer: *brave, courageous*
aufstehen: *to get up*
möglich: *possible*
möglichst: *the utmost*
die Sache: *the thing*
die Pflicht: *the duty*
sich anziehen: *to get dressed*
genießen: *to enjoy*
das Mittagessen: *the lunch*
besuchen: *to visit*
lohnen: *to reward*
sich lohnen: *to be worthwhile*
die Mühe: *the trouble, the effort*

waschen: *to wash*
sich waschen: *to wash; to get washed*
sich setzen: *to sit down*
setzen: *to place, to put*
zurzeit: *at present, at the moment*
sich begeben *(***auf** *+ accusative)***:** *to set out, start (on a journey)*
sich teilen: *to separate, to part*
trennen: *to divide, to separate*
sich trennen: *to part company*
die Straße: *the street, the road*
durch: *through*
neben: *next to, near*
gegen: *towards, against*
vor: *in front of*
der Vorschlag: *the proposal*
festhalten an *(+ dative)***:** *to stick to, to cling to*
die Meinung: *the opinion*
die Hand: *the hand*
dagegen: *against it*
darauf: *on it*
darin: *in it*
damit: *with it; so that*
dadurch: *through it*
dafür: *for it; in return for*
dabei: *close to it; by it; on the point of; present*
davon: *from it, about it*
dazu: *to it; to that end; to that purpose*
daran: *at it; on it*
daneben: *next to it, besides*
davor: *in front of it*
der Schuh: *the shoe*
die Wohnung: *the flat, the apartment*
helfen *(+ dative)***:** *to help*

Übungen/Exercises

Exercise A

BITTE BEANTWORTEN SIE DIE FOLGENDEN FRAGEN ZUM DIALOG:

Please answer the following questions about the dialogue.

1. **Kommt Monikas Freund mit?**

   ....

2. **Was bringen Monika und ihr Freund zum Picknick mit?**

   ....

3. **Was bereitet Ulrike für das Picknick zu?**

   ....

4. **Was hat Wolfgang gekauft?**

   ....

5. **Wer tut die Brathähnchen in den Korb?**

   ....

6. **Haben sie alles, was sie brauchen?**

   ....

7. **Was brauchen sie noch?**

   ....

8. **Wo will Wolfgang den Wein kaufen?**

   ....

9. **Ist der Supermarkt weit von Ulrikes Wohnung?**

   ....

10. **Wartet er oder geht er gleich?**

    ....

Exercise B

ERGÄNZEN SIE DIESE SÄTZE!

Beispiel: Ulrike <u>hat</u> gestern in der Bank <u>gearbeitet</u>. (arbeiten)

1. Herr Schmidt .... gestern Abend müde nach Hause .... (kommen)

2. Gestern .... Ulrike und Wolfgang ein Picknick .... (machen)

3. Wolfgang .... gestern Abend mit Monika .... (telefonieren)

4. Unsere Freunde .... soeben .... (eintreffen)

5. Wie lange .... Sie auf den Bus .... ? (warten)

6. .... du gestern Abend das Buch .... ? (lesen)

Exercise C

BITTE SETZEN SIE DIE GLEICHEN SÄTZE IN DIE ZUKUNFTSFORM!

Please put the same sentences into the future tense.

("**gestern**" becomes "**morgen**", "**soeben**" becomes "**bald**" – soon)

Beispiel: Ulrike <u>wird</u> morgen in der Bank <u>arbeiten</u>. (arbeiten)

1. ....

2. ....

3. ....

4. ....

5. ....

6. ....

12. Review Lessons 7-11

This review section is a revision of what you have learnt so far. Take the time to listen to the audio dialogues again and see how much you can understand without turning back to the English versions in the previous chapters! Don't forget to do the short exercise section too!

Übungen/Exercises

Exercise A

WÄHLEN SIE DEN PASSENDEN ARTIKEL: DER, DIE, DAS ODER DIE (PLURAL)!

Choose the appropriate article: der, die, das, or die (plural).

Beispiel: der Kaffee   die Tasse   das Buch   die Jahreszeiten

1. .... Brot	7. .... Städte	13. .... Telefon
2. .... Marmelade	8. .... Mittagessen	14. .... Nacht
3. .... Tee	9. .... Reservierung	15. .... Chef
4. .... Film	10. .... Stock	16. .... Zimmer
5. .... Kinos	11. .... Aufzug	17. .... Post
6. .... Trödelmarkt	12. .... Beamtin	18. .... Postkarte

19. .... Mühe	33. .... Wochenende	47. .... Salat
20. .... Paket	34. .... Auge	48. .... Wein
21. .... Flugzeug	35. .... Augenblick	49. .... Straße
22. .... Frühstück	36. .... Bus	50. .... Zeit
23. .... Briefmarken	37. .... Regenschirm	51. .... Haus
24. .... Stuhl	38. .... Wetter	52. .... Hotel
25. .... Wolke	39. .... Supermarkt	53. .... Formular
26. .... Sommer	40. .... Zeitschriften	54. .... Waage
27. .... Inhalt	41. .... Ferien	55. .... Woche
28. .... Absender	42. .... Herbst	56. .... Landschaft
29. .... Jahr	43. .... Brathähnchen	57. .... Regen
30. .... Wagen	44. .... Käse	58. .... Korb
31. .... Regenmantel	45. .... Nachtisch	59. .... Büro
32. .... Sonne	46. .... Uhr	60. .... Freundinnen

Exercise B

SETZEN SIE DIE VERBEN IN DIE GEGENWART!

Put the verbs in the present tense.

Beispiel: (trinken) Frau Schmidt trinkt Tee.

   (sprechen) Paul spricht mit Ulrike.

1. (warten) Wolfgang .... auf den Bus.

2. (anziehen) Bei kaltem Wetter .... ich warme Kleidung ....

3. (scheinen) Die Sonne .... am Himmel.

4. (machen) Was .... du da?

5. (tun) Ich .... nichts.

6. (mitkommen) Paul .... ins Kino ....

7. (zubereiten) Ulrike .... einen gemischten Salat ....

8. (geben) Paul .... der Beamtin das Paket.

9. (bleiben) Bei Regenwetter .... Herr Schmidt zu Hause.

10. (fliegen) Das Flugzeug .... nach München.

11. (kennen) .... Sie Monika?

12. (vorziehen) .... Sie Blau oder Grün .... ?

13. (können) Wie .... ich nach draußen telefonieren?

14. (müssen) Wie viel .... wir zahlen?

15. (sollen) Du .... nicht hingehen.

Exercise C

SETZEN SIE DIE SÄTZE 1 BIS 10 VON ÜBUNG B IN DIE ZUKUNFT:

Put sentences 1 to 10 in exercise B into the future tense:

Beispiel: (trinken) Frau Schmidt wird Tee trinken.

      (sprechen) Paul wird mit Ulrike sprechen.

1. ....

2. ....

3. ....

4. ....

5. ....

6. ....

7. ....

8. ....

9. ....

10. ....

Exercise D

WÄHLEN SIE DAS PASSENDE WORT!

Choose the appropriate word.

Beispiel: Ich sehe die Kinder. = Ich sehe sie.

Ich spreche mit Ulrike. = Ich spreche mit ihr.

1. **Ich rufe den Chef an. = Ich rufe** .... **an. (ihn/sie/es)**

2. **Wir fangen mit der Arbeit an. = Wir fangen** .... **an. (daran/damit/dazu)**

3. **Sie wartet auf den Bus. = Sie wartet** .... **(darauf/damit/dazu)**

4. **Ich gebe Wolfgang und Ulrike die Schlüssel. = Ich gebe** .... **die Schlüssel.**

   (sie/ihn/ihnen)

5. **Haben Sie mit Monika gesprochen? = Haben Sie mit** .... **gesprochen?**

   (ihm/ihnen/ihr)

6. **Den Wein hat er noch nicht gekauft. = Er hat** .... **noch nicht gekauft. (es/ihn/sich)**

Exercise E

SETZEN SIE DIE SÄTZE VON ÜBUNG B IN DIE VERGANGENHEIT! (NUR 1 BIS 10)

Put the sentences in exercise B into the past tense (only 1 to 10).

Beispiel: (trinken) Frau Schmidt hat Tee getrunken.

   (sprechen) Paul hat mit Ulrike gesprochen.

1. ....

2. ....

3. ....

4. ....

5. ....

6. ....

7. ....

8. ....

9. ....

10. ....

Exercise F

ANTWORTEN SIE IN DER ZUKUNFT!

Answer in the future tense.

Beispiel:

Haben Sie heute die Lektion 13 gelernt? Nein, ich werde die Lektion 13 morgen lernen.

Ist Heidi heute in Berlin gewesen? Nein, sie wird morgen in Berlin sein.

1. **Haben Sie heute mit der Empfangschefin gesprochen?**

   ....

2. **Hat der junge Mann das Paket heute verschickt?**

   ....

3. **Haben wir heute schönes Wetter gehabt?**

   ....

4. **Ist Herr Schmidt heute nach Hannover gefahren?**

   ....

13. Directions

Lesson 13 helps you to find your way around. You will delve deeper into the use of the past tense, and learn an extensive list of vocabulary, as well as how to use impersonal constructions such as *man*. Finally, you will learn how to use the verb *werden* to speak in the passive voice.

KÖNNEN SIE MIR BITTE ERKLÄREN ... CAN YOU PLEASE EXPLAIN TO ME ...

ein Tourist, in Berlin	**Entschuldigen Sie! Können Sie mir bitte erklären, wie ich am besten zum Schloss Charlottenburg komme?**
	Excuse me! Could you please explain to me how I can best get to the Charlottenburg Palace?
der Gemüsehändler	**Ja, sind Sie zu Fuß?**
	Yes, are you on foot?
der Tourist	**Ja.**
	Yes.
der Gemüsehändler	**Also, gehen Sie geradeaus, bis Sie die Bismarckstraße erreichen. Überqueren Sie die Straße. Gehen Sie nach links und dann etwa zweihundert Meter bis zum Sophie-Charlotte-Platz, dann rechts in die Schlossstraße hinein. Von dort werden Sie das Schloss schon sehen.**
	Well, go straight ahead until you reach Bismarckstraße. Cross the street. You go left and then about two hundred meters to Sophie-Charlotte-Platz. Then go right into Schlossstraße. From there you will see the palace.

der Tourist	**Ich habe es nicht ganz verstanden. Sie haben gesagt: geradeaus zur Bismarckstraße, links , und was dann?**
	I didn't quite get that. You said straight ahead to Bismarckstraße, left and then what?
der Gemüsehändler	**Nachdem Sie die Hauptstraße überquert haben, gehen Sie etwa zweihundert Meter zum Sophie-Charlotte-Platz. Sie werden die U-Bahn-Station sehen. Biegen Sie rechts in die Schlossstraße ein, und von dort werden Sie das Schloss schon sehen. Haben Sie es jetzt verstanden?**
	After you have crossed the main street, walk the two hundred meters or so to Sophie-Charlotte-Platz. You'll see the subway station. Turn right into Schlossstraße and from there you will see the palace. Got it?
der Tourist	**Danke, ja. Wie lange brauche ich zum Schloss?**
	Yes, thanks,. How long will it take me to get to the palace?
der Gemüsehändler	**Ungefähr fünfundzwanzig Minuten.**
	About twenty-five minutes.
der Tourist	**Kann man mit dem Bus fahren?**
	Can you go by bus?
der Gemüsehändler	**Das lohnt sich nicht. Die Bushaltestelle ist kurz vor dem Sophie-Charlotte-Platz, und dann sind Sie gleich in der Schlossstraße.**
	It's not worth it. The bus stop is just before Sophie-Charlotte-Platz and Schlossstraße is then only a little further on.
der Tourist	**Wissen Sie, ob man das Schloss heute besichtigen kann?**
	Do you know whether it's possible to look around the palace today?
der Gemüsehändler	**Ja, das Schloss ist heute geöffnet. Aber Sie sollten das Ägyptische Museum nicht vergessen! Es ist ganz nah beim Schloss. Der Besuch lohnt sich. Dort können Sie die Büste der Nofretete sehen.**
	Yes, the palace is open today. But don't forget the Egyptian Museum! It is quite close to the palace. It's worth visiting. You can see the Nofretete bust there.
der Tourist	**Ich werde auf jeden Fall Ihren Rat befolgen. Haben Sie recht schönen Dank! Auf Wiedersehen!**
	I'll certainly take your advice. Thank you very much indeed. Goodbye.
der Gemüsehändler	**Auf Wiedersehen! Viel Spaß!**
	Goodbye! Enjoy yourself!

Grammatik/Grammar

1. IMPERSONAL CONSTRUCTIONS: MAN

The German word **man** is used to express generalities, hearsay or to give information. It can mean **one**, **you**, **they**, **anyone**, but it is often translated by a passive construction into English:

Kann man mit dem Bus fahren?
Can you go by bus?/Is it possible to go by bus?

Man kann nie wissen.
One can never know./You never know.

So etwas tut man nicht.
That's not the done thing.

In diesem Restaurant kann man billig essen.
You can eat cheaply in this restaurant.

2. JEMAND

> jemand
> somebody, someone

Jemand hat mir erzählt, dass ...
Somebody told me that. . .

Es kommt jemand.
Someone's coming.

Spricht hier jemand Englisch?
Does anybody speak English here?

Sonst noch jemand?
Anybody else?

Falls jemand anrufen sollte: Ich bin nicht zu Hause.
If someone should call, I'm not at home.

Jemand becomes **jemanden** in the accusative, and **jemandem** in the dative; the genitive is usually expressed by **von jemandem**.

Sie ist mit jemandem gekommen, den wir nicht kennen.
She turned up with somebody we don't know.

Ich habe jemanden im Garten gesehen.
I have seen someone with in the garden.

Gehört dieser Mantel jemandem? (**gehören**: to belong to)
Does this coat belong to anyone?

3. JEDER, JEDE, JEDES

jeder, jede, jedes
each, every, any, all

Sie sind zu jeder Zeit willkommen. (zu jeder Zeit can be contracted to jederzeit)
You're welcome any time.

Ich werde auf jeden Fall Ihren Rat befolgen.
I will certainly take your advice.

Er kann jede Minute kommen.
He can come any minute.

Ich bin in jeder Hinsicht Ihrer Meinung.
I agree completely with you.

Ich verstehe jedes Wort!
I can understand every word.

Paul geht bei jedem Wetter spazieren.
Paul goes for a walk in all kinds of weather.

Es wird mit jedem Tag kälter.
It is getting colder by the day.

Jeder means **for every person**. **Jedem** means **to any person**. **Jeder** can also stand for **everyone** in general or every male person, while **jede** stands for every female person.

Das kann jedem passieren.
That can happen to anybody.

Jeder hat seine Schwächen.
Everyone has his weaknesses.

Everyone can also be expressed by **jedermann**.

Kochen ist nicht jedermanns Sache.
Cooking is not to everyone's liking.

4. NIEMAND

niemand
nobody, no one

The opposite of **jemand** is **niemand**.

Es ist niemand da.
There's nobody there.

Im Garten ist niemand.
There's nobody in the garden.

Es meldet sich niemand.
There's no answer. *(on the phone)*

5. ES/IT

In German, the use of the third person singular pronoun **es** to make a statement about something or someone is very common. **Es** can be used with personal and impersonal verbs as well as in passive constructions for general statements. Here are some examples:

Es schneit.
It's snowing.

Es ist kalt.
It's cold.

Es ist schönes Wetter.
The weather's nice.

Es steht nicht gut um ihn.
Things are not looking good for him.

Es wird getanzt. (**tanzen** to dance)
People are dancing.

Es kann jederzeit ein Unfall passieren/Ein Unfall kann jederzeit ausbrechen.
An accident can happen at any time.

6. PRONOUNS: WER, WEN, WESSEN, WEM

wer	wen	wessen	wem
who	whom	of whom/whose	to whom

The pronoun **wer** can be used both as an interrogative and as a relative pronoun. It declines just as definite articles do.

Wer ist da?
Who's there?

Wer hat das gesagt?
Who said that?

Wen haben Sie zur Party eingeladen?
Who did you invite to the party?

Für wen haben Sie die Tasche gekauft?

Who did you buy the bag for?

Ich weiß nicht, mit wem ich gesprochen habe.
I do not know who it was I spoke to.

Wem auch immer ich die Schlüssel gegeben habe, ich bekomme sie zurück.
Whoever I have given the keys to, I'll get them back.

Meine Schuld ist es nicht. – Wessen Schuld ist es dann?
It's not my fault. – Then whose fault is it?

7. VERBEN/VERBS

lassen to let, to make; to leave; to allow

ich lasse	ich lasse nicht	lasse ich … ?
Sie lassen	Sie lassen nicht	lassen Sie … ?
du lässt	du lässt nicht	lässt du … ?
er/sie/es lässt	er/sie/es lässt nicht	lässt er/sie/es … ?
wir lassen	wir lassen nicht	lassen wir … ?
Sie lassen	Sie lassen nicht	lassen Sie … ?
ihr lasst	ihr lasst nicht	lasst ihr … ?
sie lassen	sie lassen nicht	lassen sie … ?

Lassen can be used as an auxiliary verb, as a main verb in its own right, and as a reflexive verb. It is used in a number of idiomatic expressions.

Ich habe ihn rufen lassen.
I had him called for.

Ich habe mir einen Mantel machen lassen.
I had a new coat made *(for myself)*.

Das lässt sich machen.
That can be done.

Lassen Sie mal sehen!
Let me see!

Das lasse ich mir nicht gefallen. (gefallen to please/es gefällt mir I like it)
I won't stand for that.

Lassen Sie von sich hören!
Keep in touch!

Ich werde es Sie wissen lassen.
I'll let you know.

Er kann das Trinken nicht lassen.
He can't stop drinking.

Mein Mann lässt Sie grüßen. (der Gruß the greeting)
My husband sends you his best wishes.

Lassen Sie mich das Buch einige Tage behalten.
Let me hold onto the book for a few days.

Lasst uns ins Kino gehen.
Let's go to the movies.

Ich habe meine Schlüssel im Büro liegen gelassen.
I've left my keys in the office.

8. PASSIVE VOICE

The verb **werden** as an auxiliary verb together with the past participle of another verb, is used to express the passive voice, e.g. an action being carried out by someone or something else.

Er öffnet die Tür.	**Die Tür wird geöffnet.**	**Die Tür wird von ihm geöffnet.**
He opens the door.	The door is being opened.	The door is being opened by him.

Monika wird von ihrem Freund begleitet.
Monika is being accompanied by her friend.

You have already encountered the use of **werden** to express the future tense:

Ich werde auf jeden Fall Ihren Rat befolgen.
I'll certainly take your advice.

When combined with **wohl**, **werden** usually expresses **uncertainty** or **doubt**:

Er wird es wohl tun.
He'll probably do it.

Sie werden es wohl vergessen haben.
They'll probably have forgotten it.

Ihr werdet doch nicht schon gehen wollen?
You surely don't want to go already, do you?

Werden is also used to describe a **gradual development**.

Es wird allmählich dunkel.
It's getting dark.

Mir wird kalt.
I'm getting cold.

The past participle of **werden** is **geworden** when it is the main verb:

Er ist alt geworden.
He's got old.

Er ist Lehrer geworden.
He's become a teacher.

Das Wetter ist schön geworden.
The weather has has turned out nice.

The past participle is **worden** if it is used as an auxiliary:

Wir sind schnell bedient worden.
We were served very quickly.

9. SCHON/ALREADY

This frequently used word is used in many senses and is one of the essential words in German.

Ich habe es Ihnen schon gesagt.
I already told you.

Ich weiß schon.
I already know.

It can be used to reinforce another adverb:

Ich habe das schon immer gesagt.
I have always said that.

Ich muss schon um 8 Uhr anfangen.
I have to start as early as 8 o'clock.

Note:

Wie lange <u>sind Sie</u> schon hier? – Ich <u>bin</u> schon lange hier.
How long **have you been** here? – **I've been** here for a while.

Es ist schon lange her. (**lange** for a long time; **lange her** a long time ago)
It was a while ago.

Ich verstehe schon.
I understand/I get what you mean.

It can also mean express reassurance:

Er wird schon kommen.
He'll come all right./Don't worry, he'll come.

Es wird schon gehen.
Things will work out.

Note also:

Stimmt schon. (**stimmen** to be correct)
Keep the change.

10. NACH DEM WEG FRAGEN/ASKING THE WAY

Können Sie mir den Weg <u>zum</u> Schloss zeigen?
Can you show me the way **to** the palace?

To indicate places **within** a town or city, you use **zu** with the dative. You use **nach** to indicate **another** geographical location, e.g. a city *(see below).*

Wie komme ich dorthin?
How do I get there?

Die erste Straße links.
The first street on the left.

Fahren Sie geradeaus bis zur Ampel.
Drive straight on to the traffic lights.

Biegen Sie in die nächste Straße ein.
Turn into the next street.

Sie nehmen nach der Kreuzung die dritte Straße rechts.
Take the third street on the right, after the intersection.

Das Museum befindet sich auf der rechten Seite. (**die Seite** side)
The museum is on the right.

Es liegt gegenüber.
It's on the opposite side.

Wie komme ich auf dem kürzesten (schnellsten) Weg nach Bremen?
What's the shortest (quickest) way to Bremen?

Sie sollten in Richtung Hamburg fahren.
You should drive in the direction of Hamburg.

In welche Richtung? (**die Richtung** the direction)
In which direction?

Wohin führt diese Straße, bitte?
Where does this street lead to please?

In fünf Minuten sind Sie da.
You'll be there in five minutes.

Können Sie mir das auf der Karte zeigen?
Can you show me that on the map?

In Austria, you will often hear the word **Gasse** instead of **Straße**. It originally describes a narrow street. It is also used in this sense in Germany, though it occurs less frequently.

Wortschatz/Vocabulary

entschuldigen: *to excuse*

entschuldigen Sie: *excuse me, I beg your pardon*

der Weg: *the way*

fragen: *to ask*

erklären: *to explain*

die Erklärung: *the explanation*

das Schloss: *the palace*

das Gemüse: *the vegetable*

der Gemüsehändler: *the greengrocer*

der Fuß: *the foot*

zu Fuß: *on foot*

geradeaus: *straight ahead*

überqueren: *to cross over*

erreichen: *to reach*

links: *left, on the left*

rechts: *right, on the right*

der Meter: *the meter*

der Kilometer: *the kilometer*

der Platz: *the square, the place; the seat*

die Straße: *the street, the road*

die Hauptstraße: *the main road*

die Gasse: *the lane*

schon: *already, all right; also used just for emphasis*

ganz: *very, quite*

sehr: *very*

sagen: *to say*

verstehen: *to understand*

nachdem: *after*

die Station: *the station (for subway)*

der Bahnhof: *the station (for railway)*

ungefähr: *roughly, approximately*

man: *one, we, they, you (people in general)*

kurz: *short*

die Länge: *length*

lang: *long (in distance)*

besichtigen: *to look round, to examine, to visit (a place)*

vergessen: *to forget*

ägyptisch: *Egyptian*

das Museum: *the museum*

der Besuch: *the visit*

dort: *there*

dorthin: *to there (away from the speaker)*

die Büste: *the bust*

der Rat: *the advice, the suggestion*

befolgen: *to follow (something)*

der Spaß: *the good time; (the) fun*

geschlossen: *closed (from* **schließen** *to close)*

geöffnet: *open (from* **öffnen** *to open)*

jemand: *someone, somebody*

falls: *in case, if*

gehören (+ dative)**:** *to belong to*

die Theaterkarte: *the theater ticket*

jeder, jede, jedes: *each, every*

der Fall: *the case*

auf jeden Fall: *in any case, at all events*

das Wort: *the word*

die Hinsicht: *the regard, the respect*

passieren: *to happen*

die Schwäche: *the weakness*

die Sache: *the thing*

niemand: *nobody*

tanzen: *to dance*

der Baum: *the tree*

es schneit: *it's snowing*

der Unfall: *the accident*

einladen: *to invite*

bekommen: *to get*

die Schuld: *the fault; the guilt*	**der Weg:** *the way, the path*
lassen: *to let, to leave, to allow,*	**zeigen:** *to show*
gefallen: *to please*	**die Ampel:** *the traffic lights (plural)*
es gefällt mir: *I like it*	**erreichen:** *to reach, to come to*
das Trinken: *(the) drinking (here: of alcohol)*	**sich befinden:** *to be (located)*
bauen: *to build*	**gegenüber:** *opposite*
vergessen: *to forget*	**die Karte:** *the map*
allmählich: *gradually*	**die Richtung:** *the direction*
dunkel: *dark*	**lange:** *for a long time (adverb)*
alt: *old*	**lang:** *long (adjective)*
spät: *late*	**aufhaben:** *to be open*
stimmen: *to be correct*	

Übungen/Exercises

Exercise A

Answer the following questions, in reference to the audio dialogue.

1. Wohin will der Tourist gehen?

....

2 Mit wem hat er gesprochen?

....

3 Geht der Tourist zu Fuß oder fährt er mit dem Taxi?

....

4 Ist das Schloss von der Schlossstraße zu sehen?

....

5 Hat der Tourist die Erklärung des Gemüsehändlers verstanden? (die Erklärung the explanation)

....

6 Wie lange wird der Tourist zum Schloss brauchen?

....

7 Lohnt es sich, mit dem Bus dorthin zu fahren?

....

8 Was sollte der Tourist nicht vergessen?

....

9 Ist das Ägyptische Museum nah beim Schloss?

....

10 Wird der Tourist den Rat des Gemüsehändlers befolgen?

....

Exercise B

Complete the following sentences with the perfect tense of the verbs.

Wir haben viel Arbeit gehabt. **(haben)**

Wolfgang ist nach Dahlem gegangen. **(gehen)**

1. Monika .... ihren Freund ins Kino .... (begleiten)

2. Ich .... einen Salat für vier Personen .... (zubereiten)

3. Der Tourist .... den Gemüsehändler nach dem Weg .... (fragen)

4. Wir .... mit dem Taxi zum Bahnhof .... (fahren)

5. Wir .... um 7 Uhr morgens .... (ankommen)

6. Wir .... nach zwanzig Minuten das Museum .... (erreichen)

7. Ich .... es Ihnen schon .... (sagen)

8. Ich .... das Buch noch nicht .... (lesen)

9. Das Wetter .... schön .... (werden)

10. Der Tourist .... den Rat des Gemüsehändlers .... (befolgen)

Exercise C

Now put the verbs from exercise B into the future tense.

Wir <u>werden</u> viel Arbeit <u>haben</u>. (haben)

Wolfgang <u>wird</u> nach Dahlem <u>gehen</u>. (gehen)

1. Monika .... ihren Freund ins Kino .... (begleiten)

2. Ich .... einen Salat für vier Personen .... (zubereiten)

3. Der Tourist .... den Gemüsehändler nach dem Weg .... (fragen)

4. Wir .... mit dem Taxi zum Bahnhof .... (fahren)

5. Wir .... um 7 Uhr morgens .... (ankommen)

6. Wir .... nach zwanzig Minuten das Museum .... (erreichen)

7. Ich .... es Ihnen schon .... (sagen)

8. Ich .... das Buch noch nicht .... (lesen)

9. Das Wetter .... schön .... (werden)

10. Der Tourist .... den Rat des Gemüsehändlers .... (befolgen)

14. The Family

Lesson 14 introduces family and friends. You will learn how to speak about those closest to you. You will also learn how to make comparisons in German and the importance of the position of pronouns and how this can affect the meaning. There's also a big vocabulary booster in this lesson.

WIR SPRECHEN ÜBER DIE FAMILIE TALKING ABOUT THE FAMILY

Heute Nachmittag sind Wolfgang and Ulrike zum Kaffee bei Herrn und Frau Schmidt eingeladen. Alle vier sitzen bequem im Wohnzimmer der Familie Schmidt. Frau Schmidt serviert gerade Kaffee.

This afternoon, Wolfgang and Ulrike are being entertained to coffee at Mr. and Mrs. Schmidt's. The four of them are sitting comfortably in the Schmidt family's living room. Mrs. Schmidt is just serving coffee.

Frau Schmidt	Darf ich Ihnen noch etwas Kaffee anbieten, Frau Constanze?
	May I offer you some more coffee, Ms. Constanze?
Ulrike	Ja, gern. Ich brauche keinen Zucker, danke.
	Yes, please. I don't need any sugar, thanks.
Frau Schmidt	Und Sie, noch etwas Kaffee?
	And what about you, some more coffee?
Wolfgang	Danke. Ich trinke nicht viel Kaffee. Wissen Sie, das Koffein …
	No thanks. I don't drink a lot of coffee. The caffeine, you know …
Frau Schmidt	Da sind Sie wie mein Mann. Er trinkt nie Kaffee.
	You're like my husband. He never drinks coffee.
Herr Schmidt	Stimmt. Ich trinke lieber Tee.

That's true. I prefer to drink tea.

Frau Schmidt	**Leider enthält Tee auch Koffein, mein Schatz!**
	I'm afraid tea also contains caffeine, honey!
Herr Schmidt	**Aber nicht so viel. Immerhin muss man ja etwas trinken.**
	But not as much. After all, you have to drink something.
Ulrike	**Herr Schmidt, Sie haben gesagt, Sie stammen aus Österreich. Haben Sie noch Verwandtschaft dort?**
	Mr. Schmidt, you said you come from Austria. Do you still have family there?
Herr Schmidt	**Ja, natürlich! Mein Bruder und meine Schwester wohnen in Wien. Außerdem habe ich einen Onkel – der wohnt in Innsbruck. Mein Bruder ist noch unverheiratet. Meine Schwester ist aber verheiratet und hat drei Kinder, einen Jungen und zwei Mädchen.**
	Yes, of course! My brother and my sister live in Vienna. I also have an uncle – he lives in Innsbruck. My brother is still unmarried. My sister is married, though, and has three children – a boy and two girls.
Ulrike	**Wie alt sind die Kinder?**
	How old are the children?
Herr Schmidt	**Mein Neffe ist zwölf Jahre alt. Die eine Nichte ist acht und die andere fünf Jahre alt.**
	My nephew is twelve years old. One of my nieces is eight and the other five years old.
Frau Schmidt	**Und wo wohnen Sie, Frau Constanze?**
	And where do you live, Ms. Constanze?
Ulrike	**Ich wohne in Berlin – Frohnau, und zwar bei meinen Eltern. Mein Großvater und meine Großmutter wohnen auch bei uns.**
	I live in Berlin – in the Frohnau district, with my parents. My grandfather and my grandmother also live with us.
Herr Schmidt	**Sie arbeiten aber im Stadtzentrum von Berlin, in einer Bank, oder?**
	But you work in the center of Berlin, in a bank, don't you?
Ulrike	**Ja. Ich fahre jeden Morgen mit der S-Bahn in die Stadt. Deshalb suche ich eine Einzimmerwohnung im Zentrum. Ich schaue ständig online nach, aber ich habe noch nichts gefunden. Es muss nicht unbedingt eine Neubauwohnung sein. Eine Altbauwohnung geht auch.**
	Yes. I take the suburban train into town every morning. That's why I'm looking for a one-room apartment in the city center. I check online all the time, but I haven't found anything yet. It doesn't have to be an apartment in a new building. An apartment in an old building would do, too.
Wolfgang	**Du suchst aber eine relativ preiswerte Wohnung mitten im Zentrum. Deshalb hast du Schwierigkeiten!**
	But you're looking for a relatively cheap apartment right in the center. That's why you are having difficulties!

Ulrike	Ich weiß. Aber es eilt nicht. Momentan wohne ich bei meinen Eltern nicht schlecht. Davon abgesehen, wohnen mein Cousin and meine Cousinen auch im Norden von Berlin.
	I know. But there's no hurry. At present, I'm not badly off living with my parents. Apart from that, my cousins also live in the north of Berlin.
Frau Schmidt	Und wie steht es mit Ihnen, Herr Kraus? Wohnen Sie auch bei Ihren Eltern?
	And what about you, Mr. Kraus. Do you live with your parents, too?
Wolfgang	Nein, ich habe eine Einzimmerwohnung in Berlin-Schöneberg. Meine Eltern wohnen in Bremen. Ich telefoniere oft mit ihnen. Wenn ich Zeit habe, fahre ich mit dem ICE dorthin.
	No, I have a one-room apartment in Berlin-Schöneberg. My parents live in Bremen. I often speak to them on the phone. When I have time, I take the Intercity Express train there.
Ulrike	Leider fährt die S-Bahn bei weitem nicht so schnell!
	Unfortunately, the suburban train doesn't travel anything like as fast!

Grammatik/Grammar

1. UND ZWAR

This is a useful device to add something to a sentence that you omitted in the first place. It is usually not translated into English.

Ich wohne in Frohnau, und zwar bei meinen Eltern.
I live in Frohnau, with my parents.

Ich bin aus den USA, und zwar aus Texas.
I am from the USA, from Texas.

2. VERBEN/VERBS

trinken is an irregular strong verb.

trinkin (to drink) **present tense**

ich trinke	wir trinken
Sie trinken	Sie trinken
du trinkst	ihr trinkt
er/sie/es trinkt	sie trinken

Die Kinder dürfen keinen Wein trinken.
The children are not allowed to drink wine.

Unless we mention that a verb uses **SEIN** in the past tense, assume that it uses **HABEN**.

past tense

ich habe getrunken	ich habe nicht getrunken
Sie haben getrunken	Sie haben nicht getrunken
du hast getrunken	du hast nicht getrunken
er/sie/es hat getrunken	er/sie/es hat nicht getrunken
wir haben getrunken	wir haben nicht getrunken
Sie haben getrunken	Sie haben nicht getrunken
ihr habt getrunken	ihr habt nicht getrunken
sie haben getrunken	sie haben nicht getrunken

Ich habe heute kein Bier getrunken.
I have not had any beer today.

essen is also an irregular verb.

essen (to eat) present tense

ich esse	wir essen
Sie essen	Sie essen
du isst	ihr esst
er/sie/es isst	sie essen

Sie isst kein Fleisch.
She doesn't eat meat.

Note: er/sie/es <u>ist</u>: **he/she/it is**, but er/sie/es <u>isst</u>: **he/she/it eats**.

---

past tense

ich habe gegessen	ich habe nicht gegessen
Sie haben gegessen	Sie haben nicht gegessen
du hast gegessen	du hast nicht gegessen
er/sie/es hat gegessen	er/sie/es hat nicht gegessen
wir haben gegessen	wir haben nicht gegessen
Sie haben gegessen	Sie haben nicht gegessen
ihr habt gegessen	ihr habt nicht gegessen
sie haben gegessen	sie haben nicht gegessen

Was haben Sie zu Mittag gegessen?
What have you had for lunch?

rauchen to smoke

Ich habe heute keine einzige Zigarette geraucht.
I haven't smoked a single cigarette today.

Rauchen is a regular verb. There are a number of nouns derived from **rauchen**:

der Raucher	the smoker
der Nichtraucher	the non-smoker
Rauchen verboten!	no smoking
das Rauchen	smoking

3. VERBAL NOUNS

You can form a noun from some verbs very easily by beginning the verb with a capital letter and giving it the neuter gender. Usually we don't use the definite article **the** in the English translation, unless the word has taken on a meaning of its own.

rauchen	to smoke	das Rauchen	smoking
essen	to eat	das Essen	eating, the meal
trinken	to drink	das Trinken	drinking
schreiben	to write	das Schreiben	writing, the letter
sein	to be	das Sein	the existence
haben	to have	das Haben	the credit
wissen	to know	das Wissen	the knowledge
versprechen	to promise	das Versprechen	the promise
gehen	to go, to walk	das Gehen	walking

Er hat das Trinken aufgegeben.
He has given up drinking.

Er hat sein Versprechen gehalten.
He kept his promise.

Sie besitzt ein gutes technisches Wissen.
She possesses a good technical knowledge.

Das Essen ist fertig!
Lunch/dinner is ready!

Ihr Schreiben vom (plus date) ...
(Referring to) your letter of ... *(in formal correspondence)*

Das Gehen fällt meinem Großvater schwer.
My grandfather has difficulty in walking.
(schwer fallen *(+ dative)*: to have difficulty)

4. VERBEN/VERBS

haben – **to have** – is used in a number of common expressions that differ from the English usage.

Examples:

Ich habe Hunger.
I'm hungry.

Ich habe Durst.
I'm thirsty.

Ich habe Durst auf ein Bier.
I could do with a beer.

Sie haben Angst vor dem Hund.
They're afraid of the dog.

Sie hat es eilig.
She's in a hurry.

Was hast du? Was haben Sie?
What's wrong with you?

Haben Sie vielen Dank!
Thank you very much.

Sie hat mich sehr gern.
She likes me very much.

Ich habe es nötig.
I need it.

Ich habe es satt.
I'm fed up with it.

but: **Ich bin satt**. I've had enough to eat.

Ich habe genug davon.
I've had enough of it.

4. NICHT/NICHTS/**NOT**

Nicht means **not**. It is placed after the verb in a simple sentence.

Sie kommt <u>nicht</u>.
She's **not** coming.

Ich weiß es nicht.
I don't know.

When there is more than one verb in the sentence, **nicht** is usually placed after the direct object (and adverb of time) of the auxiliary verb.

Ich habe ihn (heute) <u>nicht</u> gesehen.
I have**n't** seen him (today).

If there is no direct object, **nicht** comes after the auxiliary verb (and adverb of time):

Wir sind (gestern) <u>nicht</u> nach München gefahren.
We did**n't** travel to Munich (yesterday).

However, where you want to negate a certain word, you place **nicht** before that word.

Ist die Antwort <u>nicht</u> richtig?
Is the answer **not** correct?

Study the following two sentences:

Wir sind <u>nicht</u> nach München gefahren, sondern nach Heilbronn.
We did**n't** drive to Munich, but to Heilbronn.
where you are negating **Munich**.

Wir sind nach München <u>nicht</u> gefahren, sondern geflogen.
We did**n't** drive to Munich, we flew there.
where you are negating **drive**.

Note that **sondern** is used for "**but**" after a negative statement:

Ich bin nicht ins Kino gegangen, <u>sondern</u> ins Theater.
I didn't go to the movies, **but** to the theater.

Sondern can also be used in the idiomatic expression **nicht nur ...**, **sondern auch** – **not only ...**, **but also**:

Er hat sich <u>nicht nur</u> eine neue Jacke gekauft, <u>sondern auch</u> neue Schuhe.
He did**n't only** buy a new jacket for himself, **but also** new shoes.

Nichts means **nothing**:

Ich weiß von <u>nichts</u>.
I know nothing about it.

Er spricht von <u>nichts</u> anderem.
He talks about **nothing** else.

Ich habe heute <u>nichts</u> Besonderes getan.
I did**n't** do **anything** special today.

<u>Nichts</u> für ungut!
Don't take it amiss!/So sorry!

Es macht <u>nichts</u>.
It doesn't matter.

5. RELATIVE PRONOUNS

We have already met some relative pronouns in previous lessons. They can be used in so-called relative clauses to mean **who**, **which**, **whose**, etc.

The relative pronouns are identical to the definite articles except in the genitive, where the masculine and neuter genitive definite article **des** becomes **dessen**, **der** in the feminine and all plural genitives becomes **deren**, and **den** in the plural datives becomes **denen**.

Examples:

<u>Die</u> Frau, <u>die</u> am Fenster steht, heißt Clara Schmidt.
The lady **who** is standing at the window is called Clara Schmidt.

<u>Das</u> kleine Kind, <u>das</u> wir in Wien gesehen haben, ist die Nichte von Herrn Schmidt.
The small child **whom**/**that** we saw in Vienna is Mr. Schmidt's niece.

<u>Das</u> Buch, <u>das</u> auf dem Tisch liegt, gehört mir.
(**gehören** (+ dative) to belong)
The book **which**/**that** is lying on the table belongs to me.

<u>Der</u> Mantel, <u>den</u> Herr Schmidt trägt, ist neu. (**tragen**: to wear; to carry)
The coat **which** Mr. Schmidt is wearing is new.

<u>Die</u> Frau, <u>deren</u> Tochter bei uns in der Bank arbeitet, hat einen Unfall gehabt.
The lady **whose** daughter works in our bank had an accident.

To summarize:

	masculine	feminine	neuter	plural
Nominative	der	die	das	die
	who, that	who, that	which, that	who, which, that
Accusative	den	die	das	die
	who(m), that	who(m), that	which, that	who(m), which, that
Genitive	dessen	deren	dessen	deren
	whose	whose	of which	whose, of which
Dative	dem	der	dem	denen
	to whom	to whom	to which	to whom, to which

The relative pronoun agrees in gender and number (singular or plural) with the noun to which it refers.

The relative part of the sentence (beginning with the relative pronoun) has its verb at the end (the middle part in all examples above). Note that in German all relative clauses are marked by commas.

Another form of the relative pronoun is **welch-**, which behaves very similarly to the relative pronouns just described. It is not used in the genitive.

	masculine	feminine	neuter	plural
Nominative	welcher	welche	welches	welche
Accusative	welchen	welche	welches	welche
Dative	welchem	welcher	welchem	welchen

Die Frau, welche am Fenster steht, heißt Clara Schmidt.
The lady **who** is standing at the window is called Clara Schmidt.

This relative clause is rare in modern German, though.

Welche etc. are much more common as interrogative pronouns:

Welche Frau?
Which lady?

Welches Buch?
Which book?

Welcher Zug?
Which train?

Welche Zeitschriften?
Which magazines?

Im welchem Buch haben Sie das gelesen?
In which book did you read that?

6. SO

The word **so**, is a very useful word in German, but it is not always used in the same way as in English.

Examples:

So geht das nicht!
That's not how you do it!

So ist das Leben!
Such is life.

Es ist nun einmal so.
That's just the way things are.

So einfach ist das auch wieder nicht.
It's not quite as easy as that.

So habe ich das nicht gemeint. (meinen to mean, to have an opinion)
I didn't mean it like that.

So was Schönes habe ich noch nie gesehen!
I've never seen anything as beautiful as that.

Ich komme so gegen sieben Uhr.
I'll be there around seven o'clock.

So ein Blödsinn!
What nonsense!

so... wie ... means a ... as ...

Er ist etwa so groß wie seine Schwester. (etwa about, approximately)
He's about **as** tall **as** his sister.

Ich mache das so schnell wie möglich. (möglich possible)
I'll do it **as** quickly **as** possible.

So gut wie ... means **virtually, practically**

Du hast ja so gut wie nichts gegessen!
You've eaten **practically** nothing!

So combines with other words:

so	+	lang(e) long	=	solang(e)	as long as, while
so	+	bald soon	=	sobald	as soon as
so	+	fern far, distant	=	sofern	so far as, provided that
so	+	mit with	=	somit	thus, therefore
so	+	fort away, gone	=	sofort	immediately
so	+	eben even, just	=	soeben	just now
eben	+	so	=	ebenso	equally

Solange es regnet, können wir kein Tennis spielen. (regnen to rain; spielen to play)
As long as it's raining, we can't play tennis.

Ich komme, sobald ich kann.
I'll come, as soon as I can.

Ich komme sofort!
I'll be right with you!

Sofern das Wetter schön bleibt, werden Wolfgang und Ulrike ein Picknick machen.
Provided the weather stays nice, Wolfgang and Ulrike will have a picnic.

Sofern nicht means **unless**

Sofern es nicht regnet, werden wir am Strand liegen. (**der Strand** the beach)
Unless it rains, we'll lie on the beach.

Soeben means **just**

Wir sind soeben in Berlin gelandet.
We've just landed in Berlin.

Ebenso ... wie: means **just… as**

Wir sind ebenso gute Freunde wie vorher.
We're just as good friends as previously.

Ebenso can be combined with other words:

Ich hatte ebenso viel Glück wie er. (ebenso viel just as much)
I was just as lucky as he was.

Sie hat mich ebenso gern wie vorher. (ebenso gern just as well)
She likes me just as much as she did before.

Wortschatz/Vocabulary

die Familie: *the family*

einladen: *to invite*

bequem: *comfortable*

das Wohnzimmer: *the living room*

gerade: *just, straight*

anbieten: *to offer*

ja, gern! *yes, please*

der Zucker: *the sugar*

das Koffein: *the caffeine*

koffeinfrei: *decaffeinated*

nie: *never*

der Schatz: *the treasure; honey (term of endearment)*

immerhin: *after all*

stammen aus (+ *dative*): *to come from (a place)*

die Verwandtschaft: *the relations, the family*

sicherlich: *surely, certainly, undoubtedly*

der Bruder: *the brother*

die Schwester: *the sister*

außerdem: *as well as that, besides, moreover*

der Onkel: *the uncle*

unverheiratet: *unmarried, single*

verheiratet: *married*

der Junge: *the boy*

das Mädchen: *the girl*

der Neffe: *the nephew*

die Nichte: *the niece*

wohnen: *to live (in a place)*

..., und zwar ...: *to be more precise ...; usually not translated*

die Eltern (*plural*): *the parents*

der Sohn: *the son*

die Tochter: *the daughter*

der Großvater: *the grandfather*

die Großmutter: *the grandmother*

trotzdem: *nevertheless, all the same*

das Stadtzentrum: *the city center*

die S-Bahn: *the suburban train*

deshalb: *therefore*

online: *online*

schauen: *to look*

die Einzimmerwohnung: *the one-room apartment*

finden: *to find (past participle* **gefunden***)*

unbedingt: *absolutely*

die Neubauwohnung: *the apartment in a new building*

die Altbauwohnung: *the apartment in an old building*

die Wiedervereinigung: *the reunification*

teuer: *expensive*

teurer: *more expensive*

preiswert: *inexpensive, cheap*

mitten in (+ *dative*): *in the middle of, in the center of*

die Schwierigkeit: *the difficulty*

eilen: *to hurry*

es eilt nicht: *there's no hurry*

momentan: *at the moment*

abgesehen davon: *apart from that*

der Cousin: *the cousin (male)*

die Cousine: *the cousin (female)*

der Norden: *the north*

im Norden (**von** + *dative*): *in the north (of)*

der Süden: *the south*

der Westen: *the west*

der Osten: *the east*

der Zug: *the train*
dorthin: *to there (away from the speaker)*
bei weitem: *by far*
bei weitem schneller: *faster by far*
bei weitem nicht so schnell *not nearly as fast*
unregelmäßig: *irregular*
regelmäßig: *regular*
die Flasche: *the bottle*
das Fleisch: *the meat*
rauchen: *to smoke*
einzig: *single*
die Zigarette: *the cigarette*
der Raucher: *the smoker*
der Nichtraucher: *the non-smoker*
das Rauchen: *(the) smoking*
das Sein: *the existence*
das Haben: *the credit*
das Soll: *the debit*
das Kochen: *(the) cooking*
das Wissen: *the knowledge*
das Versprechen: *the promise*
das Gehen: *(the) walking*
schwer fallen (+ *dative*)**:** *to have difficulty with*
aufgeben: *to abandon, to give up*
besitzen: *to possess, to own*
fertig: *ready, finished*
halten: *to hold, to keep*
bekommen: *to get*
der Hunger: *the hunger*
der Durst: *the thirst*
die Angst: *the fear*
der Hund: *the dog*
schwer: *difficult; heavy*
eilig: *urgent*
gern haben: *to like (something, somebody)*

nötig: *necessary*
genug: *enough*
das Schreiben: *(the) writing, the letter*
nichts für ungut!: *don't take it amiss!/so sorry!*
sondern: *but (after a negative statement)*
die Krawatte: *the tie*
die Jacke: *the jacket*
das Glas: *the glass*
das Bier: *the beer*
satt: *satisfied*
satt sein: *to be full*
etwas satt haben: *to be fed up with something*
nebenan: *nearby, next door*
der Blödsinn: *(the) nonsense*
meinen: *to mean, to have an opinion*
ziemlich: *fairly*
etwa: *about, approximately*
so ... wie ...: *as ... as ...*
so gut wie ...: *virtually, practically*
solang(e): *as long as, while*
spielen: *to play*
sobald: *as soon as*
somit: *thus, consequently*
sofort: *immediately*
sofern: *so far as, provided that*
der Strand: *the beach*
landen: *to land*
soeben: *just now*
ebenso viel: *just as much*
ebenso gern: *just as well*
der Anfang: *the beginning*
wohnen: *to live*

Übungen/Exercises

Exercise A

BITTE BEANTWORTEN SIE DIE FOLGENDEN FRAGEN ZUM DIALOG.

Answer the following questions in reference to the audio dialogue.

1. **Wer hat Wolfgang und Ulrike eingeladen?**

   ....

2. **Möchte Ulrike noch etwas Kaffee?**

   ....

3. **Trinkt Ulrike ihren Kaffee mit oder ohne Zucker?**

   ....

4. **Trinkt Herr Schmidt Kaffee?**

   ....

5. **Was trinkt er lieber?**

   ....

6. **Hat Herr Schmidt noch Verwandtschaft in Österreich?**

   ....

7. **Wie viele Kinder hat die Schwester von Herrn Schmidt?**

   ....

8. **Wie alt sind die Kinder?**

   ....

9. **Wohnt Ulrike mit Wolfgang zusammen?**

   ....

10. **Fährt sie jeden Tag mit der S-Bahn oder mit dem ICE?**

   ....

11. Sucht Ulrike eine Einzimmerwohnung in Frohnau?

....

12. Muss es unbedingt eine Neubauwohnung sein?

....

13. Hat sie schon etwas gefunden?

....

14. Hat Ulrike es eilig mit der Wohnung?

....

15. Sind Wohnungen in Berlin seit der Wiedervereinigung teurer geworden?

....

16. Wohnt Wolfgang bei seinen Eltern?

....

17. Wo wohnen Wolfgangs Eltern?

....

18. Fährt er mit der S-Bahn dorthin?

....

15. Official Business

Lesson 15 is all about evolving your command of the German language, both written and spoken. You will delve deeper into the agreements of nouns and verbs, as well as how to use and form reflexive verbs.

"ENDE GUT, ALLES GUT" "ALL'S WELL THAT ENDS WELL"

ein Reisender	**Entschuldigung! Haben Sie zufällig einen kleinen blauen Koffer gesehen? Ich muss ihn hier gelassen haben.** Excuse me! Have you by any chance seen a small blue suitcase? I must have left it here.
eine Reisende	**Nein, es tut mir leid. Hier ist kein Koffer.** No, I'm sorry. There's no suitcase here.
der Reisende	**Dann ist mein Koffer verloren gegangen! Das ist eine Katastrophe! Meine ganzen Kleider mitsamt meinen persönlichen Sachen sind drin.** Then my suitcase is lost. That's a disaster! All my clothes and my personal things are in it.
die Reisende	**Sie werden ihn vielleicht zurückbekommen! Denken Sie mal nach ... Wo sind Sie mit Ihrem Koffer gewesen? Können Sie sich erinnern?** Perhaps you'll get it back. Try and think. . . Where were with your suitcase? Can you remember?
der Reisende	**Ja. Als ich das Haus verließ, nahm ich meinen Koffer mit. Ich bin mit dem Bus zum Bahnhof gefahren und hatte meinen Koffer**

noch in der Hand, als ich ankam. Dann ging ich zur Wechselstube, wo ich einige Minuten Schlange gestanden habe. Ich hatte den Koffer neben mich auf den Boden gestellt. Dann ging ich zum Bahnsteig und dachte an meinen Koffer. Ich bin unverzüglich hierher zurückgekehrt, aber jetzt finde ich meinen Koffer nicht mehr.

Yes, when I left the house, I took my suitcase with me. I took the bus to the station and still had my suitcase in my hand when I arrived. After that, I went to the bureau de change, where I waited in line for a few minutes. I had put the suitcase on the ground beside me. Then I went to the platform and I remembered my suitcase. I came back here straight away, but I can't find my suitcase any more.

die Reisende	**Schauen Sie sich den Koffer vor der Treppe mal an! Kann das vielleicht Ihr Koffer sein?**
	Just look at that suitcase in front of the steps. Could that be your suitcase?
der Reisende	**Nein, mein Koffer ist nicht so groß. Die Farbe ist auch anders. Ach, wie dumm!**
	No, my suitcase isn't so big. It's also a different color. What a nuisance!
die Reisende	**Welche Farbe hat Ihr Koffer?**
	What color is your suitcase?
der Reisende	**Blau. Wo ist das Fundbüro?**
	Blue. Where's the lost and found office?
die Reisende	**Am anderen Ende des Bahnhofs. Aber sehen Sie den anderen Koffer, da, auf dem Schalter? Ist das Ihr Koffer?**
	At the other end of the station. But look at that other suitcase, there, on the counter. Is that your suitcase?
der Reisende	**Nein. Das ist nicht mein Koffer. Er hat Rollen dran, ganz wie der Koffer auf dem Gepäckkarren des Gepäckträgers. Aber ... das ist doch mein Koffer! Ein blauer Koffer mit Rollen. Ja, das ist ganz bestimmt mein Koffer! Hallo!**
	No, that's not my suitcase. Mine has wheels on it, just like that suitcase on the porter's luggage trolley. But ... that is my suitcase. A blue suitcase with wheels. Yes, that's quite definitely my suitcase. Hey!
der Gepäckträger	**Ja! Meinten Sie _mich_?**
	Yes! Did you want to speak to **me**?
der Reisende	**Ja! Der Koffer da, auf dem Gepäckkarren, wo haben Sie ihn gefunden?**
	Yes! The suitcase there on the luggage trolley. Where did you find it?
der Gepäckträger	**Bei der Wechselstube, samt den anderen Gepäckstücken.**
	At the bureau de change, together with the other items of luggage.
der Reisende	**Andere Gepäckstücke? Was für andere Gepäckstücke?**
	Other items of luggage? What other items of luggage?
der Gepäckträger	**Die Gepäckstücke, die der Reisegruppe gehören. Ich habe sie alle auf dem Karren mitgenommen.**

	The items of luggage that belong to the group of travelers. I took them all with me on the trolley.
der Reisende	**Sie haben sich wohl geirrt! Ich gehöre keiner Reisegruppe an. Sie haben meinen Koffer irrtümlich mitgenommen. Sehen Sie, mein Name steht drauf.**
	You must have made a mistake. I don't belong to any group of travelers. You've taken my suitcase by mistake. Look, my name's on it.
der Gepäckträger	**Oh! Entschuldigen Sie bitte! Das wusste ich nicht. Ich nehme Ihren Koffer sofort vom Karren herunter. Bitte sehr.**
	Oh! I'm so sorry! I didn't realize. I'll get your suitcase down from the trolley at once. Here you are.
der Reisende	**Danke. Danke. Aber es ist ja noch mal alles gut gegangen. So was kann ja passieren.**
	Thank you. Thank you. So everything turned out well after all. These things happen.
der Gepäckträger	Sehen Sie! "Ende gut, alles gut."
	There you are. "All's well that ends well."
der Reisende	**Ja. Sie haben recht. Herzlichen Dank, dass Sie so nett gewesen sind. Sagen Sie, wohnen Sie hier in Leipzig?**
	Yes, you're right. Thanks very much for being so kind. Tell me, do you live here in Leipzig?

Grammatik/Grammar

1. DAS PRÄTERITUM/THE PRETERITE

We have already studied the past tense formed in German by using the verbs haben or sein (for verbs of motion or changes of state) along with the past participle. This is known as the **perfect tense**. Refer back to **Lesson 11** if you need to refresh your memory.

Examples of the perfect tense:

Wir sind in Berlin gewesen.
We were in Berlin.

Ich habe ihn gesehen.

I've seen him./I saw him.

Another way of expressing the past is to use the **preterite** tense. In spoken German, the perfect tense is usually preferred to the preterite tense as it is felt to be livelier. The preterite tense is still prevalent in written texts such as reports. The **preterite** is often known as the **imperfect** in English.

The **preterite** of regular weak verbs is formed as follows:

-**te** is added to the verb stem except for verbs whose stem already ends in -**t** or -**d**, e.g. **arbeiten**, **antworten**, **landen**, where -**ete** is added. Here are some examples with the endings for all the persons.

bemerken to notice	lernen to learn
ich bemerkte	ich lernte
Sie bemerkten	Sie lernten
du bemerktest	du lerntest
er/sie/es bemerkte	er/sie/es lernte
wir bemerkten	wir lernten
Sie bemerkten	Sie lernten
ihr bemerktet	ihr lerntet
sie bemerkten	sie lernten

machen to do/to make	warten to wait
ich machte	ich wartete
Sie machten	Sie warteten
du machtest	du wartetest
er/sie/es machte	er/sie/es wartete
wir machten	wir warteten
Sie machten	Sie warteten
ihr machtet	ihr wartetet

The same differences between weak (in general regular) verbs and strong (irregular) verbs which were described for the formation of the past participle apply to the past tenses. The preterite constructions of strong verbs and irregular weak verbs have to be learnt separately.

It is best to learn the 3rd person of the present tense, the 3rd person of the preterite tense and the past participle of the irregular verbs together.

Irregular weak verbs

Infinitive	Present	Past	Preterite
absenden	sendet ab	sendete ab	abgesendet
bringen	bringt	brachte	gebracht
denken	denkt	dachte	gedacht
kennen	kennt	kannte	gekannt
nennen	nennt	nannte	genannt
wissen	weiß	wusste	gewusst

Strong verbs

Infinitive	Present	Past	Preterite
anbieten	bietet an	bot an	angeboten
anfangen	fängt an	fing an	angefangen
beginnen	beginnt	begann	begonnen
bekommen	bekommt	bekam	bekommen
eintragen	trägt ein	trug ein	eingetragen
eintreffen	trifft ein	traf ein	eingetroffen
entsprechen	entspricht	entsprach	entsprochen
essen	isst	aß	gegessen
fahren	fährt	fuhr	gefahren
finden	findet	fand	gefunden
fliegen	fliegt	flog	geflogen
geben	gibt	gab	gegeben
gehen	geht	ging	gegangen
genießen	genießt	genoss	genossen
kommen	kommt	kam	gekommen
lassen	lässt	ließ	gelassen
lesen	liest	las	gelesen
nehmen	nimmt	nahm	genommen
rufen	ruft	rief	gerufen
schließen	schließt	schloss	geschlossen
schreiben	schreibt	schrieb	geschrieben
sehen	sieht	sah	gesehen
sein	ist	war	gewesen
stehen	steht	stand	gestanden
trinken	trinkt	trank	getrunken
tun	tut	tat	getan
verlieren	verliert	verlor	verloren
verlassen	verlässt	verließ	verlassen
verstehen	versteht	verstand	verstanden
werden	wird	wurde	geworden
zurück-bekommen	bekommt zurück	bekam zurück	zurück-bekommen

Here are some examples of the use of the preterite tense:

Sie gaben es mir.
They gave it to me.

Ich sah ihn and sagte guten Tag.
I saw him and said hello.

Er stand auf, als ich ins Zimmer kam.
He stood up as I came into the room.

Er hatte eine Freundin in Bremen.
He had a girlfriend in Bremen.

As far as word order is concerned, verbs in the preterite tense are used in sentences like they are in the present tense. Separable verbs in the preterite tense also behave as they do in the present tense:

Als ich das Haus verließ, nahm ich meinen Koffer mit.
When I left the house, I took my suitcase with me.

Ich hatte meinen Koffer noch in der Hand, als ich am Bahnhof ankam.
I still had my suitcase in my hand, when I arrived in the station.

Ulrike bereitete einen gemischten Salat zu.
Ulrike prepared a mixed salad.

Separable verbs based on another root verb have the same preterite form as their root verb:

kommen	er/sie/es kam
mitkommen	er/sie/es kam mit
fangen	er/sie/es fing (fangen to catch)
anfangen	er/sie/es fing an
tragen	er/sie/es trug (tragen to carry)
eintragen	er/sie/es trug ein
rechnen	er/sie/es rechnete (rechnen to calculate)
zusammenrechnen	er/sie/es rechnete zusammen

Examples:

Es fing an zu regnen.
It began to rain.

Sie kamen mit ins Theater.
They came along to the theater as well.

Note: In spoken German, this position of **an** and **mit** is more common than the grammatically correct position at the end of the sentence.

Wir trugen uns ins Gästebuch ein. (das Gästebuch the guest book)
We entered our names in the guest book.

Ich bekam meine Schlüssel zurück.
I got my keys back.

Verbs (whether strong or weak) which are based on a root verb with **be-**, **emp-**, **ent-**, **er-**, **ge-**, **ver-** on the front, have the same preterite construction as the root verb:

Examples

schreiben	er/sie/es schrieb
beschreiben	er/sie/es beschrieb (**beschreiben** to describe)
sprechen	er/sie/es sprach
entsprechen	er/sie/es entsprach
lassen	er/sie/es ließ
verlassen	er/sie/es verließ
stehen	er/sie/es stand
verstehen	er/sie/es verstand
kennen	er/sie/es kannte
erkennen	er/sie/es erkannte (**erkennen** to recognise)
suchen	er/sie/es suchte (**suchen** to search)
besuchen	er/sie/es besuchte

Modal auxiliary verbs

The modal auxiliary verbs we have encountered can also be used in the preterite tense – in fact, they are more commonly used in the preterite than in the perfect tense.

Er konnte nicht schwimmen.
He **could**n't swim.

Wir sollten in Berlin sein.
We **were supposed** to be in Berlin.

Sie wollte kein Fleisch essen.
She **did not want** to eat any meat.

Reflexive verbs

Reflexive verbs in the preterite tense act in the same way as in the present tense:

Sie irren sich. (**sich irren** to make a mistake)
They are making a mistake.

Sie irrten sich. (**sich irren** to make a mistake)
They made a mistake.

Ich bedanke mich. (**sich bedanken** to say thanks)
Thanks very much.

Ich bedankte mich bei ihr.
I said thanks to her.

Wir treffen uns in Dahlem. (sich treffen to meet)
We're meeting in Dahlem.

Wir trafen uns in Dahlem.
We met in Dahlem.

The Passive Voice in the preterite tense

The **passive** can also be expressed in the past, by using the preterite tense of werden, in conjunction with the past participle of the verb concerned:

Er wurde nach seinem Vater genannt. (nennen to name)
He was named after his father.

Das neue Bürogebäude wurde 2014 eröffnet. (das Gebäude the building)
The new office building was opened in 2014.

2. THE PLUPERFECT TENSE

The preterite tense of haben and sein is also used in conjunction with the past participle of the verb concerned to form the **pluperfect** tense, which corresponds to the use of "had done" etc. in English:

Ich hatte meinen Koffer vorher auf den Boden gestellt.
I **had** previously **put** my suitcase on the ground.

Ich kam zu dem Schluss, dass ich meinen Koffer verloren hatte.
I came to the conclusion that I **had lost** my suitcase.

3. ALS

> als
> when, as, while; than

This word, used as a conjunction, has the same effect on word order as **dass** does:

Examples:

Als sie ankam, waren wir im Garten.
When she arrived, we were in the garden.

Als ich jung war, radelte ich gern.
When I was young, I enjoyed cycling.

It can also be used to mean "**as**" in the sense of "**in the capacity of**". Note that the indefinite article is not used in such cases in German:

Herr Schmidt ist als Lehrer tätig. (tätig sein to work, have a job)
Mr. Schmidt works **as a** teacher.

Als Junge ging ich oft in die Berge.

As a boy, I often went to the mountains.

It is used in expressions of comparison:

Ulrike ist älter als Paul.
Ulrike is older **than** Paul.

Das ist leichter gesagt als getan.
That's easier said **than** done.

It is used in the expression "**both ... and ...** ":

Sowohl meine Eltern als auch meine Großeltern wohnen im Haus.
Both my parents **and** my grandparents live in the house.

4. DIE FARBEN/COLORS

Welche Farbe hat Milch?
What color is milk?

Milch ist weiß.
Milk is white.

Wein ist rot oder weiß.
Wine is red or white.

Das Gras ist grün.
A lawn is green.

Der Himmel ist blau oder grau.
The sky is blue or grey.

Der Kanarienvogel ist gelb.
The canary is yellow.

Seine Lederjacke ist braun.
His leather jacket is brown.

Ich trinke meinen Kaffee schwarz.
I drink my coffee black.

Other examples:

In New York sah ich viele gelbe Taxis.
In New York I saw lots of yellow taxis.

Er besitzt eine silberne Uhr.
He owns a silver watch.

5. GANZ

> **ganz**
> whole, entire, all; quite, exactly

ganz can be used as an adjective:

Meine ganzen Kleider sind drin.
All my clothes are inside it.

Er hat die ganze Nacht nicht geschlafen.
He didn't sleep the **entire** night.

Meine ganzen Freunde waren zur Hochzeit anwesend.
All my friends were at the wedding.
(**die Hochzeit** the wedding)
(**anwesend** present)

It can also be used as an adverb:

Das ist mir ganz egal. (**egal** equal, the same)
It's **all** the same to me.

Das ist ganz bestimmt mein Koffer.
That's **quite** definitely my suitcase.

Der ist ganz wie mein Koffer.
That looks **exactly** like my suitcase.

Das gefällt mir ganz und gar nicht.
I do **not** like that **at all**.

Herr Schmidt widmet sich ganz seiner Arbeit. (**sich widmen** to devote oneself to (+ *dative*))
Mr. Schmidt devotes himself **entirely** to his work.

Es sind nur ganz kleine Unterschiede zwischen den beiden Computern.
There are only **very** small differences between the two computers.

Note: **ganz** can also be used to mean **quite**:

Das Essen im Restaurant war ganz gut.
The meal in the restaurant was **quite** good.

Wortschatz/Vocabulary

das Ende: *the end*
der Reisende: *the traveler (male)*
die Reisende: *the traveler (female)*
zufällig: *by chance*
stehen lassen: *to forget*
die Kleider(plural): *the clothes*
verloren gehen: *to get lost*
mitsamt *(+ dative)*: *together with*
die Katastrophe: *the disaster, the catastrophe*
es tut mir leid: *I'm sorry*
persönlich: *personal*
drin = darin: *inside*
sich erinnern an *(+ accusative)*: *to remember*
an etwas *(+ accusative)* **denken:** *to think of something*
verlassen: *to leave*
die Wechselstube: *the bureau de change, the currency exchange bureau*
wechseln: *to change, to exchange*
Schlange stehen: *to stand in a line, to queue up*
der Boden: *the floor; the ground*
der Bahnsteig: *platform (in a railway station)*
zurückkehren: *to return, to come back*
anschauen: *to look at*
die Treppe: *the steps (plural)*
die Farbe: *the color*
das Fundbüro: *the lost and found office, lost property office*
der Schalter: *the counter, the window*
das Rad: *the wheel*
dumm: *stupid*

die Rollen *(plural)*: *the wheels*
der Gepäckträger: *the porter*
der Gepäckkarren: *the luggage trolley*
bestimmt: *definitely*
ganz bestimmt: *quite definitely*
hallo! *hey!*
das Gepäckstück: *the item/piece of luggage*
die Reisegruppe: *the travel group, the group of travelers*
die Gruppe: *the group*
der Karren: *the trolley*
sich irren: *to make a mistake*
angehören: *to belong to*
irrtümlich: *by mistake*
mitnehmen: *to take (something) with you*
herunternehmen: *to take down*
es ist ja noch mal alles gut gegangen: *everything turned out well after all*
das kann ja passieren: *these things happen*
Ende gut, alles gut: *all's well that ends well*
sich bedanken: *to say thanks*
herzlichen Dank: *thank you very much*
früher: *previously, formerly*
die Pause: *the interval, the break*
die Mittagspause: *the lunch break*
schwimmen: *to swim*
feststellen: *to notice, to ascertain*
zum Schluss kommen: *to reach a conclusion*
nennen: *to name*
das Gebäude: *the building*
das Bürogebäude: *the office building*
regnen: *to rain*
beschreiben: *to describe*
erkennen: *to recognize*
suchen: *to search*

tragen: *to carry; to wear*	**gelb:** *yellow*
rechnen: *to calculate*	**schwarz:** *black*
das Gästebuch: *the guest book*	**grau:** *grey/gray*
schwer: *heavy; difficult*	**braun:** *brown*
sich irren: *to make a mistake*	**die Lederjacke:** *the leather jacket*
sich treffen: *to meet*	**der Rotwein:** *the red wine*
radeln: *to cycle, to ride a bicycle*	**silbern:** *silver*
tätig sein: *to work, to have a job*	**besitzen:** *to own, to possess*
die Milch: *the milk*	**die Hochzeit:** *the wedding*
das Gras: *the grass*	**anwesend:** *present*
der Kanarienvogel: *the canary*	**egal:** *equal, the same*
weiß: *white*	**ganz und gar nicht:** *not at all*
rot: *red*	**sich beziehen auf** (+ *accusative*)**:** *to refer to*
grün: *green*	**das Verkehrsmittel:** *the means of*
blau: *blue*	*transportation*

Übungen/Exercises

Exercise A

BITTE BEANTWORTEN SIE DIESE FRAGEN, DIE SICH AUF DAS GESPRÄCH AM ANFANG DER LEKTION BEZIEHEN:

Answer these questions, referring to the dialogue at the beginning of the lesson:

1. **Was sucht der Reisende?**

   ....

2. **Hat er seinen Regenschirm verloren?**

   ....

3. **Ist sein Koffer größer oder kleiner als der Koffer vor der Treppe?**

   ....

4. Ist sein Koffer grau, weiß, grün oder blau?

....

5. Was hatte er in seinem Koffer?

....

6. Mit welchem Verkehrsmittel fuhr er zum Bahnhof?

....

7. Hatte er den Koffer in der Hand, als er das Haus verließ?

....

8. Wohin hat er seinen Koffer gestellt?

....

9. Wo war er, als er an seinen Koffer dachte?

....

10. Wo ist das Fundbüro?

....

11. Wo hat er seinen Koffer gefunden?

....

12. Wo hat der Gepäckträger den Koffer gesehen?

....

13. Hat der Gepäckträger sich geirrt?

....

14. Stand der Name des Reisenden auf dem Koffer?

....

15. War die Reisende nett?

....

16. Review Lessons 13-15

This review section is a revision of what you have learnt so far. Take the time to listen to the audio dialogues again and see how much you can understand without turning back to the English versions in the previous chapters! Don't forget to do the short exercise section too!

Übungen/Exercises

Exercise A

ERGÄNZEN SIE DIESE SÄTZE MIT DEM PASSENDEN WORT.

Complete these sentences with the appropriate word.

Beispiel: Ich werde Ihnen den Weg <u>zeigen</u>. **(fragen/zeigen/gehen)**

1. Dieser .... ist Gemüsehändler. **(Mann/Frau/Wagen)**

2. Können Sie .... bitte diesen Satz erklären? **(mich/mir/meinem)**

3. Das Schloss .... heute geöffnet. **(hat/geht/sind)**

4. Wohin .... diese Straße? **(kommt/führt/fällt)**

5. Ich habe heute .... Besonderes getan. **(nicht/nichts/niemand)**

6. Monika .... von ihrem Freund begleitet. **(bist/werdet/wird)**

7. Das Museum ist nicht .... **(entfernt/weit/hoch)**

8. Darf ich Ihnen noch einen Kaffee .... ? (versprechen/anbieten/geben)

9. Wollen Sie .... oder getrennt zahlen? (damit/möglich/zusammen)

10. Der Tourist hat einige .... über Berlin gelesen. (Buch/Bücher/Büchern)

11. Wolfgang ist nicht mit Ulrike .... (unverheiratet/verlassen/verheiratet)

12. Ich trinke .... Bier. (keine/keinen/kein)

13. Ulrike trinkt ihren Kaffee .... Zucker. (noch/ohne/bei)

14. Ich werde .... dem Taxi zum Flughafen fahren. (bei/mit/in)

15. Ulrike wohnt .... ihren Eltern. (mit/bei/zusammen)

16. Wolfgang und Ulrike werden ein Picknick .... (haben/machen/essen)

17. Wolfgang .... mit dem ICE. (geht/fährt/tut)

18. Er .... nicht schwimmen. (werde/konnte/können)

19. Der Reisende musste .... stehen. (Zimmer/Wechselstube/Schlange)

20. Ich hatte den Koffer in .... Hand. (meinem/der/meine)

21. .... Sie! Ich habe mich geirrt. (Bitten/Entschuldigung/Entschuldigen)

22. Im Zug.. ich an meinen Koffer. (fand/dachte/zurückkehrte)

23. .... haben Sie diesen Koffer gefunden? (wie/wer/wo)

24. Diese Schlüssel gehören .... nicht. (ihn/mir/sie)

25. Ulrike ist älter .... Paul. (wie/als/so)

26. Ich trinke .... Tee. (lieber/viele/meiner)

27. Ich telefoniere oft .... ihnen. (zu/an/mit)

28. Was haben Sie .... Mittag gegessen? (in/bei/zu)

29. Ich .... Hunger. (bin/habe/werde)

30. Ich werde so früh .... möglich kommen. (wie/so/eben)

31. Ich .... eine Flasche Wein, bitte. (frage/konnte/möchte)

32. Ulrike geht .... Fuß. (auf/bei/zu)

Exercise B

ERGÄNZEN SIE DIESE SÄTZE MIT DEM PRÄTERITUM.

Complete these sentences with the preterite form of the verb.

Beispiel: Gestern <u>war</u> ich müde. **(sein)**

Ich <u>ging</u> mittags <u>spazieren</u>. **(spazieren gehen)**

1. Gestern .... wir viel Arbeit. (haben)

2. Wolfgang .... in die Stadt. (fahren)

3. Was .... Sie? (sagen)

4. Paul .... seinen Regenschirm .... (mitbringen)

5. Ulrike .... einen gemischten Salat .... (zubereiten)

6. Clara .... mit Heidi am Telefon. (sprechen)

7. Paul .... das Paket auf den Tisch. (stellen)

8. Der Reisende .... seinen Koffer. (verlieren)

9. Er .... seinen Koffer .... (zurückbekommen)

10. Frau Schmidt .... Ulrike einen Kaffee .... (anbieten)

11. Ich .... auf den Bus. (warten)

12. Ich .... nichts von der Sache. (wissen)

13. Ulrike .... die Brathähnchen in den Korb. (tun)

14. Er .... sein Bier. (genießen)

15. Sie *(plural)* .... das Zimmer. (verlassen)

16. Die Reise .... meinen Erwartungen. (entsprechen)

17. Er .... seinen Koffer auf dem Karren. (finden)

18. Sie *(singular)* .... mir einen schönen Brief. (schreiben)

19. Es .... zu regnen. (anfangen)

20. **Sie** *(singular)* .... zu singen. (beginnen)

21. **Sie** *(singular)* .... ihm eine Flasche Wein. (geben)

22. **Wir** .... keine Wolke am Himmel. (sehen)

Exercise C

WÄHLEN SIE DAS PASSENDE WORT!

Choose the appropriate word.

Beispiel: Ich weiß, <u>dass</u> Sie das Auto verkauft haben.

Die Kinder, <u>die</u> auf der Straße spielen, sind aus Wien.

Das Buch, <u>das</u> auf dem Tisch liegt, gehört mir.

1. **Kennen Sie den Herrn,** .... das Zimmer gerade verlassen hat?

2. **Kennen Sie den Mann,** .... dieser Koffer gehört?

3. **Ich stellte fest,** .... ich meinen Koffer nicht mehr hatte.

4. **Wie heißt der junge Mann, mit** .... du gerade gesprochen hast?

5. **Haben Sie sich mit der Frau getroffen,** .... das Auto kaufen möchte?

6. **Der Kellner brachte den Kaffee,** .... wir bestellt hatten.

7. **Hast du die Schlüssel gesehen,** .... auf dem Tisch waren?

8. **Ich habe gehört,** .... in München viel gebaut wird.

9. **Das Kino, in** .... wir gestern waren, ist heute geschlossen.

10. **Der Mantel,** .... ich gestern gekauft habe, ist verloren gegangen.

Exercise D

GEBEN SIE AUF DIE FOLGENDEN FRAGEN EINE NEGATIVE ANTWORT!

Give a negative answer to the following questions.

Beispiel: Haben Sie heute ein Bier getrunken? Nein, ich habe heute kein Bier getrunken.

Waren Sie gestern in Hamburg? Nein, ich war gestern nicht in Hamburg.

1. **Mussten Sie am Bahnhof lange warten?**

    ....

2. **Konnten Sie gestern die Berge sehen?**

    ....

3. **Wollten Sie heute ins Kino mitgehen?**

    ....

4. **Haben Sie heute mit Ihrer Mutter telefoniert?**

    ....

Exercise E

GEBEN SIE AUF DIESE FRAGEN EINE POSITIVE ANTWORT!

Give a positive answer to these questions.

Beispiel: Waren sie heute nicht in der Stadt? Doch, sie waren heute in der Stadt.

Wollten Sie gestern nicht spazieren gehen? Doch, ich wollte gestern spazieren

gehen.

1. **Hat Ulrike ihren Kaffee nicht getrunken?**

    ....

2. **Kommen Sie heute nicht ins Büro?**

    ....

3. Wurde sie nicht von ihrem Freund begleitet?

....

4. Können Sie diese Fragen nicht beantworten?

....

Exercise F

ANTWORTEN SIE MIT VOLLSTÄNDIGEN SÄTZEN!

Answer in complete sentences!

1. Ist das Flugzeug schneller als der Zug?

....

2. Ist der Winter in Deutschland kälter als der Herbst?

....

3. Fährt die S-Bahn so schnell wie der ICE?

....

4. Welche Farbe hat der Himmel bei schönem Wetter?

....

5. Nehmen Sie einen Koffer mit, wenn Sie eine Reise machen?

....

6. Gibt es einen Trödelmarkt in Ihrer Stadt?

....

17. Life in Berlin

Lesson 17 is an introduction to Berlin and the German way of life. You will learn how to talk in the immediate past and use demonstrative pronouns. You will also learn how to develop your conversation skills further.

PAUL HAT BESUCH PAUL HAS A VISITOR

Paul hat Verwandtschaft außerhalb Berlins. Silke, seine deutsche Cousine, besucht ihn von Zeit zu Zeit in Berlin. Während der Osterferien verbringt sie einige Tage bei ihm. Die beiden jungen Leute, die im gleichen Alter sind, wollen heute Abend ausgehen, um das Nachtleben Berlins auszuprobieren.

Paul has relatives outside Berlin. Silke, his German cousin, visits him now and then in Berlin. She is spending a few days with him during the Easter vacation. The two young people, who are the same age, are planning to go out this evening to sample something of Berlin's night life.

Paul	**Wie findest du Berlin diesmal?**
	What do you think of Berlin this time?
Silke	**Ich finde, in Berlin wird zu spät ins Bett gegangen.**
	I think that people in Berlin go to bed too late.
Paul	**Das trifft nicht auf alle zu! Manche Leute müssen früh aufstehen, damit sie früh bei der Arbeit sein können. Deshalb müssen sie früh ins Bett. Da wir Urlaub haben, können wir es uns leisten, etwas später ins Bett zu gehen.**
	That's not true for everyone. Some people have to get up early so they can be at work early. That's why they have to go to bed early. Since we're

on holiday, we can afford to go to bed a little later.

Silke   In unserer Kleinstadt wird früh aufgestanden. Ich bin ganz früh wach. Ich wasche mich, ich ziehe mich an, und ich frühstücke gemeinsam mit meinen Eltern, alles vor Sonnenaufgang.

In our little town, people get up early. I'm awake really early. I get washed, dressed, and I have breakfast with my parents, all before sunrise.

Paul   Dafür musst du ganz früh ins Bett gehen.

So you must have to go to bed very early.

Silke   Ja, ich gehe um halb zehn ins Bett und schlafe sofort ein.

Yes, I go to bed at half past nine and fall asleep straight away.

Paul   Ich gehe normalerweise um elf Uhr schlafen.

I normally go to bed at eleven o'clock.

Silke   Das überrascht mich nicht. In Berlin kann man viel mehr machen. Bei uns ist es sehr ruhig. Ich sehe ab und zu mal fern oder ich lese ein Buch. Unsere Internetverbindung ist ganz schlecht. Samstags gibt es eine Disko. Ein Kino gibt es leider nicht mehr. Deshalb langweile ich mich und gehe früh ins Bett.

That doesn't surprise me. There's a lot more to do in Berlin. It's very quiet where we are. I watch TV now and then or I read a book. Our internet connection is really bad. There's a disco on Saturdays. There isn't a movie house any more, unfortunately. That's why I feel bored and go to bed early.

Paul   Das glaube ich dir! Ich möchte nicht in einer solchen Kleinstadt wohnen. Das Leben dort scheint etwas eintönig zu sein.

I can believe that! I wouldn't like to live in a small town like that. Life there seems to be a bit monotonous.

Silke   Nicht immer. Im Frühling wird das Volksfest mit vielen Blumen veranstaltet, und im Herbst findet der Jahrmarkt statt. Wir haben auch eine gute Buchhandlung.

Not always. There's a village festival in spring with lots of flowers and in the fall there's the fair. We also have a good bookstore.

Paul   Was wollen wir denn heute Abend machen? Es gibt so viel zu tun. Wir könnten ins Kino gehen – oder in die Oper oder ins Theater. Oder wir können in eine Studentenkneipe gehen. Da treffen wir bestimmt einige Bekannte von mir. Was hältst du davon?

But what shall we do this evening? We could go to a movie – or to an opera or to the theater. Or we can go to a student bar. We'll certainly meet some of my acquaintances there. What do you think?

Silke   Ich schlage vor, wir gehen erst mal spazieren, dann können wir uns entscheiden.

I suggest we go out for a walk first, then we can decide on something.

Grammatik/Grammar

1. REFLEXIVE VERBEN (FORTSETZUNG)/**REFLEXIVE VERBS**

The uses of reflexive verbs can be illustrated as follows:

Der Kellner bedient die Kunden.
The waiter is serving the customers.

Die Kunden werden (vom Kellner) bedient.
The customers are being served (by the waiter).

Die Kunden bedienen sich.
The customers are helping themselves.

In the first sentence, the verb is used in the normal (active) way, with an accusative object, the customers. In the second, it is used in the passive voice, where the customers are still the logical object of the action of serving. In the third sentence, the verb is being used reflexively, that is, the subject and the object of the action are identical (the customers).

Some verbs can only be used reflexively:

Wir müssen uns beeilen. (sich beeilen to hurry up)
We must hurry up.

Er weigert sich, nach Hause zu gehen. (sich weigern to refuse)
He refuses to go home.

Ich freue mich, Sie zu sehen. (sich freuen to be glad, be pleased)
I'm glad to see you.

Der Gepäckträger hat sich geirrt. (sich irren to make a mistake)
The porter made a mistake.

Some verbs can be used both reflexively and non-reflexively.

Der Reisende erinnerte sich an seinen Koffer. (sich erinnern an + *accusative* to remember)
The traveler remembered his suitcase.

Seine Frau erinnerte ihn an seinen Koffer.
(erinnern (+ *accusative object*) an + *accusative* to remind)
His wife reminded him of his suitcase.

Silke langweilt sich in der Kleinstadt. (sich langweilen to feel bored, to be bored)
Silke feels bored in the little town.

Dieses Leben langweilt sie. (langweilen to bore)
This sort of life bores her.

Ich interessiere mich für Kunst. (sich interessieren für + *accusative* to be interested in)
I am interested in art.

Kunst interessiert mich. (interessieren to interest)
Art interests me.

Ich ziehe mich an. (sich anziehen to get dressed)
I'm getting dressed.

Sie zieht ein Kleid an. (anziehen to put on)
She's putting on a dress.

Sie öffnete die Tür.
She opened the door.

Die Tür öffnete sich. (sich öffnen to open)
The door opened.

The reflexive pronoun can often be used to mean "for me," "for himself," "for themselves," etc. In such cases there is always an accusative object, and the reflexive pronoun is in the dative:

Ich bestellte mir ein Glas Bier. (bestellen to order)
I ordered a glass of beer (**for myself**).

Sie holte sich den Mantel. (holen to fetch)
She went to fetch **her** coat.

Wir schälten uns eine Apfelsine. (die Apfelsine the orange; schälen to peel)
We peeled an orange **for ourselves**.

Notice that all reflexive verbs take "**haben**" in the past tense:

Es hat sich einen Verkehrsunfall ereignet.
(der Verkehrsunfall the traffic accident; sich ereignen to happen)
There was a traffic accident.

Some reflexive verbs always take a dative reflexive pronoun:

Ich leistete mir eine neue Armbanduhr. (sich leisten to afford, to treat oneself to)
I treated **myself** to a new wristwatch.

Du sollst dir ein paar Tage Ruhe gönnen. (sich gönnen to allow oneself, give oneself)
You should give yourself a few days' rest.

Das werde ich mir merken. (sich merken to remember, to bear in mind)
I'll bear that in mind.

Some reflexive verbs can take both an accusative and a dative reflexive pronoun. Again, the dative is always used with an accusative object:

Ich wasche mich. *(accusative)*
I am washing (myself).

Ich wasche mir die Hände. *(dative)*
I am washing my hands.

Reflexive pronouns can be used to express a reciprocal relationship:

Wolfgang und Ulrike begegneten sich und umarmten sich.
(sich begegnen to meet; sich umarmen to embrace)
Wolfgang and Ulrike met and embraced **each other**.

Sie haben sich lieb.
They're fond of each other.

Er liebt sie. Sie liebt ihn.
He loves her. She loves him.

Sie lieben sich.
They are in love.

2. VERBEN/VERBS

gehören – **to belong to** – takes the dative case and is declined like hören:

Der Mantel gehört ihr.
The coat belongs to her.

Wem gehört der Mantel?
Who does the coat belong to?

Diese Sachen gehören in den Schrank.
These things belong in the cupboard.

Sie gehört zu den großen Sängerinnen.
She is one of the great singers.

Es gehört dazu.
It's all part of the procedure.

Er gehört ins Bett.
He ought to be in bed.

Das gehört nicht zur Sache.
That's beside the point.

It can also be used reflexively in this idiomatic expression:

Das gehört sich nicht.
It's bad manners.

3. DEMONSTRATIVPRONOMEN/DEMONSTRATIVE PRONOUNS

dieser/diese/dieses/diese   jener/jene/jenes/jene
this one   that one

Dieser, diese, dieses, diese (**this one**) and jener, jene, jenes, jene (**that one**) are used as demonstrative pronouns. They are declined like the demonstrative adjectives dieser and jener.

Dieses Haus ist nicht schlecht, aber <u>jenes</u> ist viel schöner.
This house isn't bad, but **that one** is much more beautiful.

Definite articles are also used as demonstrative pronouns:

Der hat es nicht getan.
He didn't do it.

Wir haben eine Buchhandlung in der Stadt. Die ist nicht schlecht.
We have a bookstore in the town. It (the one I'm talking about) isn't bad.

Das, like **es**, with no gender connection, can stand for a whole sentence:

Sie wird morgen kommen. Das hat sie mir versprochen/Sie hat es mir versprochen.
She's coming tomorrow. She promised me **that**.

> dessen/deren
> his/her/its/their

Dessen/deren are also used as demonstrative pronouns to avoid ambiguity instead of the normal **sein, ihr**.

Ich traf meinen alten Lehrer und seinen Sohn sowie dessen Kind.
I met my old teacher and his son as well as his (the son's) child.

(**sein Kind** could refer to both, the teacher and his son.)

4. SOLCH-/SUCH

> solch-
> such

It is used as an adjective:

ein solcher Mann	eine solche Frau	ein solches Buch
such a man	such a woman	such a book

Ich wünsche mir einen solchen Mantel.
I'd like to have such a coat/a coat like that.

Eine solche Chance sollte man nicht verpassen.
Such an opportunity should not be missed.

Ich möchte nicht in einer solchen Kleinstadt wohnen.
I wouldn't like to live in such a small town.

It can be used without an article:

Solches Material ist teuer.
Such material/Material like that is expensive.

Solche Liebe kommt selten vor. (**selten** rare(ly))
Such love occurs rarely. (**vorkommen** to occur, to happen)

Solch by itself with no ending can be placed before the indefinite article:

solch ein Mann	mit solch einem Messer	solch ein Wetter
such a man	with such a knife	such weather

Mit solch einem scharfen Messer muss man vorsichtig umgehen.
You've got to be careful with such a sharp knife.
(**vorsichtig** careful, prudent)
(**umgehen** to deal with, to handle)

5. VERBEN/VERBS

wollen to want

Present	Preterite
ich will	ich wollte
Sie wollen	Sie wollten
du willst	du wolltest
er/sie/es will	er/sie/es wollte
wir wollen	wir wollten
Sie wollen	Sie wollten
ihr wollt	ihr wolltet
sie wollen	sie wollten

past participle **gewollt**

Wollen is used as an auxiliary verb:

Was ich sagen wollte, ist ...
What I meant to say is. . .

Wollen wir gleich nach dem Frühstück hingehen?
Shall we go there straight after breakfast?

Wir wollen gehen!
Let's go!

Ich will wissen, was hier los ist.
I want to know what is going on here.

Das will ich hoffen!
I should hope so!

Das will nicht viel sagen!
That doesn't mean much!

It can mean **to claim**:

Er will nichts gesehen haben.
He claims to have seen nothing.

It is also used to express a **polite wish**:

Wollen Sie sich bitte hier eintragen?
Would you please enter your name here?

It can be used as a verb on its own to mean **to want**, **to intend**

Ich will nicht.
I don't want to.

Wie Sie wollen!/Wie du willst!
As you like!

Was wollen Sie eigentlich? (eigentlich really, actually)
What do you really want?

Wollen Sie ein Bier?
Do you want a beer?

Was wollen Sie essen?
What do you want to eat?

Ich will nach Hause.
I want to go home.

Ich will meine Ruhe haben.
I want to be left in peace.

Was wollen Sie, es ist doch alles gut verlaufen? (verlaufen to end, to turn out, to go off)
What more do you want? Everything went off all right!

Sie haben es so gewollt.
That's the way you wanted it.

6. GEGENSÄTZE/CONTRASTS

SPÄT/LATE

Wir gehen spät ins Bett.
We go to bed late.

FRÜH/EARLY

Sie steht gern früh auf.
She likes getting up early.

SCHÖN

Wir hatten schönes Wetter.
Life in Berlin is pleasant.

HÄSSLICH

Das war hässlich von dir.
That was nasty of you.

BREIT

Der Fluss ist breit.
The river is wide.

ENG

Die Gasse ist eng.
The lane is narrow.

WEIT/FAR

Der Bahnhof ist 100 Meter <u>weit</u> von hier.
The station is 100 meters from here.

Das liegt in <u>weiter</u> Ferne.
That is a long way off.

NAH/NEAR

Das Dorf ist <u>nah</u>.
The village is near.

Sie ist eine <u>nahe</u> Verwandte.
She is a close relation.

SCHNELL

Der Zug fährt <u>schnell</u>.
The train travels fast.

LANGSAM

<u>Langsam</u> fahren!
Drive slowly!

AUF

Der Laden ist <u>auf</u>.
The shop is open.

ZU

Das Museum ist <u>zu</u>.
The museum is closed.

WEICH

Das Kissen ist <u>weich</u>.
The cushion is soft.

HART

Der Stein ist <u>hart</u>.
The stone is hard.

EINFACH

eine <u>einfache</u> Frage
a simple question

KOMPLIZIERT

eine <u>komplizierte</u> Aufgabe
a complicated task

LANGWEILIG

Nichtstun ist <u>langweilig</u>.
Doing nothing is boring.

UNTERHALTSAM

Karten spielen ist <u>unterhaltsam</u>.
Playing cards is entertaining.

LEICHT

Eine Feder ist <u>leicht</u>.
A feather is light.

SCHWER

Eisen ist <u>schwer</u>.
Iron is heavy.

HELL

Während des Tages ist es <u>hell</u>.
During the day it is light.

DUNKEL

Während der Nacht ist es <u>dunkel</u>.
During the night it is dark.

STARK

Sie trinkt <u>starken</u> Kaffee.
She drinks strong coffee.

SCHWACH

Das ist ein <u>schwaches</u> Argument.
That is a weak argument.

Contrasts can also be formed by adding **un-** onto an adjective:

ECHT

Die Unterschrift ist <u>echt</u>.
The signature is genuine.

UNECHT

Dieser Teppich ist <u>unecht</u>.
This carpet is not genuine.

BEQUEM/COMFORTABLE

Dieser Sessel ist <u>bequem</u>.
This armchair is comfortable.

UNBEQUEM/UNCOMFORTABLE

Die Couch ist <u>unbequem</u>.
The couch is uncomfortable.

DEUTLICH

Sie spricht <u>deutlich</u>.
She speaks clearly.

UNDEUTLICH

Er spricht <u>undeutlich</u>.
He speaks indistinctly.

GEWISS

Ich weiß es <u>gewiss</u>.
I'm sure of it.

UNGEWISS

Die Lage ist sehr <u>ungewiss</u>.
The situation is very uncertain.

GLÜCKLICH

Paul und Silke sind sehr <u>glücklich</u>.
Paul and Silke are very happy.

UNGLÜCKLICH

Unsere Nachbarn sind sehr <u>unglücklich</u>.
Our neighbours are very unhappy.

RUHIG

Wir wohnen in einer <u>ruhigen</u> Gegend.
In the city, life is hectic.

UNRUHIG

Das Leben in der Stadt ist <u>unruhig</u>.
We live in a quiet area.

MÖGLICH

Jetzt ist alles <u>möglich</u>.
Anything's possible now.

UNMÖGLICH

Das ist <u>unmöglich</u>!
That's impossible!

GERN

Ich spiele <u>gern</u> Klavier.
I like to play the piano.

UNGERN

Ich fahre <u>ungern</u> mit dem Zug.
I don't like to travel by train.

WAHRSCHEINLICH

Es wird <u>wahrscheinlich</u> regnen.
It is likely to rain./It'll probably rain.

UNWAHRSCHEINLICH

Es ist <u>unwahrscheinlich</u>, dass er kommt.
He's unlikely to come.

Wortschatz/Vocabulary

außerhalb: *(+ genitive) outside (of)*
der Besuch: *the visit*
Besuch haben: *to have a visitor(s), to have company*

von Zeit zu Zeit: *from time to time, now and then*
die Osterferien: *the Easter vacation*
Ostern: *Easter*

Weihnachten: *Christmas*
das Alter: *the age*
ausgehen: *to go out*
ausprobieren: *to sample, to get a taste of*
diesmal: *this time*
der Urlaub: *the vacation, the holiday*
spät: *late*
früh: *early*
aufstehen: *to get up*
schlafen: *to sleep*
die Kleinstadt: *the small town*
wach: *awake*
wach werden: *to wake up*
normalerweise: *normally, usually*
überraschen: *to surprise*
ruhig: *quiet*
die Karte: *the card*
Karten spielen: *to play cards*
das Wochenende: *the weekend*
sich langweilen: *to be bored, to feel bored*
glauben: *to believe, to think*
ich glaube: *I think*
solch- : *such (a/an)*
das Leben: *the life*
scheinen: *to appear*
eintönig: *monotonous*
das Volksfest: *the village festival*
die Blume: *the flower*
der Jahrmarkt: *the fair*
die Internetverbindung: *the internet connection*
statt (+ *genitive*)**:** *instead of*
nächst- : *next*
die Buchhandlung: *the bookshop*
außerdem: *as well as that*
stark: *strong, strongly*
die Oper: *the opera*

die Kneipe: *the bar*
die Studentenkneipe: *the students' bar*
treffen: *to meet*
halten: *to keep*
halten von (+ *dative*)**:** *to think of*
was halten Sie davon? *what do you think? (of the idea)*
bestimmen: *to determine, to decide on*
vorschlagen: *to suggest*
sich beeilen: *to hurry up*
sich weigern: *to refuse*
sich entscheiden: *to decide*
sich erinnern an (+ *accusative*)**:** *to remember*
erinnern an (+ *accusative*)**:** *to remind*
sich langweilen: *to feel bored, to be bored*
langweilen: *to bore (someone)*
sich interessieren für (+ *accusative*)**:** *to be interested in*
interessieren: *to interest*
das Kleid: *the dress*
bestellen: *to order*
holen: *to fetch, to get*
die Apfelsine: *the orange*
schälen: *to peel*
sich ereignen: *to happen*
empfangen: *to receive*
der Verkehrsunfall: *the traffic accident*
sich (*dative*) **leisten:** *to afford*
sich (*dative*) **gönnen:** *to allow oneself, to give oneself*
sich (*dative*) **merken:** *to remember, to bear in mind*
sich öffnen: *to open (by itself)*
füllen: *to fill*
sich begegen: *to meet*
sich umarmen: *to embrace*

lieben: *to love*
gehören *(+ dative)*: *to belong to*
der Schrank: *the cupboard, the closet*
das Material: *the material, the cloth*
die Chance: *the opportunity*
verpassen: *to let slip, to miss*
hart: *hard*
selten: *rare(ly), seldom*
vorkommen: *to occur*
die Sängerin: *the singer (female)*
wollen: *to want, to claim, to intend*
eigentlich: *really, actually*
verlaufen: *to end, to turn out*
die Ruhe: *the quiet, the peace*
der Gegensatz: *the contrast*
umgehen: *to deal with, to handle*
vorsichtig: *careful, prudent*
das Messer: *the knife*
das Leben: *the life*
schön: *lovely, beautiful*
breit: *broad*
eng: *narrow*
hässlich: *ugly, nasty*
die Situation: *the situation*
das Dorf: *the village*
nah: *near*
weich: *soft*
kompliziert: *complicated*
die Aufgabe: *the task, the exercise*
einfach: *simple*
unterhaltsam: *entertaining*
während *(+ genitive)*: *during*
das Eisen: *iron*
hell: *light, bright*
dunkel: *dark*

das Nichtstun: *doing nothing, idleness*
der Fluss: *the river*
die Unterschrift: *the signature*
der Teppich: *the carpet*
schwach: *weak*
das Argument: *the argument, the point*
die Feder: *the feather*
leicht: *light; easy*
echt: *genuine*
unecht: *false*
der Sessel: *the armchair*
bequem: *comfortable*
die Couch: *the couch*
unbequem: *uncomfortable*
die Lösung: *the solution*
deutlich: *clear(ly), distinct(ly)*
undeutlich: *indistinct(ly)*
die Vorstellung: *the idea; the performance*
gewiss: *certain*
ungewiss: *uncertain*
die Lage: *the situation*
das Klavier: *the piano*
die Kunst: *art*
glücklich: *happy*
unglücklich: *unhappy*
der Nachbar: *the neighbor*
die Ehe: *the marriage*
ruhig: *peaceful, quiet*
unruhig: *restless, hectic*
die Gegend: *the area, the district*
möglich: *possible*
unmöglich: *impossible*
das Ding: *the thing*
wahrscheinlich: *probable, likely*
unwahrscheinlich: *improbable, unlikely*

Übungen/Exercises

Exercise A

BITTE BEANTWORTEN SIE DIESE FRAGEN, DIE SICH AUF DAS GESPRÄCH AM ANFANG DER LEKTION BEZIEHEN.

Please answer these questions, which relate to the dialogue at the beginning of the lesson.

1. Wo wohnt Pauls Cousine?

   ....

2. Ist sie älter oder jünger als Paul?

   ....

3. Wann wird sie wach?

   ....

4. Was macht Silke schon vor Sonnenaufgang?

   ....

5. Um wie viel Uhr geht sie ins Bett?

   ....

6. Wann geht Paul normalerweise schlafen?

   ....

7. Ist das Leben ruhig oder unruhig in der Kleinstadt?

   ....

8. Gibt es ein Kino in der Kleinstadt?

   ....

9. Wollen Sie in eine Studentenkneipe?

   ....

10. Was schlägt Silke vor?

   ....

18. Shopping

Lesson 18 talks about shopping. You will learn the subjunctive mood , as well as interrogative and demonstrative pronouns. By now, you should be able to easily follow the flow of the audio and have a firm grasp of the grammar and a comprehensive vocabulary.

EINKAUFEN IN EINEM GROSSEN KAUFHAUS
SHOPPING IN A LARGE DEPARTMENT STORE

ein Verkäufer	Werden Sie schon bedient?
	Are you being attended to?
ein Kunde	Noch nicht. Ich möchte ein Paar Schuhe anprobieren.
	Not yet. I'd like to try on a pair of shoes.
der Verkäufer	Gerne. Welche Schuhe möchten Sie?
	Of course. Which shoes would you like?
der Kunde	Diejenigen, die dort unten rechts stehen.
	The ones that are down there on the right.
der Verkäufer	Gut. Welche Schuhgröße haben Sie?
	Fine. What size of shoe do you take?
der Kunde	Dreiundvierzig. Ich möchte die Schuhe in Braun, bitte.
	Forty-three. I'd like them in brown, please.
der Verkäufer	Größe dreiundvierzig in Braun. Ich weiß nicht, ob wir noch welche haben. Ich schaue nach.
	Size forty-three in brown. I don't know if we have any left. I'll go and have a look.

Nach kurzer Zeit kehrt der Verkäufer mit leeren Händen zurück.
After a short while the salesman comes back empty-handed.

der Verkäufer	**Es tut mir leid. Größe dreiundvierzig in Braun haben wir nicht mehr.** I'm sorry. We don't have any size forty-three in brown left.
der Kunde	**Das gibt's doch nicht! Ich suche solche Schuhe schon seit Wochen. Jetzt, wo ich sie in Ihrem Laden finde, haben Sie meine Größe nicht auf Lager!** I don't believe it! I've been looking for shoes like this for weeks now. And when I find them in your store, you don't have my size in stock!
der Verkäufer	**Ich kann sie Ihnen bestellen, und sie werden morgen da sein. Können Sie morgen Nachmittag wieder vorbeikommen?** I can order them for you and they'll be here tomorrow. Can you drop by again tomorrow afternoon?
der Kunde	**Morgen, hm ... Um wie viel Uhr schließen Sie?** Tomorrow, hm ... At what time do you close?
der Verkäufer	**Wir haben durchgehend bis zwanzig Uhr geöffnet.** We are open all day till eight p.m.
der Kunde	**Einverstanden. Ich komme morgen Nachmittag vorbei. Noch etwas: Ich hätte gern eine Krawatte. Wo finde ich die Herrenabteilung?** All right. I'll drop by tomorrow afternoon. Another thing: I'd like a tie. Where do I find the menswear department?
der Verkäufer	**Die Herrenabteilung ist eine Etage tiefer, im Erdgeschoss. Dort finden Sie alles, was Sie an Herrenbekleidung brauchen: Krawatten, Hemden, Anzüge, Sakkos, Hosen, Unterwäsche, Socken und so weiter.** The menswear department is one floor down, on the ground floor. You'll find everything you need as regards menswear: ties, shirts, suits, jackets, pants, underwear, socks, etc.
der Kunde	**Ich möchte auch gerne einige Reiseandenken an Berlin. Kann ich die hier bekommen? Ich brauche welche für meine Freunde im Ausland.** I'd also like some souvenirs of Berlin. Can I get them here? I need some for my friends abroad.
der Verkäufer	**Reiseandenken finden Sie auch im Erdgeschoss, gegenüber der Herrenabteilung. Postkarten und dergleichen bekommen Sie in der Schreibwarenabteilung in der dritten Etage.** You'll also find souvenirs on the ground floor, opposite the menswear department. You can get postcards and suchlike in the stationery department on the third floor.
der Kunde	**Aha! – Meine Frau wird vielleicht morgen mitkommen. Wo ist die Abteilung für Damenbekleidung?**

	I see. My wife might come with me tomorrow. Where's the department for ladies' clothing?
der Verkäufer	Wir haben eine ausgezeichnete Auswahl an Damenbekleidung, Damenwäsche usw. Die finden Sie in der zweiten Etage, einen Stock höher.
	We have an excellent selection of ladies' clothing, ladies' underwear, etc. You'll find this on the second floor, one level up.
die Kunde	Wo ist die Rolltreppe?
	Where's the escalator?
der Verkäufer	Die Rolltreppen befinden sich hinter Ihnen.
	The escalators are behind you.
der Kunde	Danke schön. Sie waren sehr hilfreich. Also bis morgen. Bitte vergessen Sie meine Schuhe nicht! Größe dreiundvierzig In Braun.
	Thank you. You've been very helpful. Well, see you tomorrow. Please don't forget my shoes! Size forty-three in brown.
der Verkäufer	Sie können sich auf mich verlassen! Bis morgen!
	You can rely on me. See you tomorrow.
der Kunde	Auf Wiederschauen!
	Goodbye!
der Verkäufer	Auf Wiederschauen!
	Goodbye!

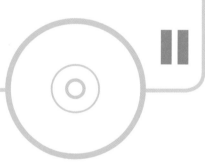

Grammatik/Grammar

1. DEMONSTRATIVE PRONOUNS

masculine	feminine	neuter	plural
derjenige	diejenige	dasjenige	diejenigen

This demonstrative pronoun is used before relative clauses to refer to an item which is then explained in more detail. The first part (**der-**, **die-**, **das-**) is declined exactly as the definite article, with **-jenige** affixed and declined as an adjective. It can mean **those**, **that one**, etc.

Examples:

Welche Schuhe möchten Sie?
Which shoes would you like?

Ich möchte diejenigen, die unten rechts stehen.
I'd like the ones *(i.e. the pair)* that are down on the right.

Welches Kind meinen Sie?
Which child do you mean?

Dasjenige, das mit dem Hund spielt.
The one that's playing with the dog.

Mit welchen Leuten hat er gesprochen?
Which people did he speak with?

Er sprach nur mit denjenigen, die er kannte.
He spoke only with those that he knew.

2. INTERROGATIVE PRONOUNS

masculine	feminine	neuter	plural
welcher?	welche?	welches?	welche?

Welch- is used as an interrogative pronoun meaning **which/what**.

Examples:

Welchen Mantel möchten Sie?
Which coat would you like?

Welche Krawatte gefällt Ihnen?
Which tie do you like?

Welches Buch meinen Sie?
Which book do you mean?

Welche Größe haben Sie?
What size do you take?

Welch- can be used as an interrogative adjective. The ending of welch- must agree with the gender of the noun it refers to:

Welcher ist der kürzeste Weg?
Which is the shortest way?

Welche ist die beste Lösung?
Which is the best solution?

Welches ist das treffende Wort?
Which is the appropriate word?

Mit welchem Zug fahren wir?
Which train are we traveling on?

Aus welcher Stadt kommen Sie?
Which town do you come from?

Für welches Kleid haben Sie sich entschieden?
Which dress have you decided on?

3. WAS FÜR?/WHAT, WHAT SORT OF?

When asking a question with **was für, a more general answer** is expected.

Was für Möglichkeiten gibt es?
What possibilities are there?

Was für Schuhe haben Sie?
What sort of shoes do you have?

with a preposition:

Mit was für einem Auto fahren wir?
What sort of car will we be taking?

also:

Was für eine herrliche Aussicht! (die Aussicht: the view; herrlich: splendid)
What a splendid view!

4. WAS/WHAT/WHICH/WHATEVER

Was can be used to mean **what?**

Was machst du?
What are you doing?

It can also be used as a relative pronoun to mean **that** or **which** after **alles, einiges, vieles,** and after superlative adjectives used as nouns.

Da finden Sie alles, was Sie brauchen.
You'll find everything (**that**) you need there.

Er tat alles, was zu tun war.
He did everything that had to be done.

Das ist das Schönste, was ich je gehört habe.
That is the most beautiful thing (**that**) I have ever heard.

Note that adjectives are given capital letters when they are used as nouns:

das Schönste   das Größte
the most beautiful thing   the biggest thing

Er ist der Beste.
He is the best.

5. DER KONJUNKTIV/THE SUBJUNCTIVE MOOD

So far, we have used sentences to express actions or state facts which happen or have happened. We have been using the **indicative mood** in the present and the past tenses. A mood is a form of a verb used to express the mode or manner of an action or state of being.

The **subjunctive mood** indicates that something is uncertain, dubious or desirable. It is also used to report something that someone said or wrote. It is used more in German than in English, especially in the written language. Its use in spoken German is becoming less common.

There are **two versions**, one based on the present tense and the other on the preterite tense introduced in lesson 15.

The subjunctive based on the present tense is called Konjunkiv I in German and consists of the stem (the part of the verb without -en) with the same present tense endings you are familiar with, except in the 'familiar' you form (singular and plural) and the third person singular:

Common verbs in the subjunctive:

kommen	haben	machen	werden
ich komme	ich habe	ich mache	ich werde
Sie kommen	Sie haben	Sie machen	Sie werden
du kommest	du habest	du machest	du werdest
er/sie/es komme	er/sie/es habe	er/sie/es mache	er/sie/es werde
wir kommen	wir haben	wir machen	wir werden
Sie kommen	Sie haben	Sie machen	Sie werden
ihr kommet	ihr habet	ihr machet	ihr werdet
sie kommen	sie haben	sie machen	sie werden

können	sein
ich könne	ich sei
Sie können	Sie seien
du könnest	du seiest
er/sie/es könne	er/sie/es sei
wir können	wir seien
Sie können	Sie seien
ihr könnet	ihr seiet
sie können	sie seien

Also, the subjunctive is used to report what someone has said or written:

(Note that the tense structure in indirect speech in German is different from English.)

Er schrieb, dass seine Schwester wieder gesund sei. (gesund: healthy, well)
He wrote that his sister **was** well again.

Sie sagte uns, sie komme nächste Woche nicht.

She said to us she **was not coming** next week.

Sie sagte uns, sie <u>könne</u> nächste Woche nicht kommen.
She said to us she **could** not come next week.

Sie fragte, was er mache.
She asked what he **was doing**.

You use the subjunctive with als ob (**Konjunkiv I** here):

Er sieht aus, als ob er krank <u>sei</u>.
He looks as though he **were** sick.

Er tut, als ob er nichts <u>wisse</u>.
He behaves **as though** he **knew** nothing.

The **Konjunktiv I** form of the subjunctive is also used in polite requests:

Bitte seien Sie so gut und helfen Sie mir!
Please be so good and help me.

The **subjunctive based on the preterite** form of the indicative (called **Konjunktiv II** in German) is formed as follows (the preterite was described in Lesson 15):

The strong verbs take an umlaut where the stem vowel is an a, o or u, except for **sollen** and **wollen**.

Regular weak verbs never take an umlaut; only in the irregular weak verb does the a sometimes change to an ä. (e.g. **bringen** – **brächte**)

kommen	haben	machen	werden:
ich käme	ich hätte	ich machte	ich würde
Sie kämen	Sie hätten	Sie machten	Sie würden
du kämest	du hättest	du machtest	du würdest
er/sie/es käme	er/sie/es hätte	er/sie/es machte	er/sie/es würde
wir kämen	wir hätten	wir machten	wir würden
Sie kämen	Sie hätten	Sie machten	Sie würden
ihr kämet	ihr hättet	ihr machtet	ihr würdet
sie kämen	sie hätten	sie machten	sie würden

können	sein
ich könnte	ich wäre
Sie könnten	Sie wären
du könntest	du wärst
er/sie/es könnte	er/sie/es wäre
wir könnten	wir wären
Sie könnten	Sie wären
ihr könntet	ihr wäret
sie könnten	sie wären

(compare these forms with: **ich kam, ich hatte, ich machte, ich wurde, ich konnte, ich war**, etc., in the preterite tense)

The Konjunktiv II form of the subjunctive is used to indicate doubt or unreality:

Das dürfte richtig sein.
That **may** be correct.

It can express a wish, which may or may not be fulfilled:

Wenn wir nur schon da wären!
If only we were there already.

It is used after als ob:

Sie benahm sich, als ob sie nichts davon wüsste. (sich benehmen: to behave)
She behaved as though she knew nothing about it.

It is used in conditional sentences referring to a condition that might or might not be fulfilled:

Wenn sie mitkäme, wäre ich sehr überrascht.
If **she were to come with us I'd be** very surprised.

Wenn wir Zeit hätten, würden wir mitkommen.
If we **had** time, we **would come** with you.

Note: the use of würden ... mitkommen in the second sentence is another way of expressing the subjunctive and is very popular in spoken German.

The Konjunktiv II is also used in a number of colloquial expressions:

Wie wär's mit einem Kartenspiel?
What about a game of cards?

Das wär.
That's all. (e.g. when shopping in a store)

Ich hätte gern eine Krawatte.
I would like a tie.

There is a tendency in modern German to use Konjunktiv II instead of Konjunktiv I for reported speech:

Sie sagte, sie ginge früh ins Bett.
She said that she goes to bed early.

To express a condition which can no longer be fulfilled, the Konjunktiv II of the past is used. It is formed on the basis of the Pluperfect tense, the participle stays the same, and haben and sein take the subjunctive form:

Ich wäre gestern spazieren gegangen, wenn es nicht geregnet hätte.
I **would have** gone for a walk yesterday, if it hadn't rained.

Ich an Ihrer Stelle hätte das nicht gemacht.
If I were you, I **wouldn't have** done that.

Wenn ich Geld gehabt hätte, hätte ich mir einen neuen Anzug gekauft.
If I had had the money, **I would have** bought myself a new suit.

And also for a missed opportunity:

Sie hätten telefonieren können!
You **could have** phoned!

Ich hätte vorsichtiger sein müssen.
I **should have** been more careful.

Das hättest du vorher sagen sollen.
You **should have** said that earlier.

Note the following polite request:

Ich hätte gern Herrn Schmidt gesprochen.
I would like to speak to Mr. Schmidt.

6. SEIT/SINCE, FOR

Examples of the use of **seit** as a preposition:

Ich suche diese Schuhe schon <u>seit</u> langem.
I have been looking for these shoes **for** a long time.

Ich kenne sie <u>seit</u> einem Jahr.
I have known her **for** a year.

Wir sind <u>seit</u> letzter Woche hier.
We've been here **since** last week.

Seit takes the dative case:

<u>seit</u> zwei Jahren   <u>seit</u> einigen Wochen
for two years   **for** some weeks

As a conjunction:

Es ist einen Monat her, seit er bei uns war.
It's a month since he stayed with us.

Compare the same sentence with **seit** as a preposition:

Seit seinem Besuch bei uns ist ein Monat vergangen.
A month has passed since his visit to our place.

7. HOCH/TIEF/HIGH/LOW

Examples:

Wie <u>hoch</u> ist der Baum?
How **tall** is the tree?

Wie <u>hoch</u> sind unsere Verluste?
How **high** are our losses?

Note: **hoch** changes to **hoh-** when it is declined:

Wir haben hohe Schulden.
We have high debts.

Es liegt noch Schnee in höheren Lagen.
There's still snow on **higher** ground.

Der Mont Blanc ist der höchste Berg in Europa.
Mont Blanc is the **highest** mountain in Europe.

Es waren höchstens zwanzig Leute im Saal.
There were **at most** twenty people in the hall.

Die Sonne steht tief am Himmel.
The sun is **low** in the sky.

Es liegt tiefer Schnee am Boden.
There's **deep** snow on the ground.

Sie stecken tief in Schulden.
They're **deeply** in debt.

Paul arbeitete bis tief in die Nacht hinein.
Paul worked **deep** into the night.

Die tiefsten Werte dieses Jahres wurden in der vergangenen Nacht gemessen.
The **lowest** temperatures of the year were recorded last night.

Wortschatz/Vocabulary

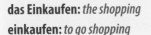

das Einkaufen: *the shopping*
einkaufen: *to go shopping*
das Kaufhaus: *the department store*
der Verkäufer: *the salesman*
der Kunde: *the customer (male)*
die Kundin: *the customer (female)*
bedienen: *to serve*
werden Sie schon bedient?: *are you being attended to?*
wünschen: *to wish, to desire*
noch nicht: *not yet*
derjenige, diejenige, dasjenige: *the one*
diejenigen (plural): *the ones*
die Größe: *the size*
die Schuhgröße: *the shoe size*
nachschauen: *to go and have a look*

seit: *since; for*
der Laden: *the store, the shop*
das Lager: *the warehouse*
... auf Lager haben: *to have ... in stock*
die Krawatte: *the tie*
die Herrenabteilung: *the menswear department*
der Stock: *the floor*
im ersten Stock: *on the first floor*
tief: *deep, low*
die Herrenbekleidung: *the menswear, men's clothing*
das Hemd: *the shirt*
der Anzug: *the suit*
die Hose: *the pants/the trousers*
die Unterwäsche: *the underwear*

die Socke: *the sock*

das Reiseandenken: *the souvenir*

etliche: *some*

die Postkarte: *the postcard*

die Schreibwarenabteilung: *the stationery department*

die Etage: *the floor (of a building)*

die Damenbekleidung: *the ladies' clothing*

ausgezeichnet: *excellent*

die Auswahl: *the selection, the choice*

Damenwäsche: *ladies' underwear*

usw. (= und so weiter): *etc.*

aha: *I understand, I see*

die Rolltreppe: *the escalator*

hinter Ihnen: *behind you*

hilfreich: *helpful*

vergessen: *to forget*

bis: *until*

verlassen: *to leave*

sich verlassen auf *(+ accusative):* **to depend on, to rely on**

verlassen Sie sich darauf!: *you can depend on it!*

auf Wiederschauen!: *goodbye! (a variant of* **auf Wiedersehen!***)*

die Tänzerin: *the dancer (female)*

kurz: *short*

treffend: *appropriate*

die Katze: *the cat*

die Möglichkeit: *the possibility*

die Geschichte: *the story, the history*

sich entscheiden: *to decide (on), to make up one's mind*

der Zug: *the train*

die Aussicht: *the view*

herrlich: *splendid*

was für: *what, what sort of*

sorgfältig: *carefully*

je: *ever*

erklären: *to explain*

gesund: *healthy*

krank: *ill, poorly*

arm: *poor*

als ob: *as though (+ subjunctive)*

der Zucker: *the sugar*

helfen: *to help*

aufhören: *to cease, to stop*

anrufen: *to call, to ring up*

das Kartenspiel: *the game of cards*

der Besuch: *the visit*

die Mauer: *the wall*

der Verlust: *the loss*

der Baum: *the tree*

der Schnee: *the snow*

der Berg: *the mountain*

der Saal: *the hall*

die Schuld: *the guilt; the debt*

der Wert: *the value*

messen: *to measure*

darüber: *about it, about this*

Übungen/Exercises

Exercise A

BITTE BEANTWORTEN SIE DIESE FRAGEN, DIE SICH AUF DAS GESPRÄCH AM ANFANG DER LEKTION BEZIEHEN.

Please answer these questions, which refer to the dialogue at the beginning of the lesson.

1. **Wo war der Kunde?**

   ....

2. **Wurde der Kunde schon bedient?**

   ....

3. **Was wollte der Kunde?**

   ....

4. **Welche Schuhgröße hatte der Kunde?**

   ....

5. **Kehrte der Verkäufer mit den Schuhen zurück?**

   ....

6. **Hatte das Kaufhaus diese Schuhe noch auf Lager?**

   ....

7. **War der Kunde glücklich darüber?** (darüber: **about this**)

   ....

8. **Seit wann suchte er solche Schuhe?**

   ....

9. **Konnte der Verkäufer die Schuhe bestellen?**

   ....

10. **Würde der Kunde am nächsten Tag vorbeikommen?**

....

11. Was hätte der Kunde noch gern gehabt?

....

12. Wo ist die Herrenabteilung?

....

13. Für wen brauchte der Kunde die Reiseandenken?

....

14. Wo könnte der Kunde Postkarten kaufen?

....

15. Was meinte der Kunde: War der Verkäufer hilfreich?

....

19. Celebrations

Lesson 19 introduces celebrations. You will learn how to use reported speech. You will learn how to distinguish the gender of nouns and you will learn a final, extended list of vocabulary. Take the time to absorb this information before continuing on to the final lesson.

EINE FEIER, BEVOR MAN AUSEINANDERGEHT
A CELEBRATION BEFORE PARTING

Frau Schmidt	**Alles Gute zum Geburtstag, Herr Kraus!**
	Happy birthday, Mr Kraus!
die anderen	**Ja. Alles Gute!**
	Yes, happy birthday!

Sie stoßen mit den Gläsern an und trinken etwas Sekt.
They clink glasses and they drink some sparkling wine.

Frau Schmidt	**Wir wollen auch Paul beglückwünschen.**
	We should also congratulate Paul!
Paul	**Mich? Weswegen? Was habe ich getan?**
	Me? Why? What have I done?
Frau Schmidt	**Sie haben große Fortschritte beim Deutschlernen gemacht. Sie sind ein ausgezeichneter Student.**
	You have made great progress in the German language. You're an excellent student.
Paul	**Ich weiß nicht, was ich sagen soll. Auf jeden Fall haben Sie viel**

dazu beigetragen. Sie sind wirklich ein talentierter Lehrer.
I don't know what to say. In any case you've played a big part. You really are a talented teacher.

Frau Schmidt
Die machen sich gegenseitig Komplimente! – Vielleicht sollten wir das Thema wechseln ... Fahren Sie in Urlaub, Paul?
They're paying each other compliments! – Perhaps we should change the subject? Are you going away on vacation, Paul?

Paul
Noch nicht. Ich bleibe vorerst in Berlin. Später will ich eventuell meine Cousine Silke besuchen. Was machen Sie, Frau Schmidt? Fahren Sie in Urlaub?
Not yet, I'm staying in Berlin for the time being. Later on, I might visit my cousin Silke. What are you doing Mrs. Schmidt? Are you going away on holiday?

Frau Schmidt
Ja, ich fliege mit meinem Mann nach Österreich. Unsere beiden Tiere, der Hund und die Katze, bleiben in Berlin. Ein befreundetes Ehepaar wird für sie sorgen. Und Sie, Frau Constanze?
Yes, I'm flying to Austria with my husband. Our two pets, the dog and the cat, are staying in Berlin. A couple we are friendly with are going to look after them. What about you, Ms. Constanze?

Ulrike
Ich will ein paar Tage bei meinen Eltern in Frohnau verbringen, und dann fahre ich nach Oldenburg, um meine Tante zu besuchen.
I want to spend a few days with my parents in Frohnau and then I'm going to Oldenburg to visit my aunt.

Wolfgang
Ich fahre mit dem Zug nach Bremen, und dann verbringe ich zwei Wochen mit ein paar Freunden in Cuxhaven. Einer der Freunde hat einen Onkel, der eine Jacht besitzt. Wir werden nicht nur baden, sondern auch segeln können. Übrigens, Oldenburg ist gar nicht so weit, Ulrike. Du könntest uns ja in Cuxhaven besuchen.
I'm taking the train to Bremen and then I'm spending two weeks with some friends in Cuxhaven. One of my friends has an uncle who owns a yacht. We'll be able not only to go swimming, but also to go sailing. By the way, Oldenburg isn't really too far away, Ulrike. You could come and visit us in Cuxhaven.

Ulrike
Ich möchte gern, aber es ist unmöglich. Es ist alles zu kompliziert. Erstens habe ich kein eigenes Auto, und zweitens habe ich nur wenige Tage zur Verfügung.
I'd like to, but it's not possible. It's all too complicated. Firstly, I don't have a car of my own and secondly, I've only got a few days.

Frau Schmidt
Würden Sie ihn besuchen, wenn Sie ein Auto hätten? Wenn Sie wollen, kann ich Ihnen mein Auto zur Verfügung stellen. Das Auto würde ich sowieso in Berlin lassen, und ich weiß, wie vorsichtig Sie fahren.
Would you visit him if you had a car? If you like, I can let you have my car.

	I'd be leaving the car in Berlin anyway and I know how carefully you drive.
Ulrike	Danke, Sie sind sehr großzügig. Aber ich muss am zwölften August nach Berlin zurückkehren, damit ich mich meiner neuen Wohnung widmen kann, und dann lohnt es sich nicht, ein Auto mitzunehmen.
	Thank you, that's very generous of you. But I have to return to Berlin on the 12th of August, so I can get started on my new apartment, and then it's not worth taking a car.
Frau Schmidt	Haben Sie endlich eine Wohnung gefunden?
	Have you found an apartment at last?
Ulrike	Ja. Ich habe monatelang eine eigene Wohnung gesucht und habe neulich eine umgebaute Einzimmerwohnung mit Küche und Bad in einem Altbau gefunden. Die Wohnung ist nicht weit von der Bank entfernt, wo ich arbeite.
	Yes. I was looking for my own apartment for months and recently I found a converted one-room apartment with a kitchen and bathroom in an old building. The apartment isn't far away from the bank where I work.
Wolfgang	Herzlichen Glückwunsch, Ulrike! Wann lädst du uns ein?
	Congratulations, Ulrike! When are you going to invite us?
Ulrike	Wenn du Lust dazu hättest, Wolfgang, könntest du mir helfen, die Wohnung einzurichten, sobald du aus Cuxhaven zurückgekehrt bist.
	If you'd like, Wolfgang, you could come and help me to decorate it as soon as you get back from Cuxhaven.
Wolfgang	Gerne. Das würde mir Spaß machen.
	Sure. I'd enjoy doing that.
Paul	Sagen Sie mir Bescheid, wenn Sie auch meine Hilfe brauchen.
	Let me know if you need my help as well.
Ulrike	Das ist nett, Paul. Aber wir sind heute Abend hier, um Wolfgangs Geburtstag zu feiern. Frau Schmidt hat uns wieder Sekt eingeschenkt. Wolfgang, wir trinken auf dein Wohl! Alles Gute zum neunundzwanzigsten Geburtstag! Auf dein Wohl!
	That's nice of you, Paul. But we're here this evening to celebrate Wolfgang's birthday. Mrs. Schmidt has filled up our glasses with sparkling wine again. Wolfgang, to your health! Many happy returns on your 29th birthday! Here's to you!

Sie stoßen nochmals mit den Gläsern an und trinken.
They clink glasses again and drink.

Grammatik/Grammar

1. BEIDE/BOTH

beide can be used as an adjective:

Beide Schwestern sind schön.
Both sisters are good-looking.

Meine beiden Brüder studieren.
Both my brothers are at university.

To express "**either**":

Sie können beide Straßen nehmen.
You can take **either** road.

As a pronoun:

Alle beide sind schön.
Both of them are good-looking.

In spoken German, **beide** on its own often becomes **beides**:

Welche Lösung ist richtig?
Which solution is correct?

Beides ist richtig. Beides ist möglich. or: Beide sind richtig. Beide sind möglich.
Both are correct. **Either** is possible.

2. EIN PAAR/A FEW, SOME

Schade – ich habe nur ein paar Euro in der Tasche.
What a pity – I only have **a few** euros in my pocket.

Ulrike kommt in ein paar Tagen zurück.
Ulrike's coming back in **a few** days.

To say "**a pair**" use **ein Paar**.

Ich möchte ein Paar Schuhe anprobieren.
I'd like to try on **a pair of** shoes.

Ein Paar Würstchen mit Senf und Brot, bitte!
Two sausages with mustard and bread, please.

Note however:

eine Hose	a pair of trousers/pants
eine Brille	a pair of (eye)glasses
eine Schere	a pair of scissors

As an adverb:

Sie hatte ihm ein paar Mal geschrieben.
She had written to him **several** times.

3. SONST/OTHERWISE, ELSE

Sonst noch etwas?
Anything **else**? *(e.g. in a shop)*

Danke, sonst nichts.
Nothing **else**, thanks.

Kann ich Ihnen sonst behilflich sein?
Can I help you **in any other way**?

Sonst noch jemand?
Anyone **else**? *(e.g. on a bus)*

Wie geht's sonst?
How are things **otherwise**?

used as a conjunction:

Wir müssen uns beeilen, sonst kommen wir zu spät an.
We must hurry, **otherwise** we'll be late.

4. NOCH/STILL, YET; OTHER

Wir haben noch viel Arbeit.
We **still** have a lot of work to do.

Ich habe das Buch noch nicht gelesen.
I haven't read the book **yet**.

Sie hat nur noch 2 Euro.
She **only** has 2 euros **left**.

Noch ein Bier, bitte.
Another beer, please.

Geben Sie mir bitte noch ein Kilo Äpfel.
Give me **another** kilo of apples, please.

Wird es noch lange dauern?
Will it take **much** longer?

Wir hatten den Zug gerade noch erreicht.
We only **just** managed to catch the train.

Möchten Sie noch etwas Kuchen?
Would you like some **more** cake?

Das wäre noch besser.
That would be **even** better.

weder ... noch ... means **neither ... nor ...**

Ich habe <u>weder</u> Zeit <u>noch</u> Lust dazu.
I have **neither** the time **nor** the inclination.

5. VERBEN/VERBS

HELFEN – **to help** – is an irregular strong verb and takes the dative:

present	preterite	Konjunktiv I
ich helfe	ich half	ich helfe
Sie helfen	Sie halfen	Sie helfen
du hilfst	du halfst	du helfest
er/sie/es hilft	er/sie/es half	er/sie/es helfe
wir helfen	wir halfen	wir helfen
Sie helfen	Sie halfen	Sie helfen
ihr helfet	ihr halfet	ihr helfet
sie helfen	sie halfen	sie helfen
future:	ich werde helfen, *etc.*	
past participle:	geholfen	
imperative:	Hilf! Helfen Sie!	

Examples:

Er will ihr <u>helfen</u>, die Wohnung einzurichten.
He wants to **help** her to decorate her apartment.

Sie weiß sich zu <u>helfen</u>.
She knows **how to take care of** herself.

Ich kann mir nicht <u>helfen</u>.
I can't **help** it.

Es <u>hilft</u> nichts, ich muss nach Hause.
It **can't be helped**, I must go home.

Der Lehrer <u>hatte</u> den Kindern beim Lernen <u>geholfen</u>.
The teacher **had been helping** the children with their studies.

6. REPORTED SPEECH

The following examples illustrate how reported speech is used in German. Note the need to use the subjunctive in reported speech, even where it is absent in direct speech.

Present:

Er hilft mir.
He's helping me.

Er glaubt, er helfe mir.
He thinks he's helping me.

In spoken German, it's more common to say: **Er glaubt, er würde mir helfen**.

Past:

Er hat mir geholfen.
He helped me.

Er sagte, er habe mir geholfen.
He said he had helped me.

In spoken German, it's more common to say: **Er sagte, er hätte mir geholfen.**

Future:

Er wird mir helfen.
He'll help me.

Er sagte, er werde mir helfen.
He said he'd help me.

Auxiliary verbs: **können**:

Present:

Sie kann mir helfen.
She can help me.

Sie sagt, sie könne mir helfen.
She says she can help me.

Past:

Sie konnte mir helfen. = Sie hat mir helfen können.
She was able to help me.

Sie sagte, sie habe mir helfen können.
She said she could help me.

Future:

Sie wird mir helfen können.
She'll be able to help me.

Sie sagt, sie werde mir helfen können.
She says she'll be able to help me.

The other auxiliary verbs, such as **müssen**, follow the same pattern:

Sie sagte, sie habe ihm helfen müssen.
She said she had to help him.

Sie sagte, sie werde ihm helfen müssen.
She says she would have to help him.

7. VERBEN/VERBS

REDEN – to speak, to talk, to converse – is a regular weak verb.

present	preterite	Konjunktiv I	Konjunktiv II
ich rede	ich redete	ich rede	ich redete
Sie reden	Sie redeten	Sie reden	Sie redeten
du redest	du redetest	du redest	du redetest
er/sie/es redet	er/sie/es redete	er/sie/es rede	er/sie/es redete
wir reden	wir redeten	wir reden	wir redeten
Sie reden	Sie redeten	Sie reden	Sie redeten
ihr redet	ihr redetet	ihr redet	ihr redetet
sie reden	sie redeten	sie reden	sie redeten
future:	ich werde reden, *etc.*		
past participle:	geredet		
imperative:	Rede!		
	Reden Sie!		

Examples:

Reden wir von etwas anderem!
Let's talk about something else!

Wir redeten gestern über ihn.
We were talking about him yesterday.

Sie reden nicht mehr miteinander.
They're no longer on speaking terms.

Du hast gut reden.
It's easy for you to talk.

Er lässt mit sich reden.
He's willing to listen to reason.

8. VOR/BEFORE, IN FRONT OF; AGO

Vor dem Essen haben sie eine Flasche Sekt geöffnet.
Before the meal they opened a bottle of sparkling wine.

Wir waren **vor** Ihnen da!
We were there **before** you!

Die Bushaltestelle ist direkt **vor** dem Bahnhof.
The bus stop is right **in front of** the station.

Heute **vor** vierzehn Tagen kamen wir aus New York zurück.
We came back from New York two weeks **ago** today.

Sie weinte **vor** Freude.
She wept **with** joy.

Er murmelte **vor sich hin**.
He muttered **away to himself**.

9. NACH/AFTER; TO

Bitte **nach** Ihnen!
After you!

Nach dem Essen trinken wir einen Schnaps.
After the meal we'll have a brandy.

Nach Ablauf dieser Frist ist die volle Summe zu zahlen.
After expiry of this period, the whole amount is payable.

Morgen fliegen wir **nach** Düsseldorf.
Tomorrow we're flying **to** Düsseldorf.

Ich werde mich **nach** dem Weg erkundigen.
I'll ask **for** directions.

Aller Wahrscheinlichkeit **nach** ist er jetzt in Südamerika.
In all probability he's in South America by now.

Nach diesem Brief zu urteilen ist er in Kanada.
To judge **by** this letter he is in Canada.

Nach dem, was Sie sagen, müsste er schon hier sein.
From what you say, he should be here by now.

Nach und nach wurde ich müde.
I **gradually** got tired.

10. EIGEN (FORTSETZUNG)/OWN

eigen is an adjective:

Sie hat kein <u>eigenes</u> Auto.
She doesn't have a car **of her own**.

Ich habe die Sonnenfinsternis mit <u>eigenen</u> Augen gesehen.
I saw the eclipse of the sun with **my own** eyes.

Er geht seinen <u>eigenen</u> Weg.
He goes **his own** way.

So etwas sollten Sie im <u>eigenen</u> Interesse nicht tun.
You should not do that, in **your own** interest.

Sie fahren auf <u>eigene</u> Gefahr.
You travel at **your own** risk.

Das kann ich aus <u>eigener</u> Erfahrung sagen.
I can say that from **my own** experience.

Wir fliegen auf <u>eigene</u> Kosten nach Amerika.
We're flying to America at **our own** expense.

Es ist so laut hier, dass man sein <u>eigenes</u> Wort nicht versteht.
It's so noisy here that you can't hear yourself speak.

eigens means **especially**:

Sie ist eigens nach Oldenburg gefahren, um ihre Tante zu besuchen.
She went to Oldenburg especially to see her aunt.

The noun derived from **eigen** is **die Eigenschaft**, meaning the **characteristic** or **quality**:

Herr Schmidt ist ein Mann mit vielen guten Eigenschaften.
Mr. Schmidt is a man with many good qualities.

11. HOW TO RECOGNIZE THE GENDERS OF NOUNS

There are no real hard and fast rules; these are only indications to help you recognize some of them.

Masculine nouns are generally:

nouns ending in **-er, -el, -ig, -ling**:

der Teller:	the plate	der Sprudel:	the sparkling mineral water
der Essig:	the vinegar	der Pflänzling:	the seedling

the seasons, months, days of the week, points of the compass and weather conditions:

der Frühling:	the spring	der Mai:	May
der Osten:	the east	der Schnee:	the snow
der Nebel:	the fog	der Montag:	Monday

words of foreign origin ending in **-är, -ent, -iker, -ismus, -ist**:

der Tourismus:	the tourism	der Aktionär:	the shareholder
der Politiker:	the politician	der Student:	the student
der Optimist:	the optimist		

(exception: das Kompliment: the compliment)

Feminine nouns are usually:

nouns ending in **-ei, -in, -heit, -keit, -schaft, -ung**:

die Partei:	the (political) party	die Wirtin:	the landlady
die Gewohnheit:	the custom, the habit	die Schönheit:	the beauty
die Höflichkeit:	the politeness	die Wirklichkeit:	the reality
die Leidenschaft:	the passion	die Eigenschaft:	the characteristic
die Neigung:	the inclination	die Leistung:	the achievement, the performance

nouns ending in **-age, -aille, -enz** which keep their original French gender:

die Etage:	the floor	die Medaille:	the medal
die Prominenz:	high society		

the names of trees and flowers:

die Eiche:	the oak	die Ulme:	the elm
die Rose:	the rose	die Nelke:	the carnation

Neuter nouns are usually:

nouns ending in **-chen, -lein, -icht, -tum**:

das Rädchen:	the little wheel	das Schäfchen:	the little lamb
das Röslein:	the little rose	das Dickicht:	the thicket
das Eigentum:	the property		

exceptions: der Reichtum: the wealth, der Irrtum: the mistake

words of foreign origin ending in **-ett, -in, -um**:

das Etikett:	the label, ticket	das Benzin:	the gasoline
das Gymnasium:	the high school/the grammar school		

many abstract nouns derived from verbs and ending in **-nis**:

das Gedächtnis:	the memory	das Geschehnis:	the event, the occurrence
das Verständnis:	the understanding	die Finsternis:	the darkness

many words beginning with **Ge-** that express a collection of things:

das Gebirge:	the mountain-range	das Gesetz:	the law
das Geräusch:	the noise, sound	das Gedicht:	the poem

exceptions: die Geschichte: the history/the story, die Gefahr: the danger

infinitives used as nouns:

das Essen:	the meal	das Singen:	the singing
das Zögern:	the hesitation	das Gehen:	the walking

Wortschatz/Vocabulary

die Feier: *the celebration*
auseinandergehen: *to part company*
herzlich: *hearty*
mit den Gläsern anstoßen: *to clink glasses*
der Geburtstag: *the birthday*
beglückwünschen: *to congratulate*
wünschen: *to wish, to desire*
der Glückwunsch: *the congratulations*
der Wunsch: *the wish, the desire*
weswegen: *why, for what reason*
der Fortschritt: *the progress*
das Deutschlernen: *learning German*
reden: *to talk, to speak*
beitragen: *to contribute*
wirklich: *really*
talentiert: *talented, gifted*
gegenseitig: *mutual*
das Kompliment: *the compliment*
das Thema: *the theme, the topic*
vorerst: *for the present, for the moment*
eventuell: *perhaps, possibly*
der Hund: *the dog*
später: *later*
die Jacht: *the yacht*
besitzen: *to possess, to own*
beider, beide, beides: *both, two*
das Tier: *the animal*
befreundet: *friendly*
sorgen für (+ *accusative*)**:** *to take care of*
die Tante: *the aunt*
baden: *to go swimming*
übrigens: *by the way*
kompliziert: *complicated*
erstens: *in the first place, firstly*
zweitens: *secondly*

zur Verfügung stellen: *to make something available*
sowieso: *in any case, anyway*
großzügig: *generous*
widmen: *to dedicate, to devote*
endlich: *final(ly)*
monatelang: *for months*
die Küche: *the kitchen*
das Bad: *the bath, the bathroom*
eigen: *own, of one's own*
umgebaut: *converted*
umbauen: *to reconstruct, to rebuild*
neulich: *recently*
die Einzimmerwohnung: *the one-room apartment*
der Altbau: *the old building*
der Bau: *the building*
entfernt: *remote, distant*
zurückkehren: *to return*
die Lust: *the pleasure, the enjoyment*
Lust haben zu (+ *dative*)**:** *to feel like doing*
die Einrichtung: *the furnishings (plural)*
einrichten: *to furnish, to decorate*
der Sekt: *the sparkling wine*
einschenken: *to fill (someone's glass)*
die Hilfe: *the help*
wohl: *well*
das Wohl: *the well-being, the happiness*
auf Ihr Wohl!: *your health, here's to you!*
die Lösung: *the solution*
die Tasche: *the bag, the pocket*
schade: *what a pity*
ein paar: *a few, some*
die Brille: *the (eye)glasses (plural)*
die Schere: *the scissors (plural)*

darauf ankommen: *to matter, to make a difference*

darauf kommt es an: *that's just the point*

es kommt darauf an: *it depends*

das Paar: *the pair*

der Schrank: *the closet, the cupboard*

das Würstchen: *the sausage*

sonst: *otherwise, else, besides*

sich beeilen: *to hurry*

behilflich sein: *to be of assistance*

der Kuchen: *the cake*

übrig: *left over, remaining*

weder ... noch: *neither ... nor*

die Rede: *the speech*

indirekt: *indirect*

das Hilfsverb: *the auxiliary verb*

miteinander: *with each other*

vor vierzehn Tagen: *a fortnight ago*

murmeln: *to mutter*

die Freude: *the joy*

weinen: *to weep*

der Schnaps: *the brandy*

die Summe: *the sum, the total*

die Frist: *the period*

der Ablauf: *the expiration*

sich erkundigen nach (+ dative)**:** *to make inquiries (about)*

die Wahrscheinlichkeit: *the probability*

urteilen: *to judge*

nach und nach: *gradually*

die Sonne: *the sun*

die Sonnenfinsternis: *the eclipse*

die Finsternis: *the darkness*

das Interesse: *the interest*

die Gefahr: *the danger*

die Erfahrung: *the experience*

die Kosten (plural): *the costs, the expense*

das Genus: *the gender (of nouns)*

erkennen: *to recognize*

der Teller: *the plate*

der Essig: *the vinegar*

der Sprudel: *the sparkling mineral water*

der Pflänzling: *the seedling*

der Tourismus: *the tourism*

der Student: *the student*

der Politiker: *the politician*

der Aktionär: *the shareholder*

der Optimist: *the optimist*

das Licht: *the light*

die Liebe: *the love*

die Partei: *the political party*

die Wirtin: *the landlady*

der Wirt: *the landlord*

die Gewohnheit: *the custom, the habit*

die Schönheit: *the beauty*

die Höflichkeit: *the politeness*

die Eigenschaft: *the characteristic, the quality*

die Wirklichkeit: *the reality*

die Leidenschaft: *the passion*

die Leistung: *the achievement, the performance*

die Neigung: *the inclination, the preference*

die Medaille: *the medal*

die Prominenz: *the high society*

die Eiche: *the oak*

die Ulme: *the elm*

die Rose: *the rose*

die Nelke: *the carnation*

das Röslein: *the little rose*

das Schäfchen: *the little sheep, the lamb*

das Dickicht: *the thicket*

das Eigentum: *the property*

das Etikett: *the label*

das Benzin: *the gasoline/the petrol*
das Gymnasium: *the high school/the grammar school*
das Gedächtnis: *the memory*
das Verständnis: *the understanding, the comprehension*
das Gesetz: *the law*
das Gebirge: *the mountain range*

das Geräusch: *the noise, the sound*
das Gedicht: *the poem*
die Geschichte: *the history, the story*
das Zögern: *the hesitation*
verstehen: *to understand*
das Angebot: *the offer*
die Küste: *the coast*

Übungen/Exercises

Exercise A

BITTE BEANTWORTEN SIE DIESE FRAGEN, DIE SICH AUF DAS GESPRÄCH AM ANFANG DER LEKTION BEZIEHEN.

1. **Wer war bei der Feier anwesend?**

....

2. **Hatte jeder etwas zu essen?**

....

3. **Was hatten sie vor dem Essen getrunken?**

....

4. **Wer feierte seinen Geburtstag?**

....

5. **Warum wollten sie Paul beglückwünschen?**

....

6. **Ist Paul ein ausgezeichneter Student?**

....

7. Wohin wollen Herr und Frau Schmidt fliegen?

....

8. Kommen der Hund und die Katze mit?

....

9. Wo will Paul seinen Urlaub verbringen?

....

10. Was will er eventuell später machen?

....

11. Wo wird Ulrike die ersten paar Tage ihres Urlaubs verbringen?

....

12. Wohin will Wolfgang mit dem Zug fahren?

....

13. Wo will er die anderen zwei Wochen seines Urlaubs verbringen?

....

14. Was meinen Sie: Ist Cuxhaven an der Küste? (die Küste: the coast)

....

15. Wer besitzt eine Jacht?

....

16. Hat Ulrike ein eigenes Auto?

....

17. Warum bleibt das Auto der Schmidts in Berlin?

....

18. Warum wird Ulrike am 12. August nach Berlin zurückkehren müssen?

....

19. Was für eine Wohnung hat sie gefunden?

   ....

20. Wie lange hat sie eine eigene Wohnung gesucht?

   ....

21. Ist die Wohnung weit von ihrem Arbeitsplatz entfernt?

   ....

22. Was könnte Wolfgang tun, sobald er von Cuxhaven zurückgekehrt ist?

   ....

23. Wer sonst hat Ulrike seine Hilfe angeboten?

   ....

24. Wie alt ist Wolfgang?

   ....

20. Review Lessons 17-19

Well done, you have reached the end of the course! This review section is a revision of the last few chapters. Take the time to listen to the audio dialogues again and see how far you have come. The language should flow more naturally now, with easy comprehension and a solid foundation in grammar and vocabulary.

Übungen/Exercises

Exercise A

WÄHLEN SIE DAS PASSENDE WORT!

Beispiel: Silke besucht Berlin von Zeit zu <u>Zeit</u>. (Urlaub/Kleinstadt/Zeit)

1. Wir haben etliche Tage am Strand .... (gekommen/verbracht/besucht)

2. Paul und Silke sind im gleichen .... (Wohnung/Familie/Alter)

3. Wir gehen mit   Freunden ins Kino. .... (ein Paar/ein paar/einige)

4. Wenn ich .... habe, trinke ich oft ein Glas Bier. (Flasche/Durst/Wirtin)

5. Silke geht nie spät .... Bett.(in/im/ins)

6. Paul hat kein Geld in der ....(Tasche/Kauf/Kosten)

7. Paul sagt, das Leben in einer Kleinstadt .... langweilig. (war/seien/sei)

8. Wenn ich .... bin, schlafe ich. (müde/langweilig/spät)

9. Herr Schmidt ist .... als Paul. (Lehrer/älter/höher)

10. Welche Krawatte .... Sie vor? (bieten/treffen/ziehen)

11. Der Kunde musste bis zum nächsten Tag .... (warten/kommen/ankommen)

12. Um wie viel Uhr .... der Laden? (feiert/schließt/kommt)

13. Wenn ich Geld .... , würde ich mir ein Auto kaufen. (habe/hatte/hätte)

14. Ich werde ein paar Tage bei meiner Tante ....

(besuchen/einrichten/verbringen)

15. Wolfgang .... seinen Geburtstag. (hatte/verbrachte/feierte)

16. Ulrike wird ihre neue Wohnung .... (eintragen/einrichten/einladen)

17. Es kommt .... an. (daran/darin/darauf)

18. Er ist .... nach Berlin gekommen, um seinen Onkel zu besuchen.

(willkommen/herzlich/eigens)

19. Sie sagte, sie .... kein Auto. (habe/führt/feiert)

20. Welche Schuhgröße .... Sie? (haben/nehmen/bekommen)

21. Er .... mit sich reden. (hat/lässt/ist)

22. Das ist das .... , was ich je gehört habe. (schönste/Schönste/beste)

23. Ich hätte .... sein müssen. (gelegentlich/vorsichtiger/persönlich)

24. Sie stecken .... in Schulden. (unten/hoch/tief)

25. Er .... sich ein Glas Wein. (trank/bestellte/bestimmte)

26. Ich kann mir keinen neuen Mantel .... (schenken/leisten/mitnehmen)

27. Ich fuhr .... dem Bus zum Bahnhof. (bei/mit/auf)

28. Ich möchte ein Paar Schuhe ....

(nachschauen/wünschen/anprobieren)

Exercise B

BITTE BENUTZEN SIE IN DEN FOLGENDEN SÄTZEN DIE KONJUNKTIVFORM DES VERBS!

Please use the subjunctive form of the verb in the following sentences:

Beispiel: a) Die Freunde haben viel gegessen und getrunken.

Sie sagte, die Freunde hätten viel gegessen und getrunken.

b) Die beiden Eheleute sind ins Stadtzentrum gegangen.

Sie sagt, die beiden Eheleute seien ins Stadtzentrum gegangen. (die Eheleu-

te: husband and wife)

1. **Das Flugzeug aus Hamburg ist schon gelandet. Sie sagt,** ....

....

2. **Der Kunde kommt aus Saarbrücken. Sie sagt,** ....

....

3. **Herr und Frau Schmidt mussten eine halbe Stunde warten. Sie sagte,** ....

....

4. **Paul hilft Ulrike in der neuen Wohnung. Ulrike sagte,** ....

....

5. **Ulrike bereitet einen gemischten Salat zu. Sie sagt,** ....

....

6. **Wolfgang kann leider nicht helfen. Sie sagt,** ....

....

Exercise C

BITTE STELLEN SIE DIE FRAGEN!

Please write out the questions:

Beispiel: Ich komme aus <u>Italien</u>.   **Frage:** <u>Wo kommen Sie her?</u>

1. Das Essen wird <u>um 8 Uhr</u> serviert.

....

2. Ich bin zwanzig Jahre <u>alt</u>.

....

3. Das Kaufhaus schließt <u>um zwanzig Uhr</u>.

....

4. Es ist <u>zwanzig Minuten vor zehn</u>.

....

5. Wir sind <u>seit gestern</u> in Berlin.

....

Exercise D

SETZEN SIE DAS VERB IN DIE RICHTIGE FORM!

Put the verb into the right form:

present, future, preterite, perfect, present subjunctive, past subjunctive, passive, pluperfect.

Beispiel: Als ich jung war, <u>wohnte</u> ich bei meinen Eltern. (wohnen)

　　　　Jetzt <u>essen</u> wir zu Mittag. (essen)

　　　　Sie sagt, er <u>müsse</u> ein Jahr in Berlin verbringen. (müssen)

　　　　Ulrike <u>hat</u> endlich eine Wohnung gefunden. (finden)

1. Morgen .... wir eine Stadtrundfahrt .... (machen)

　　(die Stadtrundfahrt: the guided tour of the city)

2. Er sagt, das Flugzeug .... verspätet. (sein)

3. Gestern .... Paul mit Silke .... (telefonieren)

4. Er .... kein Fleisch, sondern nur Gemüse. (essen)

5. Nächste Woche .... er nach Frankfurt .... (fahren)

6. Der Gepäckträger sagt, er .... von der Sache nichts .... (wissen)

7. Wenn wir Urlaub ...., würden wir nach Spanien fahren. (haben)

8. Wenn ich schwimmen ...., würde ich ins Wasser gehen. (können)

9. .... ich Ihnen einen Kaffee anbieten? (dürfen)

10. Letztes Jah .... wir sehr trockenes Wetter .... (haben)

11. Bevor sie nach Berlin ...., wohnten sie in München. (kommen)

12. Der Koffer .... mir. (gehören)

13. Gestern .... ich mit der S-Bahn nach Frohnau .... (fahren)

14. Letzte Woche .... sie von ihrem Freund begleitet. (werden)

15. Wir .... ihn diese Woche noch nicht .... (sehen)

16. Gestern .... wir von unseren Freunden zum Essen .... (einladen)

17. Es .... mir leid, die Ware ist nicht auf Lager. (tun)

18. Hier .... nur Deutsch .... (passive) (sprechen)

19. Man .... nie, was passieren kann. (wissen)

20. Ich .... meine Schlüssel .... (zurückbekommen)

BITTE LERNEN SIE DIESE WÖRTER!

die Eheleute: *the married couple*

die Stadtrundfahrt: *the guided tour of the city*

verspätet: *delayed, late*

die Ware: *the article, the merchandise*

das Wasser: *the water*

Bravo! Sie haben es geschafft!

Well done! You've made it to the end!

Answer Key

Lesson 1

A. DER, DIE ODER DAS?

1. der Stuhl
2. die Frage
3. der Schreibtisch
4. das Gespräch
5. die Schachtel
6. der Bleistift
7. das Buch
8. der Herr
9. die Antwort
10. der Kugelschreiber

B. DAS IST ODER DAS IST NICHT?

1. Ja, das ist Paul!
2. Nein, das ist nicht Ulrike!
3. Ja, das ist Herr Schmidt!
4. Ja, das ist der Lehrer!
5. Nein, das ist nicht Frau Schmidt!

C. WAS IST DAS?

1. a pen: ein Kugelschreiber
2. a box: eine Schachtel
3. a gentleman: ein Herr
4. a book: ein Buch
5. an answer: eine Antwort

Lesson 2

A. BITTE ANWORTEN SIE!

1. Nein, ich komme nicht aus Berlin.
2. Nein, ich komme nicht aus Wien.
3. Nein, ich bin kein Deutscher./Nein, ich bin keine Deutsche.
4. Nein, ich arbeite nicht in Hamburg.
5. Ja, ich lerne Deutsch.
6. Nein, ich spreche kein Spanisch./Ja, ich spreche Spanisch.

B. WÄHLEN SIE DAS PASSENDE WORT!

1. Carmen ist Spanierin.
2. Herr Giuseppe Rossini ist kein Engländer.
3. Ist Frau Schmidt eine Deutsche?
4. Sie lesen ein deutsches Buch.
5. Ist sie eine kluge Frau?
6. Berlin ist eine sehr große Stadt.

Lesson 3

A. BITTE ANTWORTEN SIE!

1. Sie fliegt nach München.
2. Nein, sie reist morgen.
3. Sie reist morgen Nachmittag.
4. Sie fliegt um zehn Uhr.
5. Sie hat einen Personalausweis.
6. Ja, sie hat einen Koffer.
7. Nein, sie hat einen großen Koffer.
8. Nein, Paul will nicht mit Ulrike fliegen.
9. Ja, Ulrike hat ein Ticket.
10. Das Ticket ist in der Tasche.
11. Nein, sie will nicht mit der U-Bahn zum Flughafen fahren.
12. Sie fährt mit dem Taxi.
13. Sie kommt in einer Woche aus München zurück.
14. Er sagt gute Reise und auf Wiedersehen.

Lesson 4

A. ZÄHLEN SIE VON EINS BIS ZEHN (NATÜRLICH AUF DEUTSCH):

eins – zwei – drei – vier – fünf – sechs – sieben – acht – neun – zehn

B. WIE VIEL UHR IST ES?

1. Viertel vor zehn
2. halb acht
3. fünf Minuten vor eins
4. zwanzig Minuten nach fünf
5. fünfundzwanzig Minuten vor neun/fünf nach halb neun

C. BITTE ANTWORTEN SIE!

1. Frau Schmidt ist zu Hause.
2. Sie telefoniert mit einer Bekannten.
3. Ja, sie ist mit einigen Bekannten verabredet.
4. Sie ist abends verabredet.
5. Ja, die Kollegen sind sehr nette Leute.
6. Sie gehen ins Theater.
7. Das Restaurant ist am Ku'damm.
8. Die Kollegen kommen um halb sieben (abends).

Lesson 5

A. ZÄHLEN SIE VON EINS BIS ZWANZIG!

eins – zwei – drei – vier – fünf – sechs – sieben – acht – neun
zehn – elf – zwölf – dreizehn – vierzehn – fünfzehn – sechzehn – siebzehn – achtzehn – neunzehn – zwanzig

B. SCHREIBEN SIE!

23: dreiundzwanzig

25: fünfundzwanzig

30: dreißig

35: fünfunddreißig

40: vierzig

57: siebenundfünfzig

60: sechzig

64: vierundsechzig

70: siebzig

80: achtzig

90: neunzig

99: neunundneunzig

100: hundert

122: hundertzweiundzwanzig

C. BEANTWORTEN SIE DIESE FRAGEN!

1. Ja, der Büroangestellte ist sehr pünktlich.
2. Ja, er hat eine ganze Menge Arbeit.
3. Der Büroangestellte muss Briefe verschicken.
4. Es sind hundertfünfundzwanzig Briefe.
5. Ja, der Büroangestellte hat eine große Kundenliste.

Lesson 6

A. BITTE WÄHLEN SIE DEN PASSENDEN ARTIKEL: DER, DIE, DAS ODER DIE (PLURAL):

1. das Haus	13. das Buch	25. der Schreibtisch
2. die Schachtel	14. der Abend	26. die Städte
3. die Schule	15. die Restaurants	27. der Freund
4. die Lehrerin	16. der Reisepass	28. die Freundin
5. die Kundenliste	17. die Leute	29. der Wortschatz
6. der Mantel	18. die Frauen	30. das Wort
7. das Telefon	19. die Häuser	31. das Geschäft
8. die U-Bahn	20. der Stuhl	32. die Antwort
9. das Taxi	21. das Theater	33. die Sätze
10. die Uhr	22. die Arbeit	34. das Smartphone
11. die Tage	23. der Chef	
12. die Woche	24. die Briefe	

B. BITTE ERGÄNZEN SIE DIESE SÄTZE:

1. Ulrike macht eine Reise.
2. Wie viel Uhr ist es?
3. Wir fahren mit dem Taxi.
4. Ulrike geht nach Hause.
5. Ich habe viel zu tun.
6. Wo arbeiten Sie?
7. Wohin fliegt er?
8. Ich bin heute Abend mit einigen Freunden verabredet.
9. Thomas Schmidt arbeitet rund um die Uhr.
10. Muss ich Deutsch lernen?
11. Ja, Sie müssen Deutsch lernen.
12. Wann fährt Ulrike zum Flughafen?
13. Gibt er heute eine Party?
14. Können Sie diese Fragen beantworten?

C. BITTE WÄHLEN SIE DAS PASSENDE WORT:

1. Welche Staatsangehörigkeit haben Sie?
2. Ich bin keine Spanierin und auch keine Italienerin.
3. Ulrike fliegt nach München.
4. Dieser Herr hat keinen Personalausweis.
5. Wer ist dieser junge Mann?
6. Ich reise immer mit einem großen Koffer.
7. Mein Reisepass ist in der Tasche.
8. Heute ist nicht Freitag
9. Die Kollegen sind sehr nette Leute.
10. Es ist fünf vor halb zehn.

Lesson 7

A. BITTE BEANTWORTEN SIE DIESE FRAGEN!

1. Ulrike und Wolfgang sitzen zusammen in einem Café.
2. Ulrike nimmt einen Tee mit Zitrone, zwei Brötchen und Aprikosenmarmelade.
3. Wolfgang bestellt einen Kaffee, Käse und Brot.
4. Wolfgang hat nichts Besonderes vor.
5. Der Film fängt um halb drei an.
6. Wolfgang und Ulrike gehen gleich nach dem Frühstück zum Trödelmarkt.

B. WIE HEISSEN DIE WOCHENTAGE?

Sie heißen Montag
Dienstag
Mittwoch
Donnerstag

Freitag
Samstag oder Sonnabend
Sonntag

C. ERGÄNZEN SIE DIE FOLGENDEN SÄTZE!

1. Ich möchte eine Scheibe Brot.
2. Ich nehme einen Tee mit Zitrone.
3. Wissen Sie, wann der Film anfängt?
4. Ich habe nichts Besonderes vor.

D.ERGÄNZEN SIE DIESE SÄTZE MIT DEM GEGENTEIL DER UNTERSTRICHENEN WÖRTER!

1. Herr Schmidt reist wenig, aber er arbeitet viel.
2. Das ist nicht richtig! Das ist falsch.
3. Die Stadt ist nicht groß. Sie ist klein.
4. Das Buch liegt nicht unter dem Schreibtisch. Es liegt auf dem Schreibtisch.
5. Ist etwas in der Schachtel? Nein, es ist nichts in der Schachtel.

Lesson 8

A. BITTE BEANTWORTEN SIE DIESE FRAGEN!

1. Herr Schmidt ist in Hannover.
2. Er hat eine Reservierung für eine Nacht.
3. Er spricht mit der Empfangsdame.
4. Er reist morgen Vormittag ab.
5. Ja, Thomas Schmidt muss seinen Namen eintragen.
6. Nein, er hat nur einen kleinen Koffer.
7. Ja, es gibt einen Aufzug im Hotel.
8. Sie servieren das Frühstück bis zehn Uhr.

B. ERGÄNZEN SIE DIESE SÄTZE MIT DEM RICHTIGEN POSSESSIVADJEKTIV!

1. Der Chef sitzt in seinem Büro an seinem Schreibtisch.

2. Wir haben unseren Koffer und unsere Taschen.

3. Sie ist erst 18, aber sie hat ihre eigene Wohnung und ihr eigenes Auto.

C. ERGÄNZEN SIE DIESE SÄTZE:

1. Die Lektion Nummer 1 ist die erste Lektion.

2. Die Frage Nummer 9 ist die neunte Frage.

3. Die Antwort Nummer 3 ist die dritte Antwort.

Lesson 9

A. BITTE BEANTWORTEN SIE DIESE FRAGEN ZUM TEXT:

1. Nein, er will keine Postkarte kaufen.

2. Er muss zwei Briefe absenden.

3. Er sendet einen Brief nach England. Er sendet den anderen Brief in die USA.

4. Die Beamtin wiegt die Briefe auf der Waage.

5. Das Paket geht nach Kanada.

6. Er muss ein Formular ausfüllen.

7. Er muss seinen Namen und seine Adresse sowie den Namen und die Adresse des Empfängers auf das Formular schreiben.

8. Ja, die Beamtin kann seine Handschrift lesen.

B. BITTE SETZEN SIE DIE ENTSPRECHENDEN PRONOMEN EIN!

1. Sie fährt ohne ihn in die Stadt.

2. Sie gehen mit ihm ins Kino.

3. Sie hat zwei Pakete für uns.

4. Er gibt ihr seine Telefonnummer.

C. SETZEN SIE DIE VERBEN IN DIE ZUKUNFT!

1. Paul wird einige Briefe schreiben.

2. Wir werden heute Abend ins Theater gehen.

3. Wann werden Sie nach München fliegen?

4. Ich werde heute nicht in die Stadt gehen.

5. Ich werde keine Zeit haben.

Lesson 10

A. BITTE BEANTWORTEN SIE DIE FOLGENDEN FRAGEN ZUM DIALOG:

1. Nein, Paul wird am Wochenende nicht ins Grüne fahren.

2. Ja, Paul zieht es vor, in Berlin zu bleiben.

3. Bei Regenwetter zieht Paul seinen Regenmantel an, er nimmt seinen Regenschirm mit und geht spazieren.

4. Paul fährt billiger mit dem Bus.

5. Wenn er bei Regenwetter spazieren geht, nimmt Paul seinen Regenschirm mit.

6. Der Wetterbericht sagt Regen fürs Wochenende voraus.

7. Im Winter ist es am kältesten.

8. Wenn es kühl wird, geht Paul trotzdem weg.

9. Ja, Paul hat viele Freunde in Berlin.

10. Diese jungen Leute reden, sie sehen fern, hören Musik oder trinken etwas.

11. Paul verbringt die Ferien in Berlin und Umgebung.

12. Nein, er verbringt seine Ferien weit entfernt von Berlin.

B. BENUTZEN SIE "DASS", "WENN" ODER "OB" IN DEN FOLGENDEN SÄTZEN:

1. Ich höre, dass Herr Schmidt in die Berge fahren wird.

2. Wolfgang bemerkt, dass Ulrike ihren Pullover auszieht.

3. Ich weiß nicht, ob Paul mitkommt/mitkommen wird.

4. Vielleicht wird es ein Konzert im Park geben. Wir gehen hin, wenn es ein Konzert gibt.

Lesson 11

A. BITTE BEANTWORTEN SIE DIE FOLGENDEN FRAGEN ZUM DIALOG.

1. Ja, Monikas Freund kommt mit.

2. Monika und ihr Freund werden den Nachtisch zum Picknick mitbringen.

3. Ulrike bereitet einen gemischten Salat für das Picknick zu.

4. Wolfgang hat zwei Brathähnchen gekauft.

5. Ulrike tut die Brathähnchen in den Korb.

6. Nein, sie haben noch nicht alles, was sie brauchen.

7. Sie brauchen noch Wein und Brot.

8. Wolfgang will den Wein im Supermarkt kaufen.

9. Nein, der Supermarkt ist nicht weit von Ulrikes Wohnung.

10. Er geht gleich.

B. ERGÄNZEN SIE DIESE SÄTZE!

1. Herr Schmidt ist gestern Abend müde nach Hause gekommen.

2. Gestern haben Ulrike und Wolfgang ein Picknick gemacht.

3. Wolfgang hat gestern Abend mit Monika telefoniert.

4. Unsere Freunde sind soeben eingetroffen.

5. Wie lange haben Sie auf den Bus gewartet?

6. Hast du gestern Abend das Buch gelesen?

C. BITTE SETZEN SIE DIE GLEICHEN SÄTZE IN DIE ZUKUNFTSFORM!

1. Herr Schmidt wird morgen Abend müde nach Hause kommen.

2. Morgen werden Ulrike und Wolfgang ein Picknick machen.

3. Wolfgang wird morgen Abend mit Monika telefonieren.

4. Unsere Freunde werden bald eintreffen.

5. Wie lange werden Sie auf den Bus warten?

6. Wirst du das Buch morgen lesen?

Lesson 12

A. WÄHLEN SIE DEN PASSENDEN ARTIKEL: DER, DIE, DAS ODER DIE (PLURAL)!

1. das Brot
2. die Marmelade
3. der Tee
4. der Film
5. die Kinos
6. der Trödelmarkt
7. die Städte
8. das Mittagessen
9. die Reservierung
10. der Stock
11. der Aufzug
12. die Beamtin
13. das Telefon
14. die Nacht
15. der Chef

16. das Zimmer	31. der Regenmantel	46. die Uhr
17. die Post	32. die Sonne	47. der Salat
18. die Postkarte	33. das Wochenende	48. der Wein
19. die Mühe	34. das Auge	49. die Straße
20. das Paket	35. der Augenblick	50. die Zeit
21. das Flugzeug	36. der Bus	51. das Haus
22. das Frühstück	37. der Regenschirm	52. das Hotel
23. die Briefmarken	38. das Wetter	53. das Formular
24. der Stuhl	39. der Supermarkt	54. die Waage
25. die Wolke	40. die Zeitschriften	55. die Woche
26. der Sommer	41. die Ferien	56. die Landschaft
27. der Inhalt	42. der Herbst	57. der Regen
28. der Absender	43. das Brathähnchen	58. der Korb
29. das Jahr	44. der Käse	59. das Büro
30. der Wagen	45. der Nachtisch	60. die Freundinnen

B. SETZEN SIE DIE VERBEN IN DIE GEGENWART!

1. Wolfgang wartet auf den Bus.
2. Bei kaltem Wetter ziehe ich warme Kleidung an.
3 Die Sonne scheint am Himmel.
4. Was machst du da?
5. Ich tue nichts.
6. Paul kommt ins Kino mit.
7. Ulrike bereitet einen gemischten Salat zu.
8. Paul gibt der Beamtin das Paket.
9. Bei Regenwetter bleibt Herr Schmidt zu Hause.
10. Das Flugzeug fliegt nach München.
11. Kennen Sie Monika?
12. Ziehen Sie Blau oder Grün vor?
13. Wie kann ich nach draußen telefonieren?
14. Wie viel müssen wir zahlen?
15. Du sollst nicht hingehen.

C. SETZEN SIE DIE SÄTZE 1 BIS 10 VON ÜBUNG 2 IN DIE ZUKUNFT:

1. Wolfgang wird auf den Bus warten.
2. Bei kaltem Wetter werde ich warme Kleidung anziehen.
3. Die Sonne wird am Himmel scheinen.
4. Was wirst du da machen?
5. Ich werde nichts tun.
6. Paul wird ins Kino mitkommen.
7. Ulrike wird einen gemischten Salat zubereiten.
8. Paul wird der Beamtin das Paket geben.
9. Bei Regenwetter wird Herr Schmidt zu Hause bleiben.
10. Das Flugzeug wird nach München fliegen.

D. WÄHLEN SIE DAS PASSENDE WORT!

1. Ich rufe ihn an.
2. Wie fangen damit an.
3. Sie wartet darauf.
4. Ich gebe ihnen die Schlüssel.
5. Haben Sie mit ihr gesprochen?
6. Er hat ihn noch nicht gekauft.

E. SETZEN SIE DIE SÄTZE VON ÜBUNG 2 IN DIE VERGANGENHEIT! (NUR 1 BIS 10)

1. Wolfgang hat auf den Bus gewartet.
2. Bei kaltem Wetter habe ich warme Kleidung angezogen.
3. Die Sonne hat geschienen.
4. Was hast du da gemacht?
5. Ich habe nichts getan.
6. Paul ist ins Kino mitgekommen.
7. Ulrike hat einen gemischten Salat zubereitet.
8. Paul hat der Beamtin das Paket gegeben.
9. Bei Regenwetter ist Herr Schmidt zu Hause geblieben.
10. Das Flugzeug ist nach München geflogen.

F. ANTWORTEN SIE IN DER ZUKUNFT!

1. Nein, ich werde morgen mit der Empfangschefin sprechen.
2. Nein, der junge Mann wird das Paket morgen verschicken.
3. Nein, wir werden morgen schönes Wetter haben.
4. Nein, Herr Schmidt wird morgen nach Hannover fahren.

Lesson 13

A. BEANTWORTEN SIE DIE FOLGENDEN FRAGEN ZUM DIALOG.

1. Der Tourist will zum Schloss Charlottenburg gehen.
2. Er hat mit dem Gemüsehändler gesprochen.
3. Der Tourist geht zu Fuß.
4. Ja, das Schloss ist von der Schlossstraße zu sehen.
5. Nein, der Tourist hat die Erklärung des Gemüsehändlers nicht ganz verstanden.
6. Er wird ungefähr fünfundzwanzig Minuten brauchen.
7. Nein, es lohnt sich nicht, mit dem Bus dorthin zu fahren.
8. Er sollte das Ägyptische Museum nicht vergessen.
9. Ja, das Ägyptische Museum ist nah beim Schloss.
10. Ja, er wird auf jeden Fall den Rat des Gemüsehändlers befolgen.

B. BITTE ERGÄNZEN SIE DIE FOLGENDEN SÄTZE MIT DER VERGANGENHEITSFORM DER VERBEN!

1. Monika hat ihren Freund ins Kino begleitet.
2. Ich habe einen Salat für vier Personen zubereitet.
3. Der Tourist hat den Gemüsehändler nach dem Weg gefragt.
4. Wir sind mit dem Taxi zum Bahnhof gefahren.
5. Wir sind um 7 Uhr morgens angekommen.
6. Wir haben nach zwanzig Minuten das Museum erreicht.
7. Ich habe es Ihnen schon gesagt.
8. Ich habe das Buch noch nicht gelesen.
9. Das Wetter ist schön geworden.
10. Der Tourist hat den Rat des Gemüsehändlers befolgt.

C. JETZT SETZEN SIE DIE VERBEN VON ÜBUNG B IN DIE ZUKUNFTSFORM!

1. Monika wird ihren Freund ins Kino begleiten.
2. Ich werde einen Salat für vier Personen zubereiten.
3. Der Tourist wird den Gemüsehändler nach dem Weg fragen.
4. Wir werden mit dem Taxi zum Bahnhof fahren.
5. Wir werden um 7 Uhr morgens ankommen.
6. Wir werden in zwanzig Minuten das Museum erreichen.

7. Ich werde es Ihnen schon sagen.
8. Ich werde das Buch noch nicht lesen.
9. Das Wetter wird schön werden.
10. Der Tourist wird den Rat des Gemüsehändlers befolgen.

Lesson 14

A. BITTE BEANTWORTEN SIE DIE FOLGENDEN FRAGEN ZUM DIALOG.

1. Herr und Frau Schmidt haben Wolfgang und Ulrike eingeladen.
2. Ja, Ulrike möchte noch Kaffee.
3. Ulrike trinkt ihren Kaffee ohne Zucker.
4. Nein, Herr Schmidt trinkt nie Kaffee.
5. Er trinkt lieber Tee.
6. Ja, Herr Schmidt hat noch Verwandtschaft in Österreich.
7. Sie hat drei Kinder.
8. Ihr Sohn ist zwölf Jahre alt, die eine Tochter ist acht, und die andere ist fünf Jahre alt.
9. Nein, Ulrike wohnt nicht mit Wolfgang zusammen.
10. Sie fährt jeden Tag mit der S-Bahn.
11. Nein, Ulrike sucht eine Einzimmerwohnung im Stadtzentrum.
12. Nein, es muss nicht unbedingt eine Neubauwohnung sein. Eine Altbauwohnung geht auch.
13. Nein, sie hat noch nichts gefunden.
14. Nein, Ulrike hat es nicht eilig.
15. Ja, Wohnungen in Berlin sind seit der Wiedervereinigung teurer geworden.
16. Nein, Wolfgang wohnt nicht bei seinen Eltern.
17. Wolfgangs/Seine Eltern wohnen in Bremen.
18. Nein, er fährt mit dem ICE dorthin.

Lesson 15

A. BITTE BEANTWORTEN SIE DIESE FRAGEN, DIE SICH AUF DAS GESPRÄCH AM ANFANG DER LEKTION BEZIEHEN:

1. Der Reisende sucht seinen Koffer.
2. Nein, er hat nicht seinen Regenschirm verloren, sondern seinen Koffer.
3. Sein Koffer ist nicht so groß wie/ist kleiner als der Koffer vor der Treppe.
4. Sein Koffer ist blau.
5. In seinem Koffer hatte er seine ganzen Kleider mitsamt seinen persönlichen Sachen.
6. Er fuhr mit dem Bus zum Bahnhof.
7. Ja, er hatte seinen Koffer in der Hand, als er das Haus verließ.
8. Er hat seinen Koffer neben sich auf den Boden gestellt.
9. Er war am Bahnsteig, als er an seinen Koffer dachte.
10. Das Fundbüro befindet sich am anderen Ende des Bahnhofs.
11. Er hat seinen Koffer auf dem Gepäckkarren des Gepäckträgers gefunden.
12. Der Gepäckträger hat den Koffer bei der Wechselstube gesehen.
13. Ja, der Gepäckträger hat sich geirrt.
14. Ja, der Name des Reisenden stand auf dem Koffer.
15. Ja, die Reisende war nett.

A. BITTE ERGÄNZEN SIE DIESE SÄTZE MIT DEM PASSENDEN WORT:

1. Dieser Mann ist Gemüsehändler.
2. Können Sie mir bitte diesen Satz erklären?
3. Das Schloss ist heute geöffnet.
4. Wohin führt diese Straße?
5. Ich habe heute nichts Besonderes getan.
6. Monika wird von ihrem Freund begleitet.
7. Das Museum ist nicht weit.
8. Darf ich Ihnen noch einen Kaffee anbieten?
9. Wollen Sie zusammen oder getrennt zahlen?
10. Der Tourist hat einige Bücher über Berlin gelesen.
11. Wolfgang ist nicht mit Ulrike verheiratet.
12. Ich trinke kein Bier.
13. Ulrike trinkt ihren Kaffee ohne Zucker.
14. Ich werde mit dem Taxi zum Flughafen fahren.
15. Ulrike wohnt bei ihren Eltern.
16. Wolfgang und Ulrike werden ein Picknick machen.
17. Wolfgang fährt mit dem ICE.
18. Er konnte nicht schwimmen.
19. Der Reisende musste Schlange stehen.
20. Ich hatte den Koffer in der Hand.
21. Entschuldigen Sie! Ich habe mich geirrt.
22. Im Zug dachte ich an meinen Koffer.
23. Wo haben sie diesen Koffer gefunden?
24. Diese Schlüssel gehören mir nicht.
25. Ulrike ist älter als Paul.
26. Ich trinke lieber Tee.
27. Ich telefoniere oft mit ihnen.
28. Was haben Sie zu Mittag gegessen?
29. Ich habe Hunger.
30. Ich werde so früh wie möglich kommen.
31. Ich möchte eine Flasche Rotwein, bitte.
32. Ulrike geht zu Fuß.

B. ERGÄNZEN SIE DIESE SÄTZE MIT DEM PRÄTERITUM:

1. Gestern hatten wir viel Arbeit.
2. Wolfgang fuhr in die Stadt.
3. Was sagten Sie?
4. Paul brachte seinen Regenschirm mit.
5. Ulrike bereitete einen gemischten Salat zu.
6. Clara sprach mit Heidi am Telefon.
7. Paul stellte das Paket auf den Tisch.
8. Der Reisende verlor seinen Koffer.
9. Er bekam seinen Koffer zurück.
10. Frau Schmidt bot Ulrike einen Kaffee an.
11. Ich wartete auf den Bus.
12. Ich wusste nichts von der Sache.
13. Ulrike tat die Brathähnchen in den Korb.
14. Er genoss sein Bier.
15. Sie verließen das Zimmer.
16. Die Reise entsprach meinen Erwartungen.
17. Er fand seinen Koffer auf dem Karren.
18. Sie schrieb mir einen schönen Brief.
19. Es fing an zu regnen.
20. Sie begann zu singen.
21. Sie gab ihm eine Flasche Wein.
22. Wir sahen keine Wolke am Himmel.

C. WÄHLEN SIE DAS PASSENDE WORT!

1. Kennen Sie den Herrn, der das Zimmer gerade verlassen hat?
2. Kennen Sie den Mann, dem dieser Koffer gehört?
3. Ich stellte fest, dass ich meinen Koffer nicht mehr hatte.
4. Wie heißt der junge Mann, mit dem du gerade gesprochen hast?
5. Haben Sie sich mit der Frau getroffen, die das Auto kaufen möchte?

6. Der Kellner brachte den Kaffee, den wir bestellt hatten.

7. Hast du die Schlüssel gesehen, die auf dem Tisch waren?

8. Ich habe gehört, dass in München viel gebaut wird.

9. Das Kino, in dem wir gestern waren, ist heute geschlossen.

10. Der Mantel, den ich gestern gekauft habe, ist verloren gegangen.

D. GEBEN SIE AUF DIE FOLGENDEN FRAGEN EINE NEGATIVE ANTWORT!

1. Nein, ich musste am Bahnhof nicht lange warten.

2. Nein, ich konnte gestern die Berge nicht sehen.

3. Nein, ich wollte heute nicht ins Kino mitgehen.

4. Nein, ich habe heute nicht mit meiner Mutter telefoniert.

E. GEBEN SIE AUF DIESE FRAGEN EINE POSITIVE ANTWORT!

1. Doch, Ulrike hat ihren Kaffee getrunken.

2. Doch, ich komme heute ins Büro.

3. Doch, sie wurde von ihrem Freund begleitet.

4. Doch, ich kann diese Fragen beantworten.

F. ANTWORTEN SIE MIT VOLLSTÄNDIGEN SÄTZEN!

1. Ja, das Flugzeug ist schneller als der Zug.

2. Ja, der Winter in Deutschland ist kälter als der Herbst.

3. Nein, die S-Bahn fährt nicht so schnell wie der ICE.

4. Bei schönen Wetter ist der Himmel blau./Der Himmel ist bei schönem Wetter blau.

5. Ja, ich nehme einen Koffer mit, wenn ich eine Reise mache./Nein, ich nehme keinen Koffer mit, wenn ich eine Reise mache.

6. Ja, es gibt einen Trödelmarkt in meiner Stadt./Nein, es gibt keinen Trödelmarkt in meiner Stadt.

Lesson 17

A. BITTE BEANTWORTEN SIE DIESE FRAGEN, DIE SICH AUF DAS GESPRÄCH AM ANFANG DER LEKTION BEZIEHEN:

1. Pauls Cousine wohnt in einer Kleinstadt außerhalb Berlins.

2. Paul und seine Cousine sind im gleichen Alter/sind gleich alt.

3. Sie wird sehr früh wach.

4. Silke wäscht sich, zieht sich an und frühstückt gemeinsam mit ihren Eltern vor Sonnenaufgang.

5. Sie geht um halb zehn ins Bett.

6. Paul geht normalerweise um elf Uhr schlafen.

7. Das Leben in der Kleinstadt ist ruhig.

8. Nein, es gibt kein Kino in der Kleinstadt.

9. Nein, ich will nicht in eine Studentenkneipe./Ja, ich will in eine Studentenkneipe.

10. Silke schlägt vor, sie gehen erst mal spazieren, dann können sie sich entscheiden. Silke schlägt vor, erst mal spazieren zu gehen; dann können sie sich entscheiden.

Lesson 18

A. BITTE BEANTWORTEN SIE DIESE FRAGEN, DIE SICH AUF DAS GESPRÄCH AM ANFANG DER LEKTION BEZIEHEN:

1. Der Kunde befand sich/war in der Schuhabteilung eines großen Kaufhauses.
2. Nein, der Kunde wurde noch nicht bedient.
3. Der Kunde wollte ein Paar Schuhe anprobieren.
4. Der Kunde hatte Größe dreiundvierzig.
5. Nein, der Verkäufer kehrte mit leeren Händen zurück.
6. Nein, das Kaufhaus hatte diese Schuhe nicht auf Lager.
7. Nein, der Kunde war nicht glücklich darüber.
8. Er suchte solche Schuhe schon seit einigen Wochen.
9. Ja, der Verkäufer konnte die Schuhe bestellen.
10. Ja, der Kunde würde am nächsten Tag vorbeikommen.
11. Der Kunde hätte auch gern eine Krawatte gehabt.
12. Die Herrenabteilung ist eine Etage tiefer, im Erdgeschoss.
13. Der Kunde brauchte die Reiseandenken für seine Freunde im Ausland.
14. Er könnte Postkarten in der Schreibwarenabteilung kaufen.
15. Der Kunde meinte, dass der Verkäufer sehr hilfreich (gewesen) sei.

Lesson 19

A. BITTE BEANTWORTEN SIE DIESE FRAGEN, DIE SICH AUF DAS GESPRÄCH AM ANFANG DER LEKTION BEZIEHEN:

1. Paul, Ulrike, Wolfgang, Herr und Frau Schmidt waren bei der Feier anwesend.
2. Ja, jeder hatte etwas zu essen.
3. Sie hatten Sekt vor dem Essen getrunken.
4. Wolfgang feierte seinen Geburtstag.
5. Sie wollten Paul beglückwünschen, weil er große Fortschritte beim Deutschlernen gemacht hatte.
6. Ja, Paul ist ein ausgezeichneter Student.
7. Herr und Frau Schmidt wollen nach Österreich fliegen.
8. Nein, der Hund und die Katze kommen nicht mit.
9. Paul will vorerst in Berlin bleiben.
10. Später will er eventuell seine Cousine Silke besuchen.
11. Ulrike will die ersten paar Tage bei ihren Eltern in Frohnau verbringen.
12. Wolfgang will mit dem Zug nach Bremen fahren.
13. Er wird die anderen zwei Wochen seines Urlaubs in Cuxhaven verbringen.
14. Ja, Cuxhaven ist an der Küste.
15. Der Onkel von Wolfgangs Freund besitzt eine Jacht.
16. Nein, Ulrike hat kein eigenes Auto.
17. Das Auto der Schmidts bleibt in Berlin, weil die Schmidts nach Österreich fliegen.
18. Sie muss am zwölften August nach Berlin zurückkehren, damit sie sich ihrer neuen Wohnung widmen kann.
19. Sie hat eine umgebaute Einzimmerwohnung mit Küche und Bad in einem Altbau gefunden.
20. Sie hat monatelang eine eigene Wohnung gesucht.
21. Nein, die Wohnung ist nicht weit von ihrem Arbeitsplatz entfernt.
22. Wolfgang könnte Ulrike helfen, die Wohnung einzurichten.
23. Paul hat Ulrike seine Hilfe angeboten.
24. Wolfgang ist neunundzwanzig Jahre alt.

A. WÄHLEN SIE DAS PASSENDE WORT!

1. Wir haben etliche Tage am Strand verbracht.
2. Paul und Silke sind im gleichen Alter.
3. Wir gehen mit ein paar Freunden ins Kino.
4. Wenn ich Durst habe, trinke ich oft ein Glas Bier.
5. Silke geht nie spät ins Bett.
6. Paul hat kein Geld in der Tasche.
7. Paul sagt, das Leben in einer Kleinstadt sei langweilig.
8. Wenn ich müde bin, schlafe ich.
9. Herr Schmidt ist älter als Paul.
10. Welche Krawatte ziehen Sie vor?
11. Der Kunde musste bis zum nächsten Tag warten.
12. Um wie viel Uhr schließt der Laden?
13. Wenn ich Geld hätte, so kaufte ich mir ein Auto.
14. Ich werde ein paar Tage bei meiner Tante verbringen.
15. Wolfgang feierte seinen Geburtstag.
16. Ulrike wird ihre neue Wohnung einrichten.
17. Es kommt darauf an.
18. Er ist eigens nach Berlin gekommen, um seinen Onkel zu besuchen.
19. Sie sagte, sie habe kein Auto.
20. Welche Schuhgröße haben Sie?
21. Er lässt mit sich reden.
22. Das ist das Schönste, was ich je gehört habe.
23. Ich hätte vorsichtiger sein müssen.
24. Sie stecken tief in Schulden.
25. Er bestellte sich ein Glas Wein.
26. Ich kann mir keinen neuen Mantel leisten.
27. Ich fuhr mit dem Bus zum Bahnhof.
28. Ich möchte ein Paar Schuhe anprobieren.

B. BITTE BENUTZEN SIE IN DEN FOLGENDEN SÄTZEN DIE KONJUNKTIVFORM DES VERBS!

1. Sie sagt, das Flugzeug aus Hamburg sei schon gelandet.
2. Sie sagt, der Kunde komme aus Saarbrücken.
3. Sie sagte, Herr und Frau Schmidt hätten eine halbe Stunde warten müssen.
4. Ulrike sagte, Paul helfe ihr in der neuen Wohnung.
5. Sie sagt, Ulrike bereite einen gemischten Salat zu.
6. Sie sagt, Wolfgang könne leider nicht helfen.

C. BITTE STELLEN SIE DIE FRAGEN!

1. Wann/Um wie viel Uhr wird das Essen serviert?
2. Wie alt sind Sie?
3. Um wie viel Uhr schließt das Kaufhaus?
4. Wie viel Uhr ist es?
5. Seit wann sind Sie in Berlin?

D. SETZEN SIE DAS VERB IN DIE RICHTIGE FORM!

1. Morgen werden wir eine Stadtrundfahrt machen.
2. Er sagt, das Flugzeug sei verspätet.
3. Gestern hat Paul mit Silke telefoniert.
4. Er isst kein Fleisch, sondern nur Gemüse.
5. Nächste Woche wird er nach Frankfurt fahren.
6. Der Gepäckträger sagt, er habe von der Sache nichts gewusst.
7. Wenn wir Urlaub hätten, würden wir nach Spanien fahren.
8. Wenn ich schwimmen könnte, würde ich ins Wasser gehen.
9. Darf ich Ihnen einen Kaffee anbieten?
10. Letztes Jahr haben wir sehr trockenes Wetter gehabt.

11. Bevor sie nach Berlin kamen, wohnten sie in München.
12. Der Koffer gehört mir.
13. Gestern bin ich mit der S-Bahn nach Frohnau gefahren.
14. Letzte Woche wurde sie von ihrem Freund begleitet.
15. Wir haben ihn diese Woche noch nicht gesehen.
16. Gestern wurden wir von unseren Freunden zum Essen eingeladen.
17. Es tut mir leid, die Ware ist nicht auf Lager.
18. Hier wird nur Deutsch gesprochen.
19. Man weiß nie, was passieren kann.
20. Ich bekam meine Schlüssel zurück./Ich habe meine Schlüssel zurückbekommen.

Verbs

This verb list includes all the basic verbs introduced in the text, plus a few other useful ones. They are classified into:

Strong verbs

Irregular weak verbs

Auxiliary verbs

Regular weak verbs are not included.

The infinitive, the third person singular of the present and preterite, the past participle, and the irregularly formed imperative, familiar form, are all given.

All other forms and tenses can be derived from these forms.

Where the past participle is preceded by **ist** (third person singular of **sein**), the tenses of the verb are conjugated with the appropriate form of **sein**. Otherwise the tenses of the verb are conjugated with the appropriate form of **haben**.

The singular familiar form of the imperative is given only where the stem vowel changes.

Many other verbs can be formed by the addition of a separable or inseparable prefix to the basic verb. These compound verbs are conjugated like the basic verb and are thus not listed.

STRONG VERBS

Infinitive	Present	Preterite	Past Participle	Imperative
befehlen (to order)	befiehlt	befahl	befohlen	befiehl
beginnen (to begin)	beginnt	begann	begonnen	
bergen (to hide)	birgt	barg	geborgen	birg
bewegen (to move)	bewegt	bewog	bewogen	

Infinitive	Present	Preterite	Past Participle	Imperative
biegen (to bend)	biegt	bog	gebogen	
bieten (to offer)	bietet	bot	geboten	
binden (to bind)	bindet	band	gebunden	
bitten (to ask)	bittet	bat	gebeten	
bleiben (to remain)	bleibt	blieb	(ist) geblieben	
brechen (to break)	bricht	brach	gebrochen	brich
dringen (to penetrate)	dringt	drang	(ist) gedrungen	
einladen (to invite)	lädt ein	lud ein	eingeladen	
empfehlen (to recommend)	empfiehlt	empfahl	empfohlen	empfiehl
erwerben (to acquire)	erwirbt	erwarb	erworben	erwirb
essen (to eat)	isst	aß	gegessen	iss
fahren (to drive, to go)	fährt	fuhr	(ist) gefahren	
fallen (to fall)	fällt	fiel	(ist) gefallen	
fangen (to catch)	fängt	fing	gefangen	
finden (to find)	findet	fand	gefunden	
fliegen (to fly)	fliegt	flog	(ist) geflogen	
fliehen (to flee)	flieht	floh	(ist) geflohen	
fließen (to flow)	fließt	floss	(ist) geflossen	
frieren (to freeze)	friert	fror	gefroren	
geben (to give)	gibt	gab	gegeben	gib
gedeihen (to thrive)	gedeiht	gedieh	(ist) gediehen	
gehen (to go; to work)	geht	ging	(ist) gegangen	
gelingen (to succeed)	gelingt	gelang	(ist) gelungen	
gelten (to be valid)	gilt	galt	gegolten	
genesen (to recover)	genest	genas	(ist) genesen	
genießen (to enjoy)	genießt	genoss	genossen	
geschehen (to happen)	geschieht	geschah	(ist) geschehen	
gewinnen (to win)	gewinnt	gewann	gewonnen	
gleichen (to resemble)	gleicht	glich	geglichen	
greifen (to seize)	greift	griff	gegriffen	
halten (to hold)	hält	hielt	gehalten	

Infinitive	Present	Preterite	Past Participle	Imperative
hängen (to hang)	hängt	hing	gehangen	
heben (to lift)	hebt	hob	gehoben	
heißen (to be called)	heißt	hieß	geheißen	
helfen (to help)	hilft	half	geholfen	hilf
klingen (to sound)	klingt	klang	geklungen	
kommen (to come)	kommt	kam	(ist) gekommen	
laden (to load)	lädt	lud	geladen	
lassen (to let)	lässt	ließ	gelassen	
laufen (to run)	läuft	lief	(ist) gelaufen	
leiden (to suffer)	leidet	litt	gelitten	
leihen (to lend)	leiht	lieh	geliehen	
lesen (to read)	liest	las	gelesen	lies
liegen (to lie)	liegt	lag	gelegen	
meiden (to avoid)	meidet	mied	gemieden	
messen (to measure)	misst	maß	gemessen	miss
misslingen (to fail)	misslingt	misslang	(ist) misslungen	
nehmen (to take)	nimmt	nahm	genommen	nimm
preisen (to praise)	preist	pries	gepriesen	
raten (to advise)	rät	riet	geraten	
reißen (to tear)	reißt	riss	gerissen	
reiten (to ride)	reitet	ritt	(ist) geritten	
rufen (to call)	ruft	rief	gerufen	
schaffen (to create)	schafft	schuf	geschaffen	
scheiden (to part)	scheidet	schied	(ist) geschieden	
scheinen (to appear; to shine)	scheint	schien	geschienen	
schieben (to push)	schiebt	schob	geschoben	
schlafen (to sleep)	schläft	schlief	geschlafen	
schlagen (to hit)	schlägt	schlug	geschlagen	
schließen (to shut)	schließt	schloss	geschlossen	
schneiden (to cut)	schneidet	schnitt	geschnitten	
schreiben (to write)	schreibt	schrieb	geschrieben	

Infinitive	Present	Preterite	Past Participle	Imperative
schweigen (to be silent)	schweigt	schwieg	geschwiegen	
schwimmen (to swim)	schwimmt	schwamm	(ist) geschwommen	
schwinden (to vanish)	schwindet	schwand	(ist) geschwunden	
sehen (to see)	sieht	sah	gesehen	sieh
sein (to be)	ist	war	(ist) gewesen	sei
singen (to sing)	singt	sang	gesungen	
sinken (to sink)	sinkt	sank	(ist) gesunken	
sinnen (to think, to reflect)	sinnt	sann	gesonnen	
sitzen (to sit)	sitzt	saß	gesessen	
sprechen (to speak)	spricht	sprach	gesprochen	sprich
springen (to spring)	springt	sprang	(ist) gesprungen	
stehen (to stand)	steht	stand	gestanden	
stehlen (to steal)	stiehlt	stahl	gestohlen	stiehl
steigen (to go up)	steigt	stieg	(ist) gestiegen	
sterben (to die)	stirbt	starb	(ist) gestorben	stirb
stoßen (to push)	stößt	stieß	gestoßen	
streiten (to argue)	streitet	stritt	gestritten	
tragen (to carry)	trägt	trug	getragen	
treffen (to meet; to hit)	trifft	traf	getroffen	triff
treiben (to drive)	treibt	trieb	getrieben	
treten (to step)	tritt	trat	(ist) getreten	tritt
trinken (to drink)	trinkt	trank	getrunken	
tun (to do)	tut	tat	getan	
verderben (to spoil)	verdirbt	verdarb	verdorben	verdirb
vergessen (to forget)	vergisst	vergaß	vergessen	vergiss
verlieren (to lose)	verliert	verlor	verloren	
verzeihen (to pardon)	verzeiht	verzieh	verziehen	
wachsen (to grow)	wächst	wuchs	(ist) gewachsen	
waschen (to wash)	wäscht	wusch	gewaschen	
weisen (to show)	weist	wies	gewiesen	
werden (to become)	wird	wurde	(ist) geworden	werde

Infinitive	Present	Preterite	Past Participle	Imperative
wiegen (to weigh)	wiegt	wog	gewogen	
ziehen (to pull; to draw)	zieht	zog	gezogen	
zwingen (to force)	zwingt	zwang	gezwungen	

IRREGULAR WEAK VERBS

Infinitive	Present	Preterite	Past Participle	Imperative
brennen (to burn)	brennt	brannte	gebrannt	
bringen (to bring)	bringt	brachte	gebracht	
denken (to think)	denkt	dachte	gedacht	
haben (to have)	hat	hatte	gehabt	habe
kennen (to know)	kennt	kannte	gekannt	
nennen (to name, to call)	nennt	nannte	genannt	
rennen (to run)	rennt	rannte	(ist) gerannt	
senden (to send)	sendet	sendete	gesendet	
wenden (to turn)	wendet	wandte	gewandt	
wissen (to know)	weiß	wusste	gewusst	

AUXILARY VERBS

Infinitive	Present	Preterite	Past Participle	Imperative
dürfen (may; to be allowed to)	darf	durfte	gedurft	dürfen
können (can; to be able)	kann	konnte	gekonnt	können
mögen (may; to like to)	mag	mochte	gemocht	mögen
müssen (must; to have to)	muss	musste	gemusst	müssen
sollen (shall; ought to)	soll	sollte	gesollt	sollen
wollen (to want to)	will	wollte	gewollt	wollen

The first past participle is used where the auxiliary verb is being used by itself in the past.

The second participle is used where the verb is being used as an auxiliary to another verb in the past.

Glossary

A

ab und zu: *now and again*

der Abend, -e: *the evening*

guten Abend: *hello/good evening*

abends: *in the evening, p.m.*

abfahren (ist): *to leave, to set out*

abgesehen davon: *quite apart from that*

abhängen von (+ *dative*)**:** *to depend on*

der Ablauf, ¨-e: *the expiration*

das Abonnement, -s: *the subscription*

die Abo-Karte, -n: *the season ticket*

abreisen (ist): *to depart*

absenden (hat): *to send (off)*

der Absender, -: *the sender*

abwarten (hat): *to wait for, to await*

abziehen (hat): *to take off, to withdraw*

Ach so!: *Ah, O.K.! Oh, I see!*

acht: *eight*

achten: *to respect*

achtzehn: *eighteen*

achtzig: *eighty*

addieren (hat): *to add*

die Adresse, -: *the address*

ägyptisch: *Egyptian*

der Aktionär, -e: *the shareholder*

alle: *all (the)*

alles: *everything*

allmählich: *gradually*

als ob (+ *subjunctive*)**:** *as though, as if*

alt: *old*

der Altbau, -ten: *the old building*

die Altbauwohnung, -en: *the apartment in an old building*

das Alter, -: *the age*

der Amerikaner,-/die Amerikanerin, -nen: *the American man/woman*

amerikanisch: *American*

die Ampel, -n: *the traffic lights (plural)*

an (+ *dative*)**:** *on, at*

an (+*accusative*)**:** *onto*

anbieten (hat): *to offer*

ander-: *other, different*

andere: *other*

anders: *different*

der Anfang, -¨e: *the beginning*

anfangen (hat): *to begin*

anfhören (hat): *to cease, to come to a stop*

angeben (hat): *to state, specify; to boast*

das Angebot, -e: *the offer*

angehen (hat): *to concern, to regard*

was mich angeht: *as far as I'm concerned*

angehören (hat): *to belong to*

angenehm: *pleasant*

der Angestellte, -n: *the salaried employee, the white collar worker*

die Angst, -¨e: *the fear, the anxiety*

ankommen (ist): *to arrive*
annehmen (hat): *to accept*
es kommt darauf an: *it depends*
der Anruf, -e: *the (phone) call*
anrufen (hat): *to call, to ring up*
anschauen (hat): *to look at*
anschließend: *subsequently, after that*
ansehen (hat): *to look at*
die Antwort, -en: *the answer*
antworten auf *(+ accusative)*: *to answer, to reply to*
anwesend: *present*
anziehen (hat): *to put on; to attract*
sich anziehen (hat): *to get dressed*
der Anzug, -¨e: *the suit*
der Apfel, -¨e: *the apple*
die Apfelsine, -n: *the orange*
die Aprikose, -n: *the apricot*
die Arbeit, -en: *the work*
arbeiten (hat): *to work*
der Arbeiter, -/die Arbeiterin, -nen: *the worker*
das Argument, e: *the argument*
arm: *poor*
die Armbanduhr, -en: *the wristwatch*
der Arzt, -¨e: *the doctor*
auch: *also, too, even*
auf *(+ accusative)*: *on, onto, in, into, at*
auf *(+ dative)*: *on, upon, in, at*
der Aufenthalt, -e: *stay*
guten Aufenthalt!: *enjoy your stay!*
aufgeben (hat): *to abandon, to give up*
aufhaben (hat): *to be open*
aufhören (hat): *to cease, to come to an end*
aufstehen (ist): *to get up*
der Aufzug, -¨e: *the elevator, the lift*
das Auge, -n: *the eye*
der Augenblick, -e: *the moment*
einen Augenblick!: *just a moment*
aus *(+ dative)*: *out of, from*
ausblasen (hat): *to blow out*
auseinandergehen (ist): *to part company*
ausfüllen (hat): *to fill out, to fill in*
die Aufgabe, -n: *the task, the exercise*
ausgeben (hat): *to spend (money)*
ausgehen (ist): *to go out*

ausgezeichnet: *excellent*
auslachen (hat) *(+ accusative)*: *to laugh at*
das Ausland, *no pl.*: *the foreign country, overseas*
ausprobieren (hat): *to sample, to try out*
aussehen (hat): *to look, to appear*
außerdem: *as well as that, besides, moreover*
außerhalb *(+ genitive)*: *outside (of)*
die Aussicht, -en: *the view*
die Aussprache, -n: *the pronunciation*
die Auswahl, -en: *the selection, the choice*
ausziehen (hat): *to take off, to remove*
das Auto, -s: *the automobile, the car*

B

das Bad, -¨er: *the bath, the bathroom*
baden (hat): *to bathe, to go swimming*
der Bahnhof, -¨e: *the station (for railway)*
der Bahnsteig, -e: *the platform (in a railway station)*
bald: *soon*
die Bank, -en: *the bank*
der Bau, -ten: *the building, the construction*
bauen (hat): *to build*
der Baum, -¨e: *the tree*
beantworten (hat): *to answer, to reply to*
sich bedanken (hat): *to say thanks*
bedenken (hat): *to consider*
bedienen (hat): *to serve*
werden Sie bedient?: *are you being attended to?*
sich beeilen (hat): *to hurry up*
sich befinden (hat): *to be located, to be*
es befindet sich: *there is*
befinden (hat): *to consider*
befolgen (hat): *to follow (something)*
befreundet: *friendly*
sich begeben *(auf + accusative)* **(hat):** *to set out, start (on a journey)*
sich begegen (ist): *to meet*
beginnen (hat): *to begin, to start, to commence*
beglückwünschen (hat): *to congratulate*
behalten (hat): *to keep*
behandeln (hat): *to treat*
behilflich sein *(+ dative)*: *to be of assistance to*
bei *(+ dative)*: *near, by, at*
bei weitem: *by far*

bei weitem nicht so schnell: *by no means as fast*
bei weitem schneller: *faster by far*
beider, beide, beides: *both, two*
das Beispiel, -e: *the example*
beitragen (hat): *to contribute*
der Bekannte, -n: *the (male) acquaintance, someone
you know*
die Bekannte- n: *the (female) acquaintance, someone
you know*
bekommen (hat): *to get*
beliebt: *popular*
das Benzin, -e: *the gas, the petrol*
bequem: *comfortable*
der Berg -e: *the mountain*
der Bericht -e: *the report*
Bescheid sagen: *to let (someone) know*
Bescheid wissen über *(+ accusative):* *to know about
(something)*
der Bescheid, -e: *the answer, the information*
beschreiben (hat): *to describe*
besichtigen (hat): *to look round, to examine, to visit (a
place)*
besitzen (hat): *to own, to possess*
besonders: *especially*
besser: *better*
bestellen (hat): *to order*
bestimmen (hat): *to determine, to decide on*
bestimmt: *certainly, surely, definitely*
Besuch haben: *to have a visitor/visitors, to have
company*
der Besuch, -e: *the visit*
besuchen (hat): *to visit*
das Bett, -en: *the bed*
bevor: *before*
bewohnen (hat): *to occupy, to inhabit*
sich beziehen auf *(+ accusative)* **(hat):** *to relate to*
die Bibliothek, -en: *the (public) library*
billig: *cheap*
bis demnächst: *see you soon*
bis: *until*
bitten (hat): *to ask, to request*
bitte kommen Sie her!: *please come here*
bitte schön: *you're welcome*
bitte sehr!: *here you are*

bitte: *please*
blau: *blue (adjective)*
bleiben (ist): *to stay, to remain*
der Bleistift, -e: *the pencil*
der Blick, -e: *the glance*
der Blödsinn, *no pl.:* *(the) silliness, (the) nonsense*
die Blume, -n: *the flower*
der Boden, -": *the ground; the floor*
das Brathähnchen, -: *the roast chicken*
brauchen (hat): *to need, to require*
brav: *good, well-behaved*
bravo: *bravo, well done*
brechen (hat): *to break*
breit: *broad*
der Brief, -e: *the letter*
die Briefmarke, -n: *the (postage) stamp*
die Brieftasche, -n: *the wallet, the bill-fold*
die Brille, -n: *the (eye)glasses (plural)*
das Brot, -e: *the bread*
das Brötchen, -: *the bread roll*
die Bruch, -"e: *the break, the fracture*
der Bruder, -": *the brother*
die Buchhandlung, -n: *the booksellers, bookstore*
der Büroangestellte, -n: *the office worker,
the employee*
das Bürogebäude, -: *the office building*
die Büste, -n: *the bust*

C

das Café, -s: *the cafe*
die Chance, -n: *the opportunity*
der Chef, -s: *the boss*
der Computer, -: *the computer*
die Couch, -s or -en: *the couch*
der Cousin,-s; the cousin (male)
die Cousine, -n; the cousin (male)

D

da: *there*
da haben Sie viel Arbeit: *you have a lot of work there*
dabei: *close to it; by it; on the point of, in the process of*
dadurch: *through it*
dafür: *for it, in return for*

dagegen: *against it*
die Dame, -n: *the lady*
die Damenbekleidung, *no pl.:* *ladies' clothing*
die Damenwäsche *no pl.:* *ladies' underwear*
damit: *with it, so that*
daneben: *next to it, besides*
danken *(+ dative)* **(hat):** *to thank*
danke schön: *thank you*
danke: *thanks; no thank you (depending on the context)*
dann: *then, thereupon*
daran: *at it; on it*
darauf: *on it*
darauf ankommen: *to matter*
es kommt darauf an: *it depends*
darauf kommt es an: *that's just the point*
darf ich …?: *may I …?*
darf ich Ihnen … vorstellen?: *may I introduce … to you?*
darf ich Sie um Ihren Namen bitten?: *may I ask your name?*
darin: *in it*
darüber: *about it, about this*
das: *it, that*
das heißt: *that is to say, that means, i.e.*
das ist nett (von dir/von Ihnen): *that's nice (of you)*
das kann ja passieren: *these things happen*
das kann nicht sein!: *that can't be!*
das sieht gut aus: *that looks good*
dass: *that (conjunction)*
dauern (hat): *to continue, to last, take (time)*
davon: *from it, about it*
davor: *in front of it*
dazu: *to it; to that end; to that purpose*
dein: *your (familiar 'you' form)*
demnächst: *soon, shortly, in the near future*
denken (hat): *to think*
denn: *then, else (adverb)*
deren: *whose (plural), of whom (feminine or plural)*
derjenige, diejenige, dasjenige: *the one*
deshalb: *therefore, for that reason*
dessen: *whose, of whom, of which (masculine or neuter)*
deutlich: *clear*
das Deutsch *no pl.:* *German (as a language)*
deutsch: *German (adjective)*

der Deutsche, -n/die Deutsche, -n: *the German man/woman*
das Deutschlernen, *no pl.:* *learning German*
dich: *you (familiar form)*
das Dickicht, -e: *the thicket*
diejenigen (plural): *those (ones)*
der Dienstag, -e: *Tuesday*
dies: *this*
dieser/diese/dieses: *this*
diesmal: *this time*
das Ding, -e: *the thing, the object*
doch: *after all, however, still*
doch!: *yes, I do/it is (etc.)! (in reply to negative questions)*
der Donnerstag, -e: *Thursday*
das Dorf, -̈er: *the village*
dort: *there*
dort drüben: *over there*
dorthin: *to there (away from the speaker)*
drei: *three*
dreißig: *thirty*
dreizehn: *thirteen*
drin = darin: *inside*
zu dritt: *three of them, three of us*
du weißt Bescheid?: *do you know about it?*
dumm: *stupid*
dunkel: *dark*
durch *(+ accusative):* *through*
dürfen (hat): *to be allowed to*
der Durst, *no pl.:* *the thirst*

E

eben: *(adjective) even, level, plain; (adverb) exactly, precisely, quite*
die Ebene-n, : *the plain*
ebenso gut: *just as well*
ebenso viel: *just as much*
ebenso wenig: *just as little*
echt: *genuine*
die Ecke, -n: *the corner*
egal: *equal, the same*
die Ehe, -n: *the marriage*
die Eiche, -n: *the oak*
eigen: *own, of one's own*

die **Eigenschaft**, **-en**: *the characteristic, the quality*
eigentlich: *really, actually*
das **Eigentum**, *no pl.*: *the property*
eilen: *to hurry*
es eilt nicht: *there's no hurry*
eilig: *hurried, urgent*
eilt!: *urgent!*
einfach: *simple*
einige: *some, several, a few*
das **Einkaufen**, *no pl.*: *the shopping*
einkaufen (**hat**): *to go shopping*
einladen (**hat**): *to invite*
einrichten (**hat**): *to furnish, to arrange*
die **Einrichtung**, **-en**: *the arrangement, the furnishing*
eins: *one*
einschenken (**hat**): *to fill (someone's) glass*
einschlafen (**ist**): *to get to sleep, to fall asleep*
einsetzen (**hat**): *to insert*
eintönig: *monotonous*
sich **eintragen** (**hat**): *to enter one's name*
eintreffen (**ist**): *to arrive, to turn up, to appear*
einverstanden sein: *to agree to*
einverstanden!: *agreed!*
der **Einwohner**, **-**: *the inhabitant*
einzeln: *single, solitary*
einziehen (**ist**): *to enter, to move in*
die **Einzimmerwohnung**, **-en**: *the one-room apartment*
das **Eisen**, **-**: *the iron*
elf: *eleven*
die **Eltern** (**plural**): *the parents*
empfangen (**hat**): *to receive*
der **Empfänger**, **-**: *the recipient*
die **Empfangsdame**, **-n**: *the receptionist*
empfehlen (**hat**): *to recommend*
das **Ende**: *the end*
Ende gut, alles gut: *all's well that ends well*
endlich: *final*
eng: *narrow*
der **Engländer**, **-**/die **Engländerin**, **-nen**: *the Englishman/the English woman*
entfernt: *remote, distant*
entgegengesetzt: *opposite*
entleihen (**hat**): *to borrow*
sich **entscheiden** (**hat**): *to decide, to make up*

one's mind
entschuldigen (**hat**): *to excuse, pardon*
entschuldigen Sie: *excuse me/I beg your pardon*
entschuldigung: *sorry*
die **Entschuldigung**, **-en**: *the excuse, the apology*
entsprechen (+ *dative*) (**hat**): *to correspond to, to meet, to fulfill*
entsprechend: *corresponding, suitable, appropriate*
entstehen (**ist**): *to arise*
entweder . . . oder: *either . . . or*
er: *he; it*
sich **ereignen** (**hat**): *to happen*
die **Erfahrung**, **-en**: *the experience*
erinnern an (+ *accusative*) (**hat**): *to remind*
sich **erinnern an** (+ *accusative*) (**hat**): *to remember*
erkennen (**hat**): *to recognize*
erklären (**hat**): *to state, to explain*
die **Erklärung**, **-en**: *the explanation*
sich **erkundigen nach** (+ *dative*) (**hat**): *to inquire (about)*
erreichen (**hat**): *to reach, to come to*
erst: *first, at first*
zum ersten Mal: *for the first time*
erstens: *in the first place, firstly*
erwarten (**hat**): *to expect*
die **Erwartung**, **-en**: *the expectation*
es: *it*
es schneit: *it's snowing*
das **Essen**, **-**: *the meal*
essen (**hat**): *to eat*
der **Essig**, *no pl.*: *the vinegar*
die **Etage**, **-n**: *the floor (of a building)*
das **Etikett**, **-en**: *the label*
etliche: *some*
etwa: *about, approximately*
etwas: *something*
etwas anderes: *something else*
eventuell: *perhaps, possibly*

F

fahren (**ist**): *to drive, to go (in a vehicle)*
die **Fahrkarte**, **-n**: *the ticket*
der **Fall** -¨e: *the case*
auf jeden Fall: *in any case, at all events, whatever*

happens

falls: *in case, if*

falsch: *wrong, false*

die Familie, -n: *the family*

fangen: *to catch*

die Farbe, -n: *the color, the colour*

fehlen (hat): *to be missing, to be lacking*

die Feier, -n: *the celebration, the rest*

das Fenster -: *the window*

die Ferien (plural): *the holidays, the vacation*

das Fernsehen, *no pl.: the television*

fernsehen (hat): *to watch television*

fertig: *ready, finished*

festhalten an *(+ dative)* **(hat):** *to stick to, to cling to*

feststellen (hat): *to notice, to ascertain*

der Film, -e: *the movie*

finden (hat): *to find*

die Finsternis, *no pl.: the darkness*

die Flasche, -n: *the bottle*

der Fleisch, *no pl.: the meat*

fliegen (ist): *to fly, to go by plane*

der Flughafen -": *the airport*

das Flugzeug, e: *the aeroplane, the plane*

der Fluss, -¨e: *the river*

folgend: *following, subsequent*

das Formular, -e: *the form*

Sie müssen dieses Formular ausfüllen: *you have to fill out this form*

der Fortschritt, -e: *the progress, the advance*

die Fortsetzung, -en: *the continuation*

die Frage, -n: *the question*

die Frage beantworten: *to answer the question*

fragen (hat): *to ask*

der Franzose, -n/die Französin, -nen: *the Frenchman/woman*

die Frau, -en: *the woman; the wife*

frei: *free, vacant*

der Freitag, -e: *Friday*

die Freude, -n: *the joy*

sich freuen (hat): *to be glad, to be pleased*

ich freue mich.: *I'm glad*

freut mich sehr.: *pleased to meet you*

der Freund, -e: *the friend (male); the boyfriend*

die Freundin, -nen: *the friend (female); the girlfriend*

frisch: *fresh*

die Frist, -en: *the period*

früh: *early*

zu früh: *early (in arriving)*

früher: *previously, formerly*

das Frühjahr, -e: *the spring*

der Frühling, -e: *the spring*

das Frühlingswetter, *no pl.: the spring weather*

das Frühstück, -e: *the breakfast*

frühstücken (hat): *to have breakfast*

das Frühstückszimmer, -: *the breakfast room*

das Fundbüro, -s: *the lost and found office, the lost property office*

fünf: *five*

fünfundzwanzig: *twenty-five*

fünfzehn: *fifteen*

fünfzig: *fifty*

der Fuß, -¨e: *the foot*

zu Fuß: *on foot*

G

ganz: *quite*

ganz bestimmt: *quite definitely*

die Gardine, -n: *the curtain*

gar nicht: *not at all*

die Gasse, -n: *the lane*

das Gästebuch, -¨er: *the guest book*

geben (jemandem etwas) (hat): *to give (something to someone), to hand over*

es gibt: *there is/there are*

das Gebäude, -: *the building*

das Gebirge, -: *the mountain range*

gebraucht: *used*

der Geburtstag, -e: *the birthday*

das Gedächtnis, -se.: *the memory*

das Gedicht, -e: *the poem*

gehen (ist): *to go; to walk*

ich gehe schnell mal hin: *I'll just go there quickly*

geht das?: *is that all right?*

die Gefahr, -en: *the danger*

gefallen *(+ dative)* **(hat):** *to please*

es gefällt mir: *I like it*

gegen *(+ accusative):* *towards, against*

die Gegend, -en: *the area, the district*

der Gegensatz, -¨e: *the contrast*
gegenseitig: *mutual*
das Gegenteil, -e: *the contrary, the opposite*
im Gegenteil: *on the contrary, quite the reverse*
gegenüber (+ *dative*): *opposite, over the way*
das Gehen, *no pl.*: *the going, walking*
gehören (+ *dative*) (**hat**): *to belong to*
gelb: *yellow (adjective)*
gelingen (+ *dative*) (**ist**): *to succeed*
das Gemüse, -: *the vegetable*
der Gemüsehändler, -: *the greengrocer*
genau: *exact(ly)*
der Genitiv, -e: *the genitive*
genießen (**hat**): *to enjoy*
genug: *enough*
das Genus, -: *the gender (of nouns)*
geöffnet: *open (from öffnen: to open)*
das Gepäck, *no pl.*: *the luggage*
der Gepäckkarren, -: *the luggage trolley*
das Gepäckstück, -e: *the item of luggage*
der Gepäckträger, -: *the porter*
gerade: *just, precisely (adverb); straight (adjective)*
geradeaus: *straight on*
das Geräusch, -e: *the noise, the sound*
gern haben (**hat**): *to like (something, somebody)*
das Geschäft, -e: *the business*
geschehen (**ist**): *to happen*
die Geschichte, -n: *the story, the history*
geschlossen: *closed (from schließen: to close)*
das Gesetz, -e: *the law*
das Gespräch, -e: *the conversation*
gestehen (**hat**): *to confess*
gestern: *yesterday*
gesund: *healthy*
getrennt: *separate(ly)*
das Gewicht, .e: *the weight*
gewinnen (**hat**): *to gain, to obtain, to win*
gewiss: *certain*
die Gewohnheit, -en: *the custom, the habit*
das Glas, -¨er: *the glass*
glauben (**hat**): *to believe, to think*
ich glaube: *I think, I guess*
gleich: *same, identical (adjective)*
gleich: *immediately, at once (adverb)*

glücklich: *happy*
der Glückwunsch, -¨e: *the congratulation*
sich (*dative*) gönnen: *to allow oneself, to treat oneself to*
das Gras, -¨er: *the grass*
gratulieren (+ *dative*) (**hat**): *to congratulate*
grau: *grey, gray*
groß: *big, large (adjective)*
großartig!: *great!/tremendous!*
die Größe, -n: *the size*
die Großeltern (plural): *the grandparents*
die Großmutter, -¨: *the grandmother*
der Großvater -¨: *the grandfather*
großzügig: *generous*
grün: *green (adjective)*
ins Grüne fahren: *to drive out into the countryside*
die Gruppe, -n: *the group*
grüß Gott!: *hello! (in southern Germany, Austria, Switzerland)*
gültig: *valid*
gut: *good; well*
es ist ja noch mal alles gut gegangen.: *everything turned out well after all*
gute Reise!: *have a good trip!*
das Gymnasium, die Gymnasien: *the high school, the grammar school*

H

haben (**hat**): *to have*
haben Sie es passend?: *do you have the right money?*
das Haben: *the credit*
halb: *half*
hallo!: *hi!, hey!*
halten (**hat**): *to keep; to hold*
halten von (+ *dative*) (**hat**): *to think of, to consider*
was halten Sie davon?: *what do you think (of the idea)?*
die Hand, -¨e: *the hand*
handeln (**hat**): *to act, to proceed*
es handelt sich um ... (+ *accusative*): *it's a matter of/ it's about ...*
die Handschrift, -en: *the handwriting*
hart: *hard*
hässlich: *ugly, nasty*
die Hauptstraße. -n: *the main road*
das Haus, -¨er: *the house*

zu Hause: *at home*
heiß: *hot*
heißen (hat): *to be called*
er heißt Paul: *his name is Paul*
was heißt ... auf Deutsch?: *what's ... in German?*
helfen *(+ dative)* **(hat):** *to help*
hell: *light, bright*
das Hemd, -en: *the shirt*
her: *a word indicating a direction or movement towards the speaker*
der Herbst, -e: *the fall*
hereinkommen (ist): *to come in (towards the speaker)*
herkommen (ist): *to come (towards the speaker)*
der Herr, -en: *the gentleman*
die Herrenabteilung, -en: *the menswear department*
die Herrenbekleidung, *no pl.*: *menswear, men's clothing*
herrlich: *splendid*
die Herrschaften *(plural)*: *ladies and gentlemen, lady and gentleman*
herunternehmen (hat): *to take down*
herzlich: *hearty, cordial*
herzlich danken: *to thank wholeheartedly*
heute Abend: *this evening*
heute: *today*
hier: *here*
hier ist: *here is*
hier und da: *here and there*
hierher: *here (towards the speaker)*
die Hilfe, -n: *the help*
hilfreich: *helpful*
das Hilfsverb, -en: *the auxiliary verb*
hin: *a word indicating a direction or movement away from the speaker*
hingehen (ist): *to go to (somewhere away from the speaker)*
die Hinsicht, -en: *the regard, the respect*
hinter *(+ accusative or dative)*: *behind, at the back of*
die Hochzeit, -en: *the wedding*
hoffentlich: *hopefully, I hope, we hope so*
die Höflichkeit, *no pl.*: *the politeness*
holen (hat): *to fetch*
der Holländer, -/die Holländerin, -nen: *the Dutchman/ the Dutch woman*

hören (hat): *to hear*
die Hose, -n: *the trousers (plural), the pants (plural)*
hübsch: *pretty*
der Hund, -e: *the dog*
das Hundert, -e: *the hundred*
hundert: *a hundred*
hundertfünfundzwanzig: *a hundred and twenty-five*
der Hunger, *no pl.*: *the hunger*

I

die Idee, -n: *the idea*
ihn: *him*
Ihnen *(polite form)*: *to you*
Ihr *(polite form)*: *your*
ihr: *her, their; you (familiar form plural)*
immer: *always*
immerhin: *after all*
in Ordnung!: *all right!/okay!*
in: *in (with dative); into (with accusative); to (with accusative)*
indirekt: *indirect*
der Inhalt, -e: *the contents (plural)*
das Inland, *no pl.*: *the home country, the country in which you are*
interessant: *interesting*
das Interesse: *the interest*
sich interessieren für *(+ accusative)* **(hat):** *to be interested in*
interessieren (hat): *to interest*
das Internet, *no pl.*: *the internet*
die Internetverbindung, -en; *the internet connection*
sich irren (hat): *to make a mistake*
irrtümlich: *by mistake*
der Italiener, -/die Italienerin, -nen: *the Italian man/ the Italian woman*
ja: *yes*
ja, gern!: *yes, please!*

J

die Jacht, -en: *the yacht*
die Jacke, -n: *the jacket*

das Jahr, -e: *the year*
die Jahreszeit, -en: *the season*
der Jahrmarkt, -¨e: *the fair*
der Japaner, -/die Japanerin, -nen: *the Japanese man/ the Japanese woman*
japanisch: *Japanese*
je: *each*
jeder, jede, jedes: *each, every*
jemand: *someone, somebody*
jener/jene/jenes: *that*
jenes: *that*
jung: *young*
der Junge, -n: *the boy*
der junge Mann: *the young man*

K

der Kaffee, -s: *the coffee*
der Kalender, -: *the calendar*
kalt: *cold*
der Kanadier, -/die Kanadierin, -nen: *the Canadian man/the Canadian woman*
der Kanarienvogel, -¨: *the canary*
der Karren. -: *the trolley*
die Karte, -n: *the card; the map*
Karten spielen: *to play cards*
das Kartenspiel, -e: *the game of cards*
der Käse, -: *the cheese*
die Katastrophe. -n: *the disaster, the catastrophe*
der Katze- n: *the cat*
das Kaufhaus, -¨er: *the department store*
kaufen (hat): *to buy*
keineswegs: *by no means*
der Kellner, -: *the waiter*
kennen (hat): *to know (somebody, some place)*
die Kerze, -n: *the candle*
das Kilo -(s): *the kilogram (2.2 lbs)*
der Kilometer, -: *the kilometer (5/8 of a mile)*
das Kind -er: *the child*
das Klavier -e: *the piano*
kleben (hat): *to stick*
das Kleid -er: *the dress*
die Kleider: *the clothes (plural)*
klein: *small, little (adjective)*
die Kleinstadt, -¨e: *the small town*

klug: *intelligent*
die Kneipe, -n: *the bar*
kochen (hat): *to cook*
das Kochen, no pl.: *the cooking*
das Koffein, no pl.: *caffeine*
koffeinfrei: *decaffeinated*
der Koffer, -: *the suitcase*
der Kollege, -n: *the colleague, work-mate (male)*
die Kollegin, -nen: *the colleague, work-mate (female)*
kommen (ist): *to come*
der Kommilitone, -n: *the fellow student*
das Kompliment, -e: *the compliment*
kompliziert: *complicated*
können (hat): *can, to be able (to)*
das Konzert, -e: *the concert, recital*
der Korb, -¨e: *the basket*
die Kosten (plural): *the costs*
das Kraftfahrzeug, -e: *the motor vehicle*
krank: *sick*
die Krawatte, -e: *the tie, the necktie*
die Küche, -n: *the kitchen*
der Kuchen, -: *the cake, the pastry*
der Kugelschreiber, -: *the ball-pen, the ballpoint pen*
kühl: *cool*
der Kunde, -n: *the customer (male)*
die Kundenliste, -n: *the customer list*
die Kundin, -nen: *the customer (female)*
die Kunst, -¨e: *the art*
kurz: *short*
die Küste, -n: *coast*

L

der Laden, -¨: *the store*
laden (hat): *to load*
die Lage, -n: *the situation, the position*
das Lager, -: *the warehouse*
... auf Lager haben: *to have ... in stock*
das Land, -¨er: *the country*
landen (hat/ist): *to land*
die Landschaft, -en: *the countryside*
lang: *long*
die Länge, -n: *length*
lange: *for a long time*
langweilen (hat): *to bore (someone)*

sich langweilen (hat): *to feel bored, to be bored*
der Laserpointer, -: *the laser pointer*
lassen (hat): *to let; to make, to leave, to allow*
lassen Sie mal sehen: *let me see/let me have a look*
das Leben, -: *the life*
die Lederjacke, -n: *the leather jacket*
leer: *empty*
der Lehrer, -/die Lehrerin, -nen: *the teacher*
leicht: *light*
es tut mir leid: *I'm sorry*
die Leidenschaft, -en: *the passion*
sich *(dative)* leisten (hat): *to afford*
die Leistung, -en: *the achievement, the performance*
die Lektion, -en: *the lesson*
lernen (hat): *to learn (also means: to study at school)*
lesen (hat): *to read*
die Leute *(plural)*: *people*
das Licht, -er: *the light*
die Liebe, -n: *the love*
lieben (hat): *to love*
lieber: *rather*
der Likör, -e: *the brandy, the liqueur*
links: *left, on the left*
die Liste, -n: *the list*
sich lohnen (hat): *to be worthwhile*
lohnen (hat): *to reward*
losfahren (ist): *to go off, to leave (in a vehicle)*
Sie müssen aber bald los: *you'll have to be going soon*
die Lösung, -en: *the solution*
die Luft, -ꞏe: *the air*
die Lupe, -n: *the magnifying glass*
die Lust, -ꞏe: *the pleasure, the enjoyment, the delight*
Lust haben zu (+ dative): *to feel like doing*

M

machen (hat): *to make, to do*
mach schnell!: *hurry up!/be quick!*
mache ich!: *will do!*
das Mädchen, -: *the girl*
man: *one, we, they, you (people in general)*
manche: *some, many a*
manchmal: *sometimes*
der Mann, -ꞏer: *the man, the husband*
der Mantel, -": *the coat*

die Marmelade, -n : *jam*
das Material, -ien: *the material, the cloth*
die Mauer, -n: *the wall*
die Medaille -n: *the medal*
mehrere: *several*
die Mehrzahl, -en: *the plural*
mein: *my*
meinen (hat): *to think, to have an opinion; to mean*
die Meinung, -en: *the opinion*
die Menge -n: *the quantity*
eine ganze Menge: *a whole lot*
sich *(dative)* merken (hat): *to remember, to bear in mind*
messen (hat): *to measure*
das Messer -: *the knife*
der/das Meter, -: *the meter*
mich: *me*
der Mieter -: *the tenant*
die Milch, *no pl.*: *the milk*
mischen (hat): *to mix*
missachten (hat): *to disregard*
mit *(+ dative)* verabredet sein: *to have arranged to meet . . ./to have an appointment with . . .*
mit den Gläsern anstoßen: *to clink glasses*
mit *(+ dative)*: *with*
miteinander: *with each other*
mitkommen (ist): *to come along, to come with*
mitnehmen (hat): *to take (something) with*
mitsamt *(+ dative)*: *together with*
das Mittagessen, -: *the lunch*
mittags: *at lunchtime*
mittel: *moderate, medium*
mitten in *(+ dative)*: *in the middle of*
der Mittwoch, -e: *Wednesday*
möglich: *possible*
die Möglichkeit, -en: *the possibility*
möglichst: *the utmost, everything possible*
momentan: *at the moment, for the present*
der Monat, -e: *the month*
monatelang: *for months*
der Montag, -e: *Monday*
morgen Nachmittag: *tomorrow afternoon*
der Morgen, -: *the morning*
am Morgen: *in the morning*

guten Morgen!: *hello/ good morning*
morgen: *tomorrow*
morgens: *in the morning*
müde: *tired*
die Mühe, -n: *trouble, effort*
München: *Munich*
murmeln (hat): *to mutter*
das Museum, die Museen: *the museum*
die Musik, -en: *the music*
müssen (hat): *must, to have to*
die Mutter, -": *the mother*

N

nach Hause gehen: *to go home*
nach und nach: *gradually*
nach (+ dative): *after*
der Nachbar -n: *the neighbour, the neighbor*
nachdem: *after*
der Nachmittag, -e: *the afternoon*
am Nachmittag: *in the afternoon*
nachmittags: *in the afternoon, p.m.*
nachschauen (hat): *to go and look*
nachsehen (hat): *to have a look, to inspect*
ich sehe nach: *I'll have a look*
die Nachsicht, no pl.: *the consideration*
nächst . . . : *next, nearest*
am nächsten Tag: *the next day*
die Nacht, -"e: *the night*
der Nachtisch, -e: *the dessert*
nachts: *by night, at night*
nah: *near*
die Nahrung, -en: *the nourishment*
der Name, -: *the name*
natürlich: *naturally, of course*
der Nebel, -: *the fog*
neben (+ dative or accusative): *next to, near*
nebenan: *nearby, next door, close by*
der Neffe, -n: *the nephew*
nehmen (hat): *to take*
die Neigung, -en: *the inclination, the preference*
nein: *no*
die Nelke, -n: *the carnation*
nennen (hat): *to name*
nett: *nice, kind*

die Neubauwohnung, -en: *the apartment in a new building*
neulich: *recently*
neun: *nine*
neunzehn: *nineteen*
neunzig: *ninety*
nicht: *not*
die Nichte, -n: *the niece*
der Nichtraucher -: *the non-smoker*
nichts: *nothing*
nichts für ungut!: *don't take it amiss!/so sorry!*
nichts Besonderes: *nothing special*
das Nichtstun, no pl.: *idleness, doing nothinh*
nie: *never*
niemand: *nobody*
noch: *still; yet*
noch etwas?: *anything else?*
noch nicht: *not yet*
der Norden, no pl.: *the north*
im Norden (von + dative): *In the North (of)*
normalerweise: *normally, as a rule, usually*
nötig: *necessary*
die Nummer, -n: *the number*

O

ob: *whether*
oder: *or*
öffnen (hat): *to open (something)*
sich öffnen (hat): *to open (up)*
oft: *often*
ohne (+ accusative): *without*
der Onkel, -: *the uncle*
die Oper, -n: *the opera*
der Optimist, -en: *the optimist*
die Ordnung, -en: *the order, the system*
der Osten, no pl.: *the east*
die Osterferien (plural): *the Easter holidays*
(das) Ostern, -: *Easter*
der Österreicher, -/die Österreicherin, -nen: *the Austrian man/the Austrian woman*
österreichisch: *Austrian*

P

das Paar, -e: *the pair*
ein paar: *a few, some*
das Paket, -e: *the parcel*
die Partei, -en: *the (political) party*
passend: *suitable*
passieren (ist): *to happen*
die Pause, -n: *the interval, the break*
die Person, -en: *the person, the individual*
der Personalausweis, -e: *the identity card*
persönlich: *personal*
das Pferd, -e: *the horse*
die Pflanze, -n: *the plant*
der Pflänzling, -e: *the seedling*
die Pflicht, -en: *the duty*
das Picknick, -e/-s: *the picnic*
der Platz, -¨e: *the place, the space, the seat; the square*
der Politiker, -: *the politician*
die Post, no pl.: *the post, the mail; the post office*
die Postkarte, -n: *the postcard*
die Präposition, -en: *the preposition*
der Preis, -e: *the price*
die Preislage, -n: *price bracket, the price range*
der mittleren Preislage: *in the medium price range, moderately priced*
die Prominenz, no pl.: *the high society*
der Pullover, -: *the pullover*
pünktlich: *punctual, on time*

R

das Rad, -¨er: *the wheel; the bicycle*
Rad fahren (ist): *to cycle, to ride a bicycle*
radeln (ist): *to cycle, to ride a bicycle*
der Rat, -¨e: *the advice, the suggestion*
das Rauchen, no pl.: *(the) smoking*
rauchen (hat): *to smoke*
der Raucher, -: *the smoker*
das Raucherabteil, -e: *the smoking compartment*
rechnen (hat): *to calculate*
die Rechnung, -en: *the bill*
Sie haben recht: *you're right*
rechts: *right, on the right*
die Rede, -n: *the speech*
reden (hat): *to talk, to speak*

reduzieren (hat): *to reduce*
regelmäßig: *regular*
der Regen, -: *the rain*
der Regenmantel -¨: *the raincoat*
der Regenschirm, -e: *the umbrella*
das Regenwetter, no pl.: *the rainy weather*
regnen (hat): *to rain*
reichen (hat): *to reach, to hand (something to someone)*
eine Reise machen (hat): *to go on a trip*
die Reise, -n: *the journey, the trip*
das Reiseandenken, -: *the souvenir*
die Reisegruppe, -n: *the travel group*
die Reisende, -n: *the traveler (female)*
der Reisende, -n: *the traveler (male)*
der Reisepass, -¨e: *the passport*
reservieren (hat): *to reserve*
die Reservierung, -en: *the reservation*
das Restaurant, -s: *the restaurant*
richtig: *right, correct*
die Richtung, -en: *the direction*
der Rock, -¨e: *the skirt*
die Rolltreppe, -n: *the escalator*
die Rose, -n: *the rose*
das Röslein, -: *the little rose*
rot: *red (adjective)*
der Rotwein, -e: *the red wine*
rufen (hat): *to call*
die Ruhe, no pl.: *the quiet, the peace*
ruhig: *peaceful, quiet*
rund um (+ accusative): *all around, about*
rund: *round*
der Russe, -n/die Russin, -nen: *the Russian man/the Russian woman*
russisch: *Russian (adjective)*

S

die S-Bahn, no pl.: *the rapid suburban train*
der Saal, die Säle: *the hall*
die Sache, -n: *the thing, the affair*
sagen (hat): *to say*
der Salat, -e: *the salad*
der Samstag, -e: *Saturday*
samstags: *on Saturdays*
sämtliche: *all (of the)*

der Sänger, -: *the singer (male)*
die Sängerin, -nen: *the singer (female)*
satt: *satisfied, full*
satt werden (ist): *to be full*
die Schachtel, -n: *the box*
schade: *what a pity*
das Schäfchen, -: *the little sheep, the lamb*
schälen (hat): *to peel*
der Schalter, -: *the counter, the window, the office*
der Schatz, -¨e: *the treasure; honey (term of endearment)*
schätzen (hat): *to appreciate*
schauen (hat): *to look*
schauen wir mal: *let's have a look*
die Scheibe, -n: *the slice*
scheinen (hat): *to appear, to shine*
die Schere, -n: *the scissors (plural)*
das Schiff, -e: *the ship*
schlafen (hat): *to sleep*
Schlange stehen (hat): *to stand in a queue, to queue*
schlecht: *bad, badly*
schließen (hat): *to close; to end*
das Schloss, -¨er: *the palace*
der Schluss, -¨e: *the close; the conclusion*
zu dem Schluss kommen: *to reach a conclusion*
der Schlüssel, -: *the key*
der Schnaps, -¨e: *the strong liquor, brandy*
der Schnee, *no pl.*: *the snow*
schnell: *fast, quick*
die Schokolade, -n: *the chocolate*
schon: *already; all right (or used for emphasis)*
schön: *beautiful, nice, lovely*
schönen Dank: *thank you very much*
die Schönheit, -en: *the beauty*
der Schrank, -¨e: *the closet, the cupboard*
das Schreiben, -: *the writing, the letter*
der Schreibtisch, -e: *the desk*
die Schreibwarenabteilung, -en: *the stationery department*
der Schuh, -e: *the shoe*
die Schuhgröße, -n: *the shoe size*
die Schuld, *no pl.*: *the guilt, the debt; the fault*
schuldig: *guilty*
die Schule, -n: *the school*

in die Schule gehen: *to go to school*
der Schüler, -: *the schoolboy, the student*
die Schülerin, -nen: *the schoolgirl, the student*
schwach: *weak*
die Schwäche, -n: *the weakness*
schwarz: *black (adjective)*
schwer: *heavy; difficult*
schwer fallen (+ dative): *to have difficulty with*
die Schwester, -n: *the sister*
die Schwierigkeit, -en: *the difficulty*
schwimmen (hat/ist): *to swim*
sechs: *six*
sechzehn: *sixteen*
sechzig: *sixty*
sehen (hat): *to see*
sehr: *very*
sehr gut: *very well, very good*
sehr schlecht: *very bad, very badly*
das Sein, *no pl.*: *the existence*
sein: *his*
sein (ist): *to be, to exist*
seit (+ dative): *since*
die Seite, -n: *side, page*
der Sekt, -e: *the sparkling wine*
selbstverständlich: *of course*
selten: *rare(ly), seldom*
senden (hat): *to send, to transmit*
servieren (hat): *to serve*
der Sessel, -: *the easy-chair, the armchair*
sich setzen (hat): *to sit down*
setzen (hat): *to place, to put*
sicherlich: *surely, certainly, undoubtedly*
sie: *she; it; they*
Sie: *you (singular and plural, formal address)*
sie meldet sich nicht: *she's not answering her phone*
sie will: *she wants to/she's going to*
sieben: *seven*
siebzehn: *seventeen*
siebzig: *seventy*
silbern: *silver*
sinken (ist): *to sink*
die Situation, -en: *the situation*
sitzen (hat/in South Germany: ist): *to sit*
das Smartphone, -s: *the smartphone*

so … wie …: *as … as …*

so gut wie …: *virtually, practically*

sobald: *as soon as,*

die Socke, -n: *the sock*

soeben: *just now*

sofern: *so far as, inasmuch*

sofort: *immediately*

der Sohn, -¨e: *the son*

solang(e): *as long as, while*

solch-: *such (a/an)*

das Soll, -: *the debit; the quota*

sollen (hat): *shall, ought to, to have to*

somit: *thus, consequently*

der Sommer, -: *the summer*

sondern: *but (after a negative statement)*

die Sonne, -n: *the sun*

die Sonnenfinsternis, -se: *the eclipse*

der Sonntag, -e: *Sunday*

sonst noch: *apart from that, as well*

sonst: *otherwise, else, besides*

sorgen (hat): *to take care of*

sorgfältig: *careful(ly)*

sowie: *as well as*

sowieso: *in any case, anyway*

der Spanier, -/die Spanierin, -nen: *the Spanish man/woman*

spanisch: *Spanish (adjective)*

der Spaß, -¨e: *the good time, (the) fun*

spät: *late*

zu spät: *late (in arriving)*

später: *later*

spazieren gehen (ist): *to go for a walk*

spielen (hat): *to play*

die Sprache, -n: *the language*

sprechen (hat): *to speak*

der Sprudel, -: *the sparkling mineral water*

die Staatsangehörigkeit, -en: *the nationality*

die Stadt, -¨e: *the town*

das Stadtzentrum, die Stadtzentren: *the city center*

im Stadtzentrum: *down town, in the city center*

stammen (hat): *to come from (a place)*

stark: *strong, strongly*

die Station, -en: *the station (for subway)*

statt (+ genitive): *instead of*

statt zu (+ infinitive): *instead of*

stehen lassen (hat): *to leave standing, to forget*

sterben (ist): *to die*

stimmen (hat): *to be correct*

es stimmt!: *that's right!/correct!*

der Stock, -¨e: *the story, the floor*

im ersten Stock: *on the first floor (in USA: second floor)*

on welchem Stock?: *on which floor?*

stoßen (hat): *to push, to shove*

der Strand, -¨e: *the beach*

die Straße, -n: *the street, the road*

der Student, -en: *the student*

die Studentenkneipe, -n: *the bar frequented by students*

studieren (hat): *to study (at university)*

das Studium, die Studien: *studies (plural)*

der Stuhl, -¨e: *the chair*

sich umarmen (hat): *to embrace*

suchen (hat): *to search*

der Süden, no pl.: *the south*

die Summe, -n: *the sum, the total*

der Supermarkt, -¨e: *the supermarket*

T

der Tag, -e: *the day*

guten Tag!: *hello/hi*

die Tageskarte, -n: *the day ticket*

talentiert: *talented, gifted*

die Tante, -n: *the aunt*

tanzen (hat/ist): *to dance*

der Tänzer, -: *the dancer (male)*

die Tänzerin, -nen: *the dancer (female)*

tapfer: *brave, courageous*

die Tasche, -n: *the bag, pocket*

die Tasse, -n: *the cup*

tätig sein (ist): *to work, to have a job*

das Taxi, -s: *the taxi, the cab*

der Tee, -s: *the tea*

der Teil, -e: *the part*

zum Teil: *partly*

teilen (hat): *to divide*

sich teilen (hat): *to separate, to part*

das Telefon, -e: *the telephone*

ans Telefon gehen (ist): *to go and answer the phone*

am Telefon: *on the phone*

telefonieren (hat): *to telephone*
die Telefonnummer, -n: *the telephone number*
der Teller, -: *the plate*
der Teppich, -e: *the carpet*
teuer: *expensive*
teurer: *more expensive*
das Theater, -: *the theater/the theatre*
ins Theater gehen (ist): *to go to the theater/theatre*
der Theaterkarte, -n: *the theater ticket*
das Thema, die Themen: *the topic, the subject*
das Ticket, -s: *the ticket*
tief: *deep, low*
das Tier, -e: *the animal*
der Tisch, -e: *the table*
die Tochter, -": *the daughter*
das Tor, -e: *the gate*
der Tourismus, no pl.: *the tourism*
tragen (hat): *to carry*
treffen (hat): *to meet (someone)*
sich treffen (hat): *to meet*
treffend: *appropriate*
trennen (hat): *to divide, to separate*
sich trennen (hat): *to part*
die Treppe, -n: *the steps (plural)*
das Trinken, no pl.: *the drinking (here: of alcohol)*
trinken (hat): *to drink*
der Trödelmarkt, -"e: *the flea market*
trotz (+ genitive or dative): *in spite of, despite*
trotzdem: *nevertheless, all the same*
tun (hat): *to do; to place*
die Tür, -en: *the door*

U

die U-Bahn, -en: *the subway, the underground*
über etwas (accusative) Bescheid wissen: *to know about something*
überhaupt nichts: *nothing at all*
überqueren (hat): *to cross over*
überraschen (hat): *to surprise*
übrig: *left over, remaining*
übrigens: *by the way*
die Übung, -en: *the exercise*
die Uhr, -en: *the time; the clock*
die Ulme, -n: *the elm*

um die Ecke: *around the corner*
um achtzehn Uhr: *at six p.m.*
mm wie viel Uhr?: *at what time?*
um (+ accusative): *around*
umbauen (hat): *to reconstruct, to rebuild*
umgebaut: *converted*
die Umgebung, -en: *the surroundings*
umgehen (ist): *to deal with, to handle*
unbedingt: *absolutely*
unbequem: *uncomfortable*
und: *and*
undeutlich: *indistinct(ly)*
unecht: *false*
der Unfall, -"e: *the accident*
ungefähr: *roughly, approximately*
ungewiss: *uncertain*
unglücklich: *unhappy*
unmöglich: *impossible*
unregelmäßig: *irregular*
unruhig: *restless, hectic*
uns: *us*
unter (+ accusative or dative): *under*
unterhalten (hat): *to entertain*
sich unterhalten (hat): *to enjoy oneself, to have a good time*
unterhaltsam: *entertaining*
die Unterschrift, -en: *the signature*
die Unterwäsche, no pl.: *the underwear*
unverheiratet: *unmarried, single*
unwahrscheinlich: *improbable, unlikely*
der Urlaub, -e: *the leave, the vacation*
urteilen (hat): *to judge*
die USA: *the USA*
usw. = und so weiter: *etc., and so on*

V

der Vater, -": *the father*
verbringen (hat): *to spend (time)*
verehren (hat): *to admire, to look up to*
die Vereinigten Staaten (von Amerika) (plural): *the United States (of America)*
zur Verfügung stellen: *to make something available*
vergeben (hat): *to forgive*
vergessen (hat): *to forget*

das Vergnügen, *no pl.*: *the pleasure, the enjoyment*
das Verhältnis, -se: *the circumstance, the condition*
verheiratet: *married*
verkaufen (hat): *to sell*
der Verkäufer, -: *the salesman*
das Verkehrsmittel, -: *the means of transportation*
der Verkehrsunfall, -¨e: *the traffic accident*
verlassen (hat): *to leave*
sich verlassen auf (+ *accusative*): *to depend on, to rely on*
verlassen Sie sich darauf!: *you can depend on it!*
verlaufen (ist): *to end, to turn out*
verlieren (hat): *to lose*
verloren gehen (ist): *to get lost*
der Verlust, -¨e: *the loss, the damage*
verpassen (hat): *to let slip, to miss*
verreisen (ist): *to go on a trip*
das Versprechen, -: *the promise*
verständlich: *comprehensible*
das Verständnis, *no pl.*: *the understanding, the comprehension*
verstehen (hat): *to understand*
versuchen (hat): *to try, to attempt*
die Verwandtschaft, -en: *the relations, the family*
die Verzeihung, *no pl.*: *the pardon*
um Verzeihung bitten: *to ask someone's pardon*
Verzeihung!: *I'm sorry/excuse me*
viel: *a lot, much*
viel Arbeit: *a lot of work*
viel Vergnügen!: *enjoy yourself/yourselves*
viele: *many, a lot of, lots of*
viele Bücher: *a lot of books*
vielen Dank: *many thanks/thank you very much*
ich habe viel zu tun: *I have a lot (of work) to do*
vielleicht: *perhaps, maybe*
vier: *four*
zu viert: *four of them, four of us*
vierzehn: *fourteen*
vierzig: *forty*
das Volksfest, -e: *the village festival*
von (+ *dative*): *from*
vor (+ *accusative or dative*): *before, in front of*
vor vierzehn Tagen: *a fortnight ago*
voraussagen (hat): *to forecast*

vorerst: *for the present*
die Vorfahrt, -en: *the right of way*
vorkommen (ist): *to occur, to be met with*
der Vormittag, -e: *the morning*
vormittags: *in the morning, a.m.*
der Vorschlag, -¨e: *the proposal*
vorschlagen (hat): *to suggest, to propose*
vorsichtig: *careful, cautious*
vorstellen (hat): *to introduce*
die Vorstellung, -en: *the introduction; the idea, the performance*
vorwählen (hat): *to dial first, to dial beforehand*
vorziehen (hat): *to prefer*

W

die Waage, -n: *the balance, the scales (plural)*
wach: *awake*
wach werden (ist): *to wake up*
der Wagen, -: *the wagon*
wählen (hat): *to choose, to dial (a telephone number)*
während (+ *genitive*): *during*
wahr: *true, genuine*
die Wahrscheinlichkeit, -en: *the probability*
wahrscheinlich: *probable, likely*
die Wand, -¨e: *the wall*
wann: *when*
warm: *warm*
warten (hat): *to wait*
warum: *why*
warum nicht?: *why not?*
was: *what*
was für: *what, what sort of*
was darf's denn sein?: *what can I get you?*
sich waschen (hat): *to wash (oneself)*
waschen (hat): *to wash*
das Wasser, – or -": *the water*
wechseln (hat): *to change, to exchange*
die Wechselstube, -n: *the bureau de change, the currency exchange office*
weder . . . noch: *neither . . . nor*
der Weg, -e: *the way, the path, the lane*
weich: *soft*
sich weigern (hat): *to refuse*
das Weihnachten, -: *Christmas*

weil: *because*
der Wein, -e: *the wine*
weinen (hat): *to weep*
weiß: *white (adjective)*
weit: *far*
weit entfernt: *far away*
weiter-: *further, additional, more*
welch-: *which, that*
wenig: *a little*
wenn: *if; when, whenever*
wer: *who*
der Wert, -e: *the value*
der Westen, no pl.: *the west*
weswegen: *why, for what reason, on what account*
das Wetter, no pl.:: *the weather*
der Wetterbericht, -e: *the weather report*
wichtig: *important*
widmen (+ dative) (hat): *to dedicate, to devote*
auf Wiederhören!: *goodbye! (on the telephone)*
auf Wiedersehen: *goodbye!*
auf Wiederschauen!: *goodbye! (variant of auf Wiedersehen)*
die Wiedervereinigung: *the reunification*
wie: *as, like*
wie: *how (in questions), in what way*
wie lange wird das dauern?: *how long will it take?*
wie geht es Ihnen?: *how are you?*
wie geht's?: *how are things?*
wiegen (hat): *to weigh*
Wien: *Vienna*
wie viel?: *how much?*
wie viel bin ich Ihnen schuldig?: *how much do I owe you?*
wie viel macht das alles zusammen?: *how much does that all come to?*
wie viel Uhr ist es?: *what time is it?*
wie viele: *how many?*
der Winter, -: *the winter*
wir: *we*
wirklich: *really*
die Wirklichkeit, no pl.: *the reality*
der Wirt, -e: *the landlord*
die Wirtin, -nen: *the landlady*
das Wissen, no pl.: *knowledge*

wissen (hat): *to know (something)*
wo: *where*
wo gehen Sie hin?: *where are you going to?*
wo kommen Sie her?: *where do you come from?*
wo: *where*
woher?: *where from?*
wohin?: *where to?*
die Woche, -n: *the week*
in einer Woche: *in a week*
das Wochenende, -n: *the weekend*
am Wochenende: *at the weekend*
das Wohl, no pl.: *the well-being, the happiness*
wohl: *well, happy*
auf Ihr Wohl!: *to your health!*
zum Wohl!: *good health!*
wohnen (hat): *to live (in a place)*
die Wohnung, -en: *the home*
das Wohnzimmer -: *the living room*
die Wolke, -n: *the cloud*
wollen (hat): *to want, to desire; to intend, to be going to*
wollen Sie sich bitte hier eintragen?: *would you please enter your name here?*
wollen Sie …?: *do you want to?*
das Wort, -e or -¨er: *the word*
wozu: *what for?*
wunderbar: *wonderful, great*
der Wunsch, -¨e: *the wish, the desire*
wünschen (hat): *to wish, to desire, to want*
Sie wünschen?: *can I help you?*
die Wurst, -¨e: *the sausage*
das Würstchen, -: *the sausage*

Z

die Zahl, -en: *the number*
zählen (hat): *to count*
zehn: *ten*
zeigen (hat): *to show*
die Zeit, -en: *the time*
von Zeit zu Zeit: *from time to time, now and then*
zurzeit: *at present, at the moment*
die Zeitschrift, -en: *the magazine*
die Zeitung, -en: *the newspaper*
zerbrechen (hat): *to smash*
ziehen (hat): *to pull*

ziemlich: *fairly, quite*
die Zigarette, -n: *the cigarette*
das Zimmer, -: *the room*
die Zitrone, -n: *the lemon*
das Zögern, *no pl.:* *the hesitation*
zu *(+ dative):* *to, towards, up to; at, in; on*
zubereiten (hat): *to prepare*
der Zucker, -: *the sugar*
zuerst: *first of all*
zufällig: *by chance, as it happens*
der Zug, -¨e: *the train*
zurück: *back*
zurückbekommen (hat): *to get back*
zurückkehren (ist): *to return, to come back*

zurücksenden (hat): *to send back*
zusammen: *together*
zusammengesetzt *(aus + dative):* *composed of, consisting of*
zusammenrechnen (hat): *to add up*
zusammensetzen (hat): *to put together, to assemble*
zuzahlen (hat): *to pay extra*
zuziehen (hat): *to draw together; to consult*
zwanzig: *twenty*
…, und zwar … : *…, to be more precise …* *(usually not translated)*
zweitens: *secondly*
zwölf: *twelve*